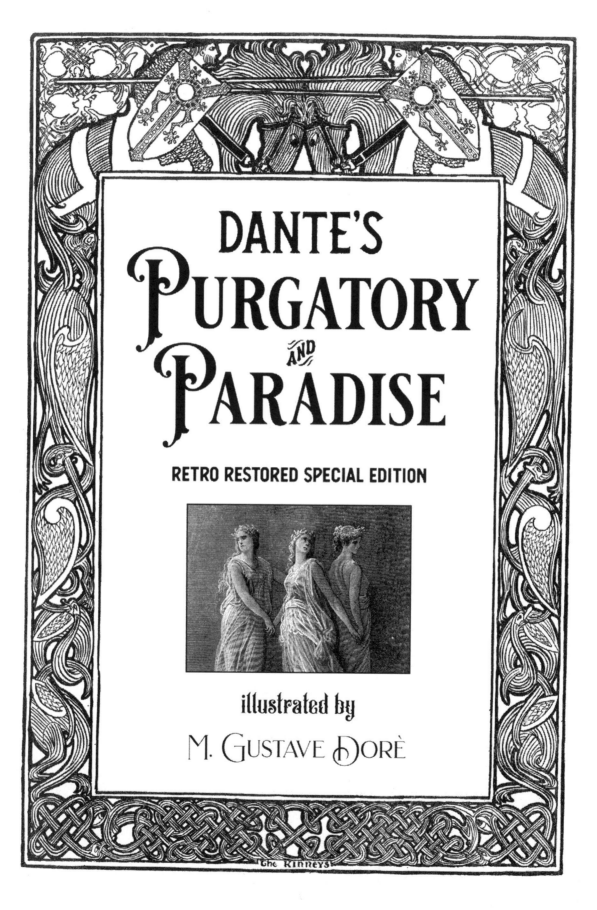

**Dante's Purgatory and Paradise:
Retro Restored Special Edition**

Written by Dante Alighieri
Translated by Henry Francis Cary
Illustrated by Gustave Doré

Restored print from 1880

Copyright © 2020 Inecom, LLC.
All Rights Reserved

No parts of this book may be reproduced or broadcast in any
way without written permission from Inecom, LLC.

www.CGRpublishing.com

P. P.—1.

Then when he knew
The pilot cried aloud, "Down, down; bend low
Thy knees; behold God's angel: fold thy hands:
Now shalt thou see true ministers indeed."

Canto II., lines 27-30.

Altemus' Edition.

Purgatory AND Paradise

Translated from the Original of Dante Alighieri

BY

HENRY FRANCIS CARY, M.A.,

AND ILLUSTRATED BY

GUSTAVE DORÉ

Edited by HENRY C. WALSH, A.M.,
Editor of American Notes and Queries.

PHILADELPHIA

DANTE'S "PURGATORY" AND "PARADISE."

"THE 'PURGATORY' OF DANTE," says the eminent Italian critic Sismondi, "is, in some respects, a fainter picture of the infernal regions. The same crimes are there corrected by punishments of a sinless nature, but limited in their duration, inasmuch as the sinner gave proofs of penitence previous to his death." The awful words, "All hope abandon, ye who enter here," however, are not written above the portals of Purgatory, and so faith and hope lighten the punishments, and here all

> " apprehend a bliss
> On which the soul may rest, the hearts of all
> Yearn after it, and to that wished bourn
> All, therefore, strive to tend."

The vision of the ideal is here, and where this is hell is not. "The theory of the poem," says Miss Blow, "is that goodness is not a dower, but an achievement. This second kingdom is one in which by effort 'the human spirit doth purge itself.' Man is a worm 'born to bring forth the angelic butterfly.' Paradise is at the top of a precipitous mountain. The climbing in the beginning is tiresome and painful, but 'aye the more one climbs, the less it hurts.' There is nowhere in the poem a trace of the heresy which confounds what man is with what he may become, and which paralyzes effort by ignoring the significance of choice."

Purgatory is divided into three parts—the base of the mountain to the first circle, the seven circles in which souls are purged from the seven capital sins, and the earthly Paradise upon the summit of the mountain. The first part forms an ante-Purgatory, and here souls are delayed until they have atoned for having postponed repentance until the very last moment. The souls are in the first process of transition toward good by turning away from evil. In a valley of this first section Dante falls asleep, and wakes to find himself at the gates of Purgatory. Here the seven circles or terraces rise one above the other, and here the marks of the seven capital sins are purged from the gradually-ascending soul. The more heinous sins, pride, envy, anger, are lowest in the scale, and consequently farthest away from the Paradise. Pride is the most heinous offence, for it is the substitution of self for God, and is punished in the first circle, as in the Inferno it is found deepest down in the frozen circle. On the next terrace the envious are punished by being clothed in sackcloth and by having their eyes sewed up with iron thread; above them, the sin of anger is purged amid a dense fog. In the fourth circle is purged the sin of slothfulness, and in the fifth the souls of the avaricious grovel along the earth. Pride, anger and envy all in greater or lesser degree insist upon self; their common characteristic is a distorted self-love, greatest in pride and least in anger. In sloth self is subordinated, but not overcome. In the sixth circle the sin of gluttony is purged, and the gluttons are condemned to suffer the tortures of hunger and thirst, and reduced to the outlines of skeletons. In the seventh and last circle the sin of incontinence is punished in flames of fire.

The symbolism of the various punishments can be readily understood. Growth in spiritual life depends upon giving and sharing; this principle presses with great weight upon the proud soul that wishes to live for itself alone, neither giving nor taking; and so the proud in the first circle are represented as bearing heavy weights. Envy blinds the eyes and anger causes the reason to become clouded, so that perception of right is dimmed. Sloth causes loss of power; avarice, setting its heart upon lucre and things of the earth, grovels and casts its eyes downward. The higher ideals are lost, and with them the stimulus to action. Hunger and thirst torture the glutton, and unholy love is tortured by burning shame.

In the sixteenth canto the poet insists upon the free agency of man, which forms one of the central ideas of the "Divina Commedia." He exemplifies the idea that the causes of error and sin must be sought for in men themselves, and repudiates the doctrine of necessity, which borders upon fatalism:

> "Light have ye still to follow evil or good,
> And of the will free power, which, if it stand
> Firm and unwearied in Heaven's first assay,
> Conquers at last, so it be cherished well,
> Triumphant over all. To mightier force,
> To better nature subject, ye abide
> Free, not constrained by that which forms in you
> The reasoning mind uninfluenced by the stars.
> If then the present race of mankind err,
> Seek in yourselves the cause, and find it there."

After passing through the seven circles Dante enters into the earthly Paradise, of which a magnificent description is given. Under figurative language the poet gives a picture of the state of the Church, drawing largely from the Revelations of St. John. Here the poet meets Beatrice, who descends upon the car of the Church—an image of divine grace. The description of the appearance of Beatrice is one of the most exquisite passages of the poem. The poet trembles with awe, and feels "the mighty influence of an ancient love." Love, the uplifting power on earth, is revealed to men in its most perfect form through woman. It is but a symbol of the higher love that exists in heaven. Goethe expresses this idea in "Faust:"

DANTE'S "PURGATORY" AND "PARADISE."

> " All things transitory
>   But as symbols are sent:
> Earth's insufficiency
>   Here grows to Event;
> The Indescribable—
>   Here it is done:
> The Woman-Soul leadeth us
>   Upward and on.

Dante, after drinking of the waters of Lethe, is led by the Woman-Soul upward and onward into the realms of the heavenly Paradise. "'Purgatory,'" to quote Miss Blow again, "traces the redemption of man out of individualism into social communion. It treats of the soul's relation to God—not directly, but as mediated by the Church—and its lesson is that in the organic relationship of the individual to the social whole is grounded the possibility of social development." Dante's flight from the earthly to the heavenly Paradise is effected in a moment under the leadership of Beatrice.

"Paradise" is the most difficult of comprehension of the three divisions of the "Divina Commedia" because it is the farthest removed from human emotions and experiences. It pictures a range of spiritual experience beyond our ken, and, being a state of sinlessness, it transcends human experience. The poet divides the heavenly Paradise into ten circles; the earth is supposed to be immovable and the centre of the universe. The seven planets—the Moon, Mercury, Venus, the Sun, Mars, Jupiter and Saturn—form the first seven circles, and are visited in turn; the fixed constellations form the eighth circle; the ninth is the empyrean, and the tenth the abode of the Divinity. This division gives evidence of a profound knowledge of the learned sciences, and of astronomy as known in that day.

Any attempt at an analysis of "Paradise" would require a volume in itself. Miss Blow's work, *A Study of Dante*, will be found very useful in arriving at a proper understanding of the poem. "The ascending insights of Paradise," she says, "are God in the universe, God in the individual, each individual in every other, all individuals in God. This final vision is the truth 'beyond which nothing true expands itself,' and in which 'all intellect finds rest.'"

In the tenth and last circle Dante is given a glimpse of the great mystery, the hypostatical union of Christ's human nature with his divine being, and arrives at the utmost boundaries of the gratification of desire; for, to quote the closing lines,

> " Here vigour failed the tow'ring fantasy:
> But yet the will roll'd onward, like a wheel
> In even motion, by the Love impell'd
> That moves the sun in heaven and all the stars."

PURGATORY.

P. P.—2.

The radiant planet, that to love invites,
Made all the orient laugh, and veil'd beneath
The Pisces' light, that in his escort came.

Canto I., lines 19-21.

THE VISION OF DANTE.

PURGATORY.

CANTO I.

ARGUMENT.

The Poet describes the delight he experienced at issuing a little before dawn from the infernal regions, into the pure air that surrounds the isle of Purgatory; and then relates how, turning to the right, he beheld four stars never seen before but by our first parents, and met on his left the shade of Cato of Utica, who, having warned him and Virgil what is needful to be done before they proceed on their way through Purgatory, disappears; and the two poets go towards the shore, where Virgil cleanses Dante's face with the dew, and girds him with a reed, as Cato had commanded.

O'ER better waves to speed her rapid course
    The light bark of my genius lifts the sail,
    Well pleased to leave so cruel sea behind;
And of that second region will I sing,
In which the human spirit from sinful blot
Is purged, and for ascent to Heaven prepares.
    Here, O ye hallow'd Nine! for in your train
I follow, here the deaden'd strain revive;
Nor let Calliope refuse to sound
A somewhat higher song, of that loud tone
Which when the wretched birds of chattering note
Had heard, they of forgiveness lost all hope.
    Sweet hue of eastern sapphire, that was spread
O'er the serene aspect of the pure air,
High up as the first circle, to mine eyes
Unwonted joy renew'd, soon as I 'scaped
Forth from the atmosphere of deadly gloom,

That had mine eyes and bosom fill'd with grief.
The radiant planet, that to love invites,
Made all the orient laugh, and veil'd beneath
The Pisces' light, that in his escort came.

 To the right hand I turn'd, and fix'd my mind
On the other pole attentive, where I saw
Four stars ne'er seen before save by the ken
Of our first parents. Heaven of their rays
Seem'd joyous. O thou northern site! bereft
Indeed, and widow'd, since of these deprived.

 As from this view I had desisted, straight
Turning a little towards the other pole,
There from whence now the wain had disappear'd,
I saw an old man standing by my side
Alone, so worthy of reverence in his look,
That ne'er from son to father more was owed.
Low down his beard, and mix'd with hoary white,
Descended, like his locks, which, parting, fell
Upon his breast in double fold. The beams
Of those four luminaries on his face
So brightly shone, and with such radiance clear
Deck'd it, that I beheld him as the sun.

 "Say who are ye, that stemming the blind stream,
Forth from the eternal prison-house have fled?"
He spoke and moved those venerable plumes.
"Who hath conducted, or with lantern sure
Lights you emerging from the depth of night,
That makes the infernal valley ever black?
Are the firm statutes of the dread abyss
Broken, or in high heaven new laws ordain'd,
That thus, condemn'd, ye to my caves approach?"

 My guide, then laying hold on me, by words
And intimations given with hand and head,
Made my bent knees and eye submissive pay

Due reverence; then thus to him replied:

"Not of myself I come; a Dame from heaven
Descending, him besought me in my charge
To bring. But since thy will implies, that more
Our true condition I unfold at large,
Mine is not to deny thee thy request.
This mortal ne'er hath seen the furthest gloom;
But erring by his folly had approach'd
So near, that little space was left to turn.
Then, as before I told, I was dispatch'd
To work his rescue; and no way remain'd
Save this which I have ta'en. I have display'd
Before him all the regions of the bad;
And purpose now those spirits to display,
That under thy command are purged from sin.
How I have brought him would be long to say.
From high descends the virtue, by whose aid
I to thy sight and hearing him have led.
Now may our coming please thee. In the search
Of liberty he journeys; that how dear,
They know who for her sake have life refused.
Thou knowest, to whom death for her was sweet
In Utica, where thou didst leave those weeds,
That in the last great day will shine so bright.
For us the eternal edicts are unmoved:
He breathes, and I of Minos am not bound,
Abiding in that circle, where the eyes
Of thy chaste Marcia beam, who still in look
Prays thee, O hallow'd spirit! to own her thine.
Then by her love we implore thee, let us pass
Through thy seven regions; for which, best thanks
I for thy favour will to her return,
If mention there below thou not disdain."

"Marcia so pleasing in my sight was found."

He then to him rejoin'd, "while I was there,
That all she ask'd me I was fain to grant.
Now that beyond the accursed stream she dwells,
She may no longer move me, by that law,
Which was ordain'd me, when I issued thence.
Not so, if Dame from heaven, as thou sayst,
Moves and directs thee; then no flattery needs.
Enough for me that in her name thou ask.
Go therefore now; and with a slender reed
See that thou duly gird him, and his face
Lave, till all sordid stain thou wipe from thence.
For not with eye, by any cloud obscured,
Would it be seemly before him to come,
Who stands the foremost minister in heaven.
This islet all around, there far beneath,
Where the wave beats it, on the oozy bed
Produces store of reeds. No other plant,
Cover'd with leaves, or harden'd in its stalk,
There lives, not bending to the water's sway.
After, this way return not; but the sun
Will show you, that now rises, where to take
The mountain in its easiest ascent."

 He disappear'd; and I myself upraised
Speechless, and to my guide retiring close,
Toward him turn'd mine eyes. He thus began:
"My son! observant thou my steps pursue.
We must retreat to rereward; for that way
The champain to its low extreme declines."

 The dawn had chased the matin hour of prime,
Which fled before it, so that from afar
I spied the trembling of the ocean stream.

 We traversed the deserted plain, as one
Who, wander'd from his track, thinks every step
Trodden in vain till he regain the path.

P. P.—3.

My guide, then laying hold on me, by words
And intimations given with hand and head,
Made my bent knees and eye submissive pay
Due reverence.

Canto I., lines 49-52.

P. P.—4. The heavenly steersman at the prow was seen,
Visibly written Blessed in his looks.

Canto II., lines 42, 43.

When we had come, where yet the tender dew
Strove with the sun, and in a place where fresh
The wind breathed o'er it, while it slowly dried;
Both hands extended on the watery grass
My master placed, in graceful act and kind.
Whence I of his intent before apprised,
Stretch'd out to him my cheeks suffused with tears,
There to my visage he anew restored
That hue which the dun shades of hell conceal'd.

Then on the solitary shore arrived,
That never sailing on its waters saw
Man that could after measure back his course,
He girt me in such manner as had pleased
Him who instructed; and, O strange to tell!
As he selected every humble plant,
Wherever one was pluck'd another there
Resembling, straightway in its place arose.

CANTO II.

ARGUMENT.

They behold a vessel under conduct of an angel, coming over the waves with spirits to Purgatory, among whom, when the passengers have landed, Dante recognizes his friend Casella; but, while they are entertained by him with a song, they hear Cato exclaiming against their negligent loitering, and at that rebuke hasten forwards to the mountain.

NOW had the sun to that horizon reach'd,
That covers, with the most exalted point
Of its meridian circle, Salem's walls;
And night, that opposite to him her orb
Rounds, from the stream of Ganges issued forth,
Holding the scales, that from her hands are dropt
When she reigns highest: so that where I was,
Aurora's white and vermeil-tinctured cheek
To orange turn'd as she in age increased.
 Meanwhile we linger'd by the water's brink,
Like men, who, musing on their road, in thought
Journey, while motionless the body rests.
When lo! as, near upon the hour of dawn,
Through the thick vapours Mars with fiery beam
Glares down in west, over the ocean floor;
So seem'd, what once again I hope to view,
A light, so swiftly coming through the sea,
No winged course might equal its career.
From which when for a space I had withdrawn
Mine eyes, to make inquiry of my guide,
Again I look'd, and saw it grown in size
And brightness: then on either side appear'd
Something, but what I knew not, of bright hue,
And by degrees from underneath it came

Another. My preceptor silent yet
Stood, while the brightness, that we first discern'd,
Open'd the form of wings: then when he knew
The pilot, cried aloud, "Down, down; bend low
Thy knees; behold God's angel: fold thy hands:
Now shalt thou see true ministers indeed.
Lo! how all human means he sets at nought;
So that nor oar he needs, nor other sail
Except his wings, between such distant shores.
Lo! how straight up to heaven he holds them rear'd,
Winnowing the air with those eternal plumes,
That not like mortal hairs fall off or change."

As more and more toward us came, more bright
Appear'd the bird of God, nor could the eye
Endure his splendour near: I mine bent down.
He drove ashore in a small bark so swift
And light, that in its course no wave it drank.
The heavenly steersman at the prow was seen,
Visibly written Blessed in his looks.
Within, a hundred spirits and more there sat.
"In Exitu Israel de Egypto,"
All with one voice together sang, with what
In the remainder of that hymn is writ.
Then soon as with the sign of holy cross
He bless'd them, they at once leap'd out on land:
He, swiftly as he came, return'd. The crew,
There left, appear'd astounded with the place,
Gazing around, as one who sees new sights.

From every side the sun darted his beams,
And with his arrowy radiance from mid heaven
Had chased the Capricorn, when that strange tribe,
Lifting their eyes toward us: "If ye know,
Declare what path will lead us to the mount."

Then Virgil answer'd: "Ye suppose, perchance,

Us well acquainted with this place: but here,
We, as yourselves, are strangers. Not long erst
We came, before you but a little space,
By other road so rough and hard, that now
The ascent will seem to us as play." The spirits,
Who from my breathing had perceived I lived,
Grew pale with wonder. As the multitude
Flock round a herald sent with olive branch,
To hear what news he brings, and in their haste
Tread one another down; e'en so at sight
Of me those happy spirits were fix'd, each one
Forgetful of its errand to depart
Where, cleansed from sin, it might be made all fair.

 Then one I saw darting before the rest
With such fond ardour to embrace me, I
To do the like was moved. O shadows vain!
Except in outer semblance: thrice my hands
I clasp'd behind it, they as oft return'd
Empty into my breast again. Surprise
I need must think was painted in my looks,
For that the shadow smiled and backward drew.
To follow it I hasten'd, but with voice
Of sweetness it enjoin'd me to desist.
Then who it was I knew, and pray'd of it,
To talk with me it would a little pause.
It answer'd: "Thee as in my mortal frame
I loved, so loosed from it I love thee still,
And therefore pause: but why walkest thou here?"

 "Not without purpose once more to return,
Thou find'st me, my Casella, where I am,
Journeying this way," I said. "But how of thee
Hath so much time been lost?" He answer'd straight:

 "No outrage hath been done to me, if he,
Who when and whom he chooses takes, hath oft

Denied me passage here; since of just will
His will he makes. These three months past indeed,
He, whoso chose to enter, with free leave
Hath taken; whence I wandering by the shore
Where Tiber's wave grows salt, of him gain'd kind
Admittance, at that river's mouth, toward which
His wings are pointed; for there always throng
All such as not to Acheron descend."

    Then I: "If new law taketh not from thee
Memory or custom of love-tuned song,
That whilom all my cares had power to 'swage;
Please thee therewith a little to console
My spirit, that encumber'd with its frame,
Travelling so far, of pain is overcome."

    "Love, that discourses in my thoughts," he then
Began in such soft accents, that within
The sweetness thrills me yet. My gentle guide,
And all who came with him, so well were pleased,
That seem'd nought else might in their thoughts have room.

    Fast fix'd in mute attention to his notes
We stood, when lo! that old man venerable
Exclaiming, "How is this, ye tardy spirits?
What negligence detains you loitering here?
Run to the mountain to cast off those scales,
That from your eyes the sight of God conceal."

    As a wild flock of pigeons to their food
Collected, blade or tares, without their pride
Accustom'd, and in still and quiet sort,
If aught alarm them, suddenly desert
Their meal, assail'd by more important care;
So I that new-come troop beheld, the song
Deserting, hasten to the mountain's side,
As one who goes, yet, where he tends, knows not.

    Nor with less hurried step did we depart.

CANTO III.

ARGUMENT.

Our Poet, perceiving no shadow except that cast by his own body, is fearful that Virgil has deserted him; but he is freed from that error, and both arrive together at the foot of the mountain. On finding it too steep to climb, they inquire the way from a troop of spirits that are coming towards them, and are by them shown which is the easiest ascent. Manfredi, King of Naples, who is one of these spirits, bids Dante inform his daughter Costanza, Queen of Arragon, of the manner in which he had died.

THEM sudden flight had scatter'd o'er the plain,
   Turn'd towards the mountain, whither reason's voice
   Drives us: I, to my faithful company
Adhering, left it not. For how, of him
Deprived, might I have sped? or who, beside,
Would o'er the mountainous tract have led my steps?
He, with the bitter pang of self-remorse,
Seem'd smitten. O clear conscience, and upright!
How doth a little failing wound thee sore.
   Soon at his feet desisted (slackening pace)
From haste, that mars all decency of act,
My mind, that in itself before was wrapt,
Its thought expanded, as with joy restored;
And full against the steep ascent I set
My face, where highest to heaven its top o'erflows.
   The sun, that flared behind, with ruddy beam
Before my form was broken; for in me
His rays resistance met. I turn'd aside
With fear of being left, when I beheld
Only before myself the ground obscured.
When thus my solace, turning him around,
Bespake me kindly: "Why distrustest thou?
Believest not I am with thee, thy sure guide?

It now is evening there, where buried lies
The body in which I cast a shade, removed
To Naples from Brundusium's wall. Nor thou
Marvel, if before me no shadow fall,
More than that in the skyey element
One ray obstructs not other. To endure
Torments of heat and cold extreme, like frames
That virtue hath disposed, which, how it works,
Wills not to us should be reveal'd. Insane,
Who hopes our reason may that space explore,
Which holds three persons in one substance knit.
Seek not the wherefore, race of human kind;
Could ye have seen the whole, no need had been
For Mary to bring forth. Moreover, ye
Have seen such men desiring fruitlessly;
To whose desires, repose would have been given,
That now but serve them for eternal grief.
I speak of Plato, and the Stagirite,
And others many more." And then he bent
Downwards his forehead, and in troubled mood
Broke off his speech. Meanwhile we had arrived
Far as the mountain's foot, and there the rock
Found of so steep ascent, that nimblest steps
To climb it had been vain. The most remote,
Most wild, untrodden path, in all the tract
'Twixt Lerice and Turbia, were to this
A ladder easy and open of access.

"Who knows on which hand now the steep declines?"
My master said, and paused; "so that he may
Ascend, who journeys without aid of wing?"
And while, with looks directed to the ground,
The meaning of the pathway he explored,
And I gazed upward round the stony height;
On the left hand appear'd to us a troop

Of spirits, that toward us moved their steps;
Yet moving seem'd not, they so slow approach'd.
   I thus my guide address'd: "Upraise thine eyes:
Lo! that way some, of whom thou mayst obtain
Counsel, if of thyself thou find'st it not."
   Straightway he look'd, and with free speech replied:
"Let us tend thither: they but softly come.
And thou be firm in hope, my son beloved."
   Now was that crowd from us distant as far,
(When we some thousand steps, I say, had past,)
As at a throw the nervous arm could fling;
When all drew backward on the massy crags
Of the steep bank, and firmly stood unmoved,
As one, who walks in doubt, might stand to look.
   "O spirits perfect! O already chosen!"
Virgil to them began: "by that blest peace,
Which, as I deem, is for you all prepared,
Instruct us where the mountain low declines,
So that attempt to mount it be not vain.
For who knows most, him loss of time most grieves."
   As sheep, that step from forth their fold, by one,
Or pairs, or three at once; meanwhile the rest
Stand fearfully, bending the eye and nose
To ground, and what the foremost does, that do
The others, gathering round her if she stops,
Simple and quiet, nor the cause discern;
So saw I moving to advance the first,
Who of that fortunate crew were at the head,
Of modest mien, and graceful in their gait.
When they before me had beheld the light
From my right side fall broken on the ground,
So that the shadow reach'd the cave; they stopp'd,
And somewhat back retired: the same did all
Who follow'd, though unweeting of the cause.

P. P.—5. And I gazed upward round the stony height;
On the left hand appear'd to us a troop
Of spirits, that toward us moved their steps;
Yet moving seem'd not, they so slow approach'd.

Canto III., lines 56-59.

"Unask'd of you, yet freely I confess,
This is a human body which ye see.
That the sun's light is broken on the ground,
Marvel not: but believe, that not without
Virtue derived from Heaven, we to climb
Over this wall aspire." So them bespake
My master; and that virtuous tribe rejoin'd:
"Turn, and before you there the entrance lies;"
Making a signal to us with bent hands.

Then of them one began. "Whoe'er thou art,
Who journey'st thus this way, thy visage turn;
Think if me elsewhere thou hast ever seen."

I towards him turn'd, and with fix'd eye beheld.
Comely and fair, and gentle of aspect
He seem'd, but on one brow a gash was mark'd.

When humbly I disclaim'd to have beheld
Him ever: "Now behold!" he said, and show'd
High on his breast a wound: then smiling spake.

"I am Manfredi, grandson to the Queen
Costanza: whence I pray thee, when return'd,
To my fair daughter go, the parent glad
Of Aragonia and Sicilia's pride;
And of the truth inform her, if of me
Aught else be told. When by two mortal blows
My frame was shatter'd, I betook myself
Weeping to Him, who of free will forgives.
My sins were horrible: but so wide arms
Hath goodness infinite, that it receives
All who turn to it. Had this text divine
Been of Cosenza's shepherd better scann'd,
Who then by Clement on my hunt was set,
Yet at the bridge's head my bones had lain,
Near Benevento, by the heavy mole
Protected; but the rain now drenches them,

And the wind drives, out of the kingdom's bounds,
Far as the stream of Verde, where, with lights
Extinguish'd, he removed them from their bed.
Yet by their curse we are not so destroy'd,
But that the eternal love may turn, while hope
Retains her verdant blossom. True it is,
That such one as in contumacy dies
Against the holy church, though he repent,
Must wander thirty-fold for all the time
In his presumption past; if such decree
Be not by prayers of good men shorter made.
Look therefore if thou canst advance my bliss;
Revealing to my good Costanza how
Thou hast beheld me, and beside, the terms
Laid on me of that interdict; for here
By means of those below much profit comes."

CANTO IV.

ARGUMENT.

Dante and Virgil ascend the mountain of Purgatory, by a steep and narrow path pent in on each side by rock, till they reach a part of it that opens into a ledge or cornice. There seating themselves, and turning to the east, Dante wonders at seeing the sun on their left, the cause of which is explained to him by Virgil; and while they continue their discourse, a voice addresses them, at which they turn, and find several spirits behind the rock, and amongst the rest one named Belacqua, who had been known to our Poet on earth, and who tells that he is doomed to linger there on account of his having delayed his repentance to the last.

WHEN by sensations of delight or pain,
    That any of our faculties hath seized,
    Entire the soul collects herself, it seems
She is intent upon that power alone;
And thus the error is disproved, which holds
The soul not singly lighted in the breast.
And therefore whenas aught is heard or seen,
That firmly keeps the soul toward it turn'd,
Time passes, and a man perceives it not.
For that, whereby we harken, is one power;
Another that, which the whole spirit hath:
This is as it were bound, while that is free.

    This found I true by proof, hearing that spirit,
And wondering; for full fifty steps aloft
The sun had measured, unobserved of me,
When we arrived where all with one accord
The spirits shouted, "Here is what ye ask."

    A larger aperture oft-times is stopt,
With forked stake of thorn by villager,
When the ripe grape imbrowns, than was the path
By which my guide, and I behind him close,
Ascended solitary, when that troop

Departing left us. On Sanleo's road
Who journeys, or to Noli low descends,
Or mounts Bismantua's height, must use his feet;
But here a man had need to fly, I mean
With the swift wing and plumes of high desire,
Conducted by his aid, who gave me hope,
And with light furnish'd to direct my way.

    We through the broken rock ascended, close
Pent on each side, while underneath, the ground
Ask'd help of hands and feet. When we arrived
Near on the highest ridge of the steep bank,
Where the plain level open'd, I exclaim'd,
"O Master! say, which way can we proceed."

    He answer'd, "Let no step of thine recede.
Behind me gain the mountain, till to us
Some practised guide appear." That eminence
Was lofty, that no eye might reach its point;
And the side proudly rising, more than line
From the mid quadrant to the centre drawn.
I, wearied, thus began: "Parent beloved!
Turn and behold how I remain alone,
If thou stay not." "My son!" he straight replied,
"Thus far put forth thy strength;" and to a track
Pointed, that, on this side projecting, round
Circles the hill. His words so spurr'd me on,
That I, behind him, clambering, forced myself,
Till my feet press'd the circuit plain beneath.
There both together seated, turn'd we round
To eastward, whence was our ascent: and oft
Many beside have with delight look'd back.

    First on the nether shores I turn'd mine eyes,
Then raised them to the sun, and wondering mark'd
That from the left it smote us. Soon perceived
That poet sage, how at the car of light

While underneath, the ground
Ask'd help of hands and feet.

Canto IV., lines 31, 32.

And there were some, who in the shady place
Behind the rock were standing, as a man
Through idleness might stand.

Canto IV., lines 100–102.

Amazed I stood, where 'twixt us and the north
Its course it enter'd. Whence he thus to me:
"Were Leda's offspring now in company
Of that broad mirror, that high up and low
Imparts his light beneath, thou mightst behold
The ruddy Zodiac nearer to the Bears
Wheel if its ancient course it not forsook.
How that may be, if thou wouldst think; within
Pondering, imagine Sion with this mount
Placed on the earth, so that to both be one
Horizon, and two hemispheres apart,
Where lies the path that Phaeton ill knew
To guide his erring chariot: thou wilt see
How of necessity by this, on one,
He passes, while by that on the other side;
If with that clear view thine intellect attend."

"Of truth, kind teacher!" I exclaim'd, "so clear
Aught saw I never, as I now discern,
Where seem'd my ken to fail, that the mid orb
Of the supernal motion (which in terms
Of art is call'd the Equator, and remains
Still 'twixt the sun and winter) for the cause
Thou hast assign'd, from hence toward the north
Departs, when those, who in the Hebrew land
Were dwellers, saw it towards the warmer part.
But if it please thee, I would gladly know,
How far we have to journey: for the hill
Mounts higher, than this sight of mine can mount."

He thus to me: "Such is this steep ascent,
That it is ever difficult at first,
But more a man proceeds, less evil grows.
When pleasant it shall seem to thee, so much
That upward going shall be easy to thee
As in a vessel to go down the tide,

Then of this path thou wilt have reach'd the end.
There hope to rest thee from thy toil. No more
I answer, and thus far for certain know."
As he his words had spoken, near to us
A voice there sounded: "Yet ye first perchance
May to repose you by constraint be led."
At sound thereof each turn'd; and on the left
A huge stone we beheld, of which nor I
Nor he before was ware. Thither we drew;
And there were some, who in the shady place
Behind the rock were standing, as a man
Through idleness might stand. Among them one,
Who seem'd to be much wearied, sat him down,
And with his arms did fold his knees about,
Holding his face between them downward bent.

"Sweet Sir!" I cried, "behold that man who shows
Himself more idle than if laziness
Were sister to him." Straight he turn'd to us,
And, o'er the thigh lifting his face, observed,
Then in these accents spake: "Up then, proceed,
Thou valiant one." Straight who it was I knew;
Nor could the pain I felt (for want of breath
Still somewhat urged me) hinder my approach.
And when I came to him, he scarce his head
Uplifted, saying, "Well hast thou discern'd,
How from the left the sun his chariot leads."

His lazy acts and broken words my lips
To laughter somewhat moved; when I began:
"Belacqua, now for thee I grieve no more.
But tell, why thou art seated upright there.
Waitest thou escort to conduct thee hence?
Or blame I only thine accustom'd ways?"
Then he: "My brother! of what use to mount,
When, to my suffering, would not let me pass

The bird of God, who at the portal sits?
Behoves so long that heaven first bear me round
Without its limits, as in life it bore;
Because I, to the end, repentant sighs
Delay'd; if prayer do not aid me first,
That riseth up from heart which lives in grace.
What other kind avails, not heard in heaven?"

   Before me now the poet, up the mount
Ascending, cried: "Haste thee: for see the sun
Has touch'd the point meridian; and the night
Now covers with her foot Marocco's shore."

CANTO V.

ARGUMENT.

They meet with others, who had deferred their repentance till they were overtaken by a violent death, when sufficient space being allowed them, they were then saved; and amongst these Giacopo del Cassero, Buonconte da Montefeltro, and Pia, a lady of Sienna.

NOW had I left those spirits, and pursued
The steps of my conductor; when behind,
Pointing the finger at me, one exclaim'd:
"See, how it seems as if the light not shone
From the left hand of him beneath, and he,
As living, seems to be led on." Mine eyes
I at that sound reverting, saw them gaze,
Through wonder, first at me; and then at me
And the light broken underneath, by turns.
"Why are thy thoughts thus riveted," my guide
Exclaim'd, "that thou hast slack'd thy pace? or how
Imports it thee, what thing is whisper'd here?
Come after me, and to their babblings leave
The crowd. Be as a tower, that, firmly set,
Shakes not its top for any blast that blows.
He, in whose bosom thought on thought shoots out,
Still of his aim is wide, in that the one
Sicklies and wastes to nought the other's strength."

What other could I answer, save "I come"?
I said it, somewhat with that colour tinged,
Which oft-times pardon meriteth for man.

Meanwhile traverse along the hill there came,
A little way before us, some who sang
The "Miserere" in responsive strains.
When they perceived that through my body I

Gave way not for the rays to pass, their song
Straight to a long and hoarse exclaim they changed;
And two of them, in guise of messengers,
Ran on to meet us, and inquiring ask'd:
"Of your condition we would gladly learn."

    To them my guide. "Ye may return, and bear
Tidings to them who sent you, that his frame
Is real flesh. If, as I deem, to view
His shade they paused, enough is answer'd them:
Him let them honour: they may prize him well."

    Ne'er saw I fiery vapours with such speed
Cut through the serene air at fall of night,
Nor August's clouds athwart the setting sun,
That upward these did not in shorter space
Return; and, there arriving, with the rest
Wheel back on us, as with loose rein a troop.

    "Many," exclaim'd the bard, "are these, who throng
Around us: to petition thee they come.
Go therefore on, and listen as thou go'st."

    "O spirit! who go'st on to blessedness,
With the same limbs that clad thee at thy birth,"
Shouting they came: "a little rest thy step.
Look if thou any one amongst our tribe
Hast e'er beheld, that tidings of him there
Thou mayst report. Ah, wherefore go'st thou on?
Ah, wherefore tarriest thou not? We all
By violence died, and to our latest hour
Were sinners, but then warn'd by light from heaven:
So that, repenting and forgiving, we
Did issue out of life at peace with God,
Who, with desire to see him, fills our heart."

    Then I: "The visages of all I scan,
Yet none of ye remember. But if aught
That I can do may please you, gentle spirits!

Speak, and I will perform it; by that peace,
Which, on the steps of guide so excellent
Following, from world to world, intent I seek."

    In answer he began: "None here distrusts
Thy kindness, though not promised with an oath;
So as the will fail not for want of power.
Whence I, who sole before the others speak,
Entreat thee, if thou ever see that land
Which lies between Romagna and the realm
Of Charles, that of thy courtesy thou pray
Those who inhabit Fano, that for me
Their adorations duly be put up,
By which I may purge off my grievous sins.
From thence I came. But the deep passages,
Whence issued out the blood wherein I dwelt,
Upon my bosom in Antenor's land
Were made, where to be more secure I thought.
The author of the deed was Este's prince,
Who, more than right could warrant, with his wrath
Pursued me. Had I towards Mira fled,
When overta'en at Oriaco, still
Might I have breathed. But to the marsh I 'sped;
And in the mire and rushes tangled there
Fell, and beheld my life-blood float the plain."

    Then said another: "Ah! so may the wish,
That takes thee o'er the mountain, be fulfill'd,
As thou shalt graciously give aid to mine.
Of Montefeltro I; Buonconte I:
Giovanna nor none else have care for me;
Sorrowing with these I therefore go." I thus:
"From Campaldino's field what force or chance
Drew thee, that ne'er thy sepulture was known?"

    "Oh!" answer'd he, "at Casentino's foot
A stream there courseth, named Archiano, sprung

In Apennine above the hermit's seat.
E'en where its name is cancel'd, there came I,
Pierced in the throat, fleeing away on foot,
And bloodying the plain. Here sight and speech
Fail'd me; and, finishing with Mary's name,
I fell, and tenantless my flesh remain'd.
I will report the truth; which thou again
Tell to the living. Me God's angel took,
Whilst he of hell exclaim'd: 'O thou from heaven:
Say wherefore hast thou robb'd me? Thou of him
The eternal portion bear'st with thee away,
For one poor tear that he deprives me of.
But of the other, other rule I make.'

"Thou know'st how in the atmosphere collects
That vapour dank, returning into water
Soon as it mounts where cold condenses it.
That evil will, which in his intellect
Still follows evil, came; and raised the wind
And smoky mist, by virtue of the power
Given by his nature. Thence the valley, soon
As day was spent, he cover'd o'er with cloud,
From Pratomagno to the mountain range;
And stretch'd the sky above; so that the air
Impregnate changed to water. Fell the rain;
And to the fosses came all that the land
Contain'd not; and, as mightiest streams are wont,
To the great river, with such headlong sweep,
Rush'd, that nought stay'd its course. My stiffen'd frame,
Laid at his mouth, the fell Archiano found,
And dash'd it into Arno; from my breast
Loosening the cross, that of myself I made
When overcome with pain. He hurl'd me on,
Along the banks and bottom of his course;
Then in his muddy spoils encircling wrapt."

"Ah! when thou to the world shalt be return'd,
And rested after thy long road," so spake
Next the third spirit; "then remember me.
I once was Pia. Sienna gave me life;
Maremma took it from me. That he knows,
Who me with jewel'd ring had first espoused."

P. P.—8.

"Many," exclaim'd the bard, "are these, who throng
Around us: to petition thee, they come.
Go therefore on, and listen as thou go'st."

Canto V., lines 42-44.

From my breast
Loosening the cross, that of myself I made
When overcome with pain.

Canto V., lines 123-125.

"Then remember me.
I once was Pia."

Canto V., lines 130, 131.

"Through every orb
Of that sad region," he replied, "thus far
Am I arrived."

Canto VII., lines 21–23.

CANTO VI.

ARGUMENT.

Many besides, who are in like case with those spoken of in the last Canto, beseech our Poet to obtain for them the prayers of their friends, when he shall be returned to this world. This moves him to express a doubt to his guide, how the dead can be profited by the prayers of the living; for the solution of which doubt he is referred to Beatrice. Afterwards he meets with Sordello, the Mantuan, whose affection, shown to Virgil, his countryman, leads Dante to break forth into an invective against the unnatural divisions with which Italy, and more especially Florence, was distracted.

WHEN from their game of dice men separate,
He who hath lost remains in sadness fix'd,
Revolving in his mind what luckless throws
He cast: but, meanwhile, all the company
Go with the other; one before him runs,
And one behind his mantle twitches, one
Fast by his side bids him remember him.
He stops not; and each one, to whom his hand
Is stretch'd, well knows he bids him stand aside;
And thus he from the press defends himself.
E'en such was I in that close-crowding throng;
And turning so my face around to all,
And promising, I 'scaped from it with pains.
    Here of Arezzo him I saw, who fell
By Ghino's cruel arm; and him beside,
Who in his chase was swallow'd by the stream.
Here Frederic Novello, with his hand
Stretch'd forth, entreated; and of Pisa he,
Who put the good Marzuco to such proof
Of constancy. Count Orso I beheld;
And from its frame a soul dismiss'd for spite
And envy, as it said, but for no crime;
I speak of Peter de la Brosse: and here,

While she yet lives, that Lady of Brabant,
Let her beware; lest for so false a deed
She herd with worse than these. When I was freed
From all those spirits, who pray'd for others' prayers
To hasten on their state of blessedness;
Straight I began: "O thou, my luminary!
It seems expressly in thy text denied,
That heaven's supreme decree can ever bend
To supplication: yet with this design
Do these entreat. Can then their hope be vain?
Or is thy saying not to me reveal'd?"

    He thus to me: "Both what I write is plain,
And these deceived not in their hope; if well
Thy mind consider, that the sacred height
Of judgment doth not stoop, because love's flame
In a short moment all fulfils, which he,
Who sojourns here, in right should satisfy.
Besides, when I this point concluded thus,
By praying no defect could be supplied;
Because the prayer had none access to God.
Yet in this deep suspicion rest thou not
Contented, unless she assure thee so,
Who betwixt truth and mind infuses light:
I know not if thou take me right; I mean
Beatrice. Her thou shalt behold above,
Upon this mountain's crown, fair seat of joy."

    Then I: "Sir! let us mend our speed; for now
I tire not as before: and lo! the hill
Stretches its shadow far." He answer'd thus:
"Our progress with this day shall be as much
As we may now dispatch; but otherwise
Than thou supposest is the truth. For there
Thou canst not be, ere thou once more behold
Him back returning, who behind the steep

Is now so hidden, that, as erst, his beam
Thou dost not break. But lo! a spirit there
Stands solitary, and toward us looks:
It will instruct us in the speediest way."

    We soon approach'd it. O thou Lombard spirit!
How didst thou stand, in high abstracted mood,
Scarce moving with slow dignity thine eyes.
It spoke not aught, but let us onward pass,
Eyeing us as a lion on his watch.
But Virgil, with entreaty mild, advanced,
Requesting it to show the best ascent.
It answer to his question none return'd;
But of our country and our kind of life
Demanded. When my courteous guide began,
"Mantua," the shadow, in itself absorb'd,
Rose towards us from the place in which it stood,
And cried, "Mantuan! I am thy countryman,
Sordello." Each the other then embraced.

    Ah, slavish Italy; thou inn of grief!
Vessel without a pilot in loud storm!
Lady no longer of fair provinces,
But brothel-house impure! this gentle spirit,
Even from the pleasant sound of his dear land
Was prompt to greet a fellow-citizen
With such a glad cheer: while now thy living ones
In thee abide not without war; and one
Malicious gnaws another; ay, of those
Whom the same wall and the same moat contains.
Seek, wretched one! around thy sea-coasts wide;
Then homeward to thy bosom turn; and mark,
If any part of thee sweet peace enjoy.
What boots it, that thy reins Justinian's hand
Refitted, if thy saddle be unprest?
Nought doth he now but aggravate thy shame.

THE VISION.

Ah, people! thou obedient still shouldst live,
And in the saddle let thy Cæsar sit,
If well thou marked'st that which God commands.
    Look how that beast to felness hath relapsed,
From having lost correction of the spur,
Since to the bridle thou hast set thine hand,
O German Albert! who abandon'st her
That is grown savage and unmanageable,
When thou shouldst clasp her flanks with forked heels.
Just judgment from the stars fall on thy blood;
And be it strange and manifest to all;
Such as may strike thy successor with dread;
For that thy sire and thou have suffered thus,
Through greediness of yonder realms detain'd,
The garden of the empire to run waste
Come, see the Capulets and Montagues,
The Filippeschi and Monaldi, man
Who carest for nought! those sunk in grief, and these
With dire suspicion rack'd. Come, cruel one!
Come, and behold the oppression of the nobles,
And mark their injuries; and thou mayst see
What safety Santafiore can supply.
Come and behold thy Rome, who calls on thee,
Desolate widow, day and night with moans,
"My Cæsar, why dost thou desert my side?"
Come, and behold what love among thy people:
And if no pity touches thee for us,
Come, and blush for thine own report. For me,
If it be lawful, O Almighty Power!
Who wast in earth for our sakes crucified,
Are thy just eyes turn'd elsewhere? or is this
A preparation, in the wondrous depth
Of thy sage counsel made, for some good end,
Entirely from our reach of thought cut off?

So are the Italian cities all o'erthrong'd
With 'tyrants, and a great Marcellus made
Of every petty factious villager.

    My Florence! thou mayst well remain unmoved
At this digression, which affects not thee;
Thanks to thy people, who so wisely speed.
Many have justice in their heart, that long
Waiteth for counsel to direct the bow,
Or ere it dart unto its aim: but thine
Have it on their lip's edge. Many refuse
To bear the common burdens: readier thine
Answer uncall'd, and cry, "Behold I stoop!"

    Make thyself glad, for thou hast reason now,
Thou wealthy! thou at peace! thou wisdom-fraught!
Facts best will witness if I speak the truth.
Athens and Lacedæmon, who of old
Enacted laws, for civil arts renown'd,
Made little progress in improving life
Toward thee, who usest such nice subtlety,
That to the middle of November scarce
Reaches the thread thou in October weavest.
How many times within thy memory,
Customs, and laws, and coins, and offices
Have been by thee renew'd, and people changed.

    If thou remember'st well and canst see clear,
Thou wilt perceive thyself like a sick wretch,
Who finds no rest upon her down, but oft
Shifting her side, short respite seeks from pain.

CANTO VII.

ARGUMENT.

The approach of night hindering further ascent, Sordello conducts our Poet apart to an eminence, from whence they behold a pleasant recess, in form of a flowery valley, scooped out of the mountain; where are many famous spirits, and among them the Emperor Rodolph, Ottocar, King of Bohemia, Philip III. of France, Henry of Navarre, Peter III. of Arragon, Charles I. of Naples, Henry III. of England, and William, Marquis of Montferrat.

AFTER their courteous greetings joyfully
    Seven times exchanged, Sordello backward drew
    Exclaiming, "Who are ye?"—"Before this mount
By spirits worthy of ascent to God
Was sought, my bones had by Octavius' care
Been buried. I am Virgil; for no sin
Deprived of heaven, except for lack of faith."
So answer'd him in few my gentle guide.
    As one, who aught before him suddenly
Beholding, whence his wonder riseth, cries,
"It is, yet is not," wavering in belief;
Such he appear'd; then downward bent his eyes,
And, drawing near with reverential step,
Caught him, where one of mean estate might clasp
His lord. "Glory of Latium!" he exclaim'd,
"In whom our tongue its utmost power display'd;
Boast of my honour'd birth-place! what desert
Of mine, what favour, rather, undeserved,
Shows thee to me? If I to hear that voice
Am worthy, say if from below thou comest,
And from what cloister's pale."—"Through every orb
Of that sad region," he replied, "thus far
Am I arrived, by heavenly influence led:
And with such aid I come. Not for my doing,

But for not doing, have I lost the sight
Of that high Sun, whom thou desirest, and who
By me too late was known. There is a place
There underneath, not made by torments sad,
But by dun shades alone; where mourning's voice
Sounds not of anguish sharp, but breathes in sighs.
There I with little innocents abide,
Who by death's fangs were bitten, ere exempt
From human taint. There I with those abide,
Who the three holy virtues put not on,
But understood the rest, and without blame
Follow'd them all. But, if thou know'st, and canst,
Direct us how we soonest may arrive,
Where Purgatory its true beginning takes."

    He answer'd thus: "We have no certain place
Assign'd us; upwards I may go, or round.
Far as I can, I join thee for thy guide.
But thou beholdest now how day declines;
And upwards to proceed by night, our power
Excels: therefore it may be well to choose
A place of pleasant sojourn. To the right
Some spirits sit apart retired. If thou
Consentest, I to these will lead thy steps:
And thou wilt know them, not without delight."

    "How chances this?" was answer'd: "whoso wish'd
To ascend by night, would he be thence debarr'd
By other, or through his own weakness fail?"

    The good Sordello then along the ground
Trailing his finger, spoke: "Only this line
Thou shalt not overpass, soon as the sun
Hath disappear'd; not that aught else impedes
Thy going upwards, save the shades of night.
These, with the want of power, perplex the will.
With them thou haply mightst return beneath,

Or to and fro around the mountain's side
Wander, while day is in the horizon shut."

   My master straight, as wondering at his speech,
Exclaim'd: "Then lead us quickly, where thou sayst
That, while we stay, we may enjoy delight."

   A little space we were removed from thence,
When I perceived the mountain hollow'd out,
Even as large valleys hollow'd out on earth.

   "That way," the escorting spirit cried, "we go,
Where in a bosom the high bank recedes:
And thou await renewal of the day."

   Betwixt the steep and plain, a crooked path
Led us traverse into the ridge's side,
Where more than half the sloping edge expires.
Refulgent gold, and silver thrice refined,
And scarlet grain and ceruse, Indian wood
Of lucid dye serene, fresh emeralds
But newly broken, by the herbs and flowers
Placed in that fair recess, in colour all
Had been surpass'd, as great surpasses less.
Nor nature only there lavish'd her hues,
But of the sweetness of a thousand smells
A rare and undistinguish'd fragrance made.

   "Salve Regina," on the grass and flowers,
Here chanting, I beheld those spirits sit,
Who not beyond the valley could be seen.

   "Before the westering sun sink to his bed,"
Began the Mantuan, who our steps had turn'd,
"'Mid those, desire not that I lead ye on.
For from this eminence ye shall discern
Better the acts and visages of all,
Than, in the nether vale, among them mix'd.
He, who sits high above the rest, and seems
To have neglected that he should have done,

"Salve Regina," on the grass and flowers,
Here chanting, I beheld those spirits sit,
Who not beyond the valley could be seen.

Canto VII., lines 82-84.

P. P.—13.

Hearing the air cut by their verdant plumes,
The serpent fled; and, to their stations, back
The angels up return'd with equal flight.

Canto VIII., lines 105–107.

And to the others' song moves not his lip,
The Emperor Rodolph call, who might have heal'd
The wounds whereof fair Italy hath died,
So that by others she revives but slowly.
He, who with kindly visage comforts him,
Sway'd in that country, where the water springs,
That Moldaw's river to the Elbe, and Elbe
Rolls to the ocean: Ottocar his name:
Who in his swaddling clothes was of more worth
Than Winceslaus his son, a bearded man,
Pamper'd with rank luxuriousness and ease.
And that one with the nose deprest, who close
In counsel seems with him of gentle look,
Flying expired, withering the lily's flower.
Look there, how he doth knock against his breast.
The other ye behold, who for his cheek
Makes of one hand a couch, with frequent sighs.
They are the father and the father-in-law
Of Gallia's bane: his vicious life they know
And foul; thence comes the grief that rends them thus.

"He, so robust of limb, who measure keeps
In song with him of feature prominent,
With every virtue bore his girdle braced.
And if that stripling, who behind him sits,
King after him had lived, his virtue then
From vessel to like vessel had been pour'd;
Which may not of the other heirs be said.
By James and Frederick his realms are held;
Neither the better heritage obtains.
Rarely into the branches of the tree
Doth human worth mount up: and so ordains
He who bestows it, that as his free gift
It may be call'd. To Charles my words apply
No less than to his brother in the song;

Which Pouille and Provence now with grief confess.
So much that plant degenerates from its seed,
As, more than Beatrix and Margaret,
Costanza still boasts of her valorous spouse.

"Behold the king of simple life and plain,
Harry of England sitting there alone:
He through his branches better issue spreads.

"That one, who, on the ground, beneath the rest,
Sits lowest, yet his gaze directs aloft,
Is William, that brave Marquis, for whose cause,
The deed of Alexandria and his war
Makes Montferrat and Canavese weep."

CANTO VIII.

ARGUMENT.

Two angels, with flaming swords broken at the points, descend to keep watch over the valley, into which Virgil and Dante entering by desire of Sordello, our Poet meets with joy the spirit of Nino, the judge of Gallura, one who was well known to him. Meantime three exceedingly bright stars appear near the pole, and a serpent creeps subtly into the valley, but flees at hearing the approach of those angelic guards. Lastly, Conrad Malaspina predicts to our Poet his future banishment.

NOW was the hour that wakens fond desire
In men at sea, and melts their thoughtful heart
Who in the morn have bid sweet friends farewell,
And pilgrim newly on his road with love
Thrills, if he hear the vesper bell from far
That seems to mourn for the expiring day:
When I, no longer taking heed to hear,
Began, with wonder, from those spirits to mark
One risen from its seat, which with its hand
Audience implored. Both palms it join'd and raised,
Fixing its stedfast gaze toward the east,
As telling God, "I care for nought beside."

"Te Lucis Ante," so devoutly then
Came from its lip, and in so soft a strain,
That all my sense in ravishment was lost.
And the rest after, softly and devout,
Follow'd through all the hymn, with upward gaze
Directed to the bright supernal wheels.

Here, reader! for the truth make thine eyes keen:
For of so subtle texture is this veil,
That thou with ease mayst pass it through unmark'd.

I saw that gentle band silently next
Look up, as if in expectation held,
Pale and in lowly guise; and from on high,

THE VISION.

I saw, forth issuing descend beneath,
Two angels, with two flame-illumined swords,
Broken and mutilated of their points.
Green as the tender leaves but newly born,
Their vesture was, the which, by wings as green
Beaten, they drew behind them, fann'd in air.
A little over us one took his stand;
The other lighted on the opposing hill;
So that the troop were in the midst contain'd.

    Well I descried the whiteness on their heads:
But in their visages the dazzled eye
Was lost, as faculty that by too much
Is overpower'd. "From Mary's bosom both
Are come," exclaim'd Sordello, "as a guard
Over the vale, 'gainst him, who hither tends,
The serpent." Whence, not knowing by which path
He came, I turn'd me round; and closely press'd,
All frozen, to my leader's trusted side.

    Sordello paused not: "To the valley now
(For it is time) let us descend; and hold
Converse with those great shadows: haply much
Their sight may please ye." Only three steps down
Methinks I measured, ere I was beneath,
And noted one who look'd as with desire
To know me. Time was now that air grew dim;
Yet not so dim, that, 'twixt his eyes and mine,
It clear'd not up what was conceal'd before.
Mutually towards each other we advanced.
Nino, thou courteous judge! what joy I felt,
When I perceived thou wert not with the bad.

    No salutation kind on either part
Was left unsaid. He then inquired: "How long,
Since thou arrived'st at the mountain's foot,
Over the distant waves?"—"Oh!" answer'd I,

PURGATORY.—CANTO VIII.

"Through the sad seats of woe this morn I came;
And still in my first life, thus journeying on,
The other strive to gain." Soon as they heard
My words, he and Sordello backward drew,
As suddenly amazed. To Virgil one,
The other to a spirit turn'd, who near
Was seated, crying: "Conrad! up with speed:
Come, see what of his grace high God hath will'd."
Then turning round to me: "By that rare mark
Of honour, which thou owest to him, who hides
So deeply his first cause it hath no ford;
When thou shalt be beyond the vast of waves,
Tell my Giovanna, that for me she call
There, where reply to innocence is made.
Her mother, I believe, loves me no more;
Since she has changed the white and wimpled folds,
Which she is doom'd once more with grief to wish.
By her it easily may be perceived,
How long in woman lasts the flame of love,
If sight and touch do not relume it oft.
For her so fair a burial will not make
The viper, which calls Milan to the field,
As had been made by shrill Gallura's bird."

He spoke, and in his visage took the stamp
Of that right zeal, which with due temperature
Glows in the bosom, My insatiate eyes
Meanwhile to heaven had travel'd, even there
Where the bright stars are slowest, as a wheel
Nearest the axle; when my guide inquired:
"What there aloft, my son, has caught thy gaze?"

I answered: "The three torches, with which here
The pole is all on fire." He then to me:
"The four resplendent stars, thou saw'st this morn,
Are there beneath; and these, risen in their stead."

THE VISION.

    While yet he spoke, Sordello to himself
Drew him, and cried: "Lo there our enemy!"
And with his hand pointed that way to look.
    Along the side, where barrier none arose
Around the little vale, a serpent lay,
Such haply as gave Eve the bitter food.
Between the grass and flowers, the evil snake
Came on, reverting oft his lifted head;
And, as a beast that smooths its polish'd coat,
Licking his back. I saw not, nor can tell,
How those celestial falcons from their seat
Moved, but in motion each one well descried.
Hearing the air cut by their verdant plumes,
The serpent fled; and, to their stations, back
The angels up return'd with equal flight.
    The spirit, (who to Nino, when he call'd,
Had come,) from viewing me with fixed ken,
Through all that conflict, loosen'd not his sight.
    "So may the lamp, which leads thee up on high,
Find, in thy free resolve, of wax so much,
As may suffice thee to the enamel'd height,"
It thus began: "If any certain news
Of Valdimagra and the neighbour part
Thou know'st, tell me, who once was mighty there.
They call'd me Conrad Malaspina; not
That old one; but from him I sprang. The love
I bore my people is now here refined."
    "In your domains," I answer'd, "ne'er was I.
But, through all Europe, where do those men dwell,
To whom their glory is not manifest?
The fame, that honours your illustrious house,
Proclaims the nobles, and proclaims the land;
So that he knows it, who was never there.
I swear to you, so may my upward route

Prosper, your honour'd nation not impairs
The value of her coffer and her sword.
Nature and use give her such privilege,
That while the world is twisted from his course
By a bad head, she only walks aright,
And has the evil way in scorn." He then:
"Now pass thee on: seven times the tired sun
Revisits not the couch, which with four feet
The forked Aries covers, ere that kind
Opinion shall be nail'd into thy brain
With stronger nails than others' speech can drive;
If the sure course of judgment be not stay'd."

CANTO IX.

ARGUMENT.

Dante is carried up the mountain, asleep and dreaming, by Lucia; and, on wakening, finds himself, two hours after sunrise, with Virgil, near the gate of Purgatory, through which they are admitted by the angel deputed by St. Peter to keep it.

NOW the fair consort of Tithonus old,
    Arisen from her mate's beloved arms,
    Look'd palely o'er the eastern cliff; her brow,
Lucent with jewels, glitter'd, set in sign
Of that chill animal, who with his train
Smites fearful nations: and where then we were,
Two steps of her ascent the night had past;
And now the third was closing up its wing,
When I, who had so much of Adam with me,
Sank down upon the grass, o'ercome with sleep,
There where all five were seated. In that hour,
When near the dawn the swallow her sad lay,
Remembering haply ancient grief, renews;
And when our minds, more wanderers from the flesh,
And ·less by thought restrain'd, are, as 'twere, full
Of holy divination in their dreams;
Then, in a vision, did I seem to view
A golden-feather'd eagle in the sky,
With open wings, and hovering for descent;
And I was in that place, methought, from whence
Young Ganymede, from his associates 'reft,
Was snatch'd aloft to the high consistory.
"Perhaps," thought I within me, "here alone
He strikes his quarry, and elsewhere disdains
To pounce upon the prey." Therewith, it seem'd,
A little wheeling in his aëry tour,

P. P.—14. Now the fair consort of Tithonus old,
Arisen from her mate's beloved arms,
Look'd palely o'er the eastern cliff.

Canto IX., lines 1–3.

There both, I thought, the eagle and myself
Did burn; and so intense the imagined flames,
That needs my sleep was broken off.

Canto IX., lines 29-31.

In visage such, as past my power to bear.

Canto IX., line 74.

The wretch appear'd amid all these to say:
"Grant vengeance, Sire! for, woe beshrew this heart,
My son is murder'd."

Canto X., lines 74-76.

Terrible as the lightning, rush'd he down,
And snatch'd me upward even to the fire.
There both, I thought, the eagle and myself
Did burn; and so intense the imagined flames,
That needs my sleep was broken off. As erst
Achilles shook himself, and round he roll'd
His waken'd eyeballs, wondering where he was,
Whenas his mother had from Chiron fled
To Scyros, with him sleeping in her arms;
(There whence the Greeks did after sunder him;)
E'en thus I shook me, soon as from my face
The slumber parted, turning deadly pale,
Like one ice-struck with dread. Sole at my side
My comfort stood: and the bright sun was now
More than two hours aloft: and to the sea
My looks were turn'd. "Fear not," my master cried,
"Assured we are at happy point. Thy strength
Shrink not, but rise dilated. Thou art come
To Purgatory now. Lo! there the cliff
That circling bounds it. Lo! the entrance there,
Where it doth seem disparted. Ere the dawn
Usher'd the day-light, when thy wearied soul
Slept in thee, o'er the flowery vale beneath
A lady came, and thus bespake me; 'I
Am Lucia. Suffer me to take this man,
Who slumbers. Easier so his way shall speed.'
Sordello and the other gentle shapes
Tarrying, she bare thee up; and, as day shone,
This summit reach'd: and I pursued her steps.
Here did she place thee. First, her lovely eyes
That open entrance show'd me; then at once
She vanish'd with thy sleep." Like one, whose doubts
Are chased by certainty, and terror turn'd
To comfort on discovery of the truth,

Such was the change in me: and as my guide
Beheld me fearless, up along the cliff
He moved, and I behind him, towards the height.

    Reader! thou markest how my theme doth rise;
Nor wonder therefore, if more artfully
I prop the structure. Nearer now we drew,
Arrived whence, in that part, where first a breach
As of a wall appear'd, I could descry
A portal, and three steps beneath, that led
For inlet there, of different colour each;
And one who watch'd, but spake not yet a word.
As more and more mine eye did stretch its view,
I mark'd him seated on the highest step,
In visage such, as past my power to bear.
Grasp'd in his hand, a naked sword glanced back
The rays so towards me, that I oft in vain
My sight directed. "Speak, from whence ye stand;"
He cried: "What would ye? Where is your escort?
Take heed your coming upward harm ye not."

    "A heavenly dame, not skilless of these things,"
Replied the instructor, "told us, even now,
'Pass that way: here the gate is.'"—"And may she,
Befriending, prosper your ascent," resumed
The courteous keeper of the gate: "Come then
Before our steps." We straightway thither came.

    The lowest stair was marble white, so smooth
And polish'd, that therein my mirror'd form
Distinct I saw. The next of hue more dark
Than sablest grain, a rough and singed block,
Crack'd lengthwise and across. The third, that lay
Massy above, seem'd porphyry, that flamed
Red as the life-blood spouting from a vein.
On this God's angel either foot sustain'd,
Upon the threshold seated, which appear'd

A rock of diamond. Up the trinal steps
My leader cheerly drew me. "Ask," said he,
"With humble heart, that he unbar the bolt."

    Piously at his holy feet devolved
I cast me, praying him for pity's sake
That he would open to me; but first fell
Thrice on my bosom prostrate. Seven times
The letter, that denotes the inward stain,
He, on my forehead, with the blunted point
Of his drawn sword, inscribed. And "Look," he cried,
"When enter'd, that thou wash these scars away."

    Ashes, or earth ta'en dry out of the ground,
Were of one colour with the robe he wore.
From underneath that vestment forth he drew
Two keys, of metal twain: the one was gold,
Its fellow silver. With the pallid first,
And next the burnish'd, he so ply'd the gate,
As to content me well. "Whenever one
Faileth of these, that in the key-hole straight
It turn not, to this alley then expect
Access in vain." Such were the words he spake.
"One is more precious: but the other needs
Skill and sagacity, large share of each,
Ere its good task to disengage the knot
Be worthily perform'd. From Peter these
I hold, of him instructed that I err
Rather in opening, than in keeping fast;
So but the suppliant at my feet implore."

    Then of that hallow'd gate he thrust the door,
Exclaiming, "Enter, but this warning hear:
He forth again departs who looks behind."

    As in the hinges of that sacred ward
The swivels turn'd, sonorous metal strong,
Harsh was the grating; nor so surlily

THE VISION.

Roar'd the Tarpeian, when by force bereft
Of good Metellus, thenceforth from his loss
To leanness doom'd. Attentively I turn'd,
Listening the thunder that first issued forth;
And "We praise thee, O God," methought I heard,
In accents blended with sweet melody.
The strains came o'er mine ear, e'en as the sound
Of choral voices, that in solemn chant
With organ mingle, and, now high and clear
Come swelling, now float indistinct away.

CANTO X.

ARGUMENT.

Being admitted at the gate of Purgatory, our Poets ascend a winding path up the rock till they reach an open and level space that extends each way round the mountain. On the side that rises, and which is of white marble, are seen artfully engraven many stories of humility, which whilst they are contemplating, there approach the souls of those who expiate the sin of pride, and who are bent down beneath the weight of heavy stones.

WHEN we had past the threshold of the gate,
(Which the soul's ill affection doth disuse,
Making the crooked seem the straighter path,)
I heard its closing sound. Had mine eyes turn'd,
For that offence what plea might have avail'd?
    We mounted up the riven rock, that wound
On either side alternate, as the wave
Flies and advances. "Here some little art
Behoves us," said my leader, "that our steps
Observe the varying flexure of the path."
    Thus we so slowly sped, that with cleft orb
The moon once more o'erhangs her watery couch,
Ere we that strait have threaded. But when free,
We came, and open, where the mount above
One solid mass retires; I spent with toil,
And both uncertain of the way, we stood,
Upon a plain more lonesome than the roads
That traverse desert wilds. From whence the brink
Borders upon vacuity, to foot
Of the steep bank that rises still, the space
Had measured thrice the stature of a man:
And, distant as mine eye could wing its flight,
To leftward now and now to right dispatch'd,
That cornice equal in extent appear'd.
    Not yet our feet had on that summit moved
When I discover'd that the bank, around,

Whose proud uprising all ascent denied,
Was marble white; and so exactly wrought
With quaintest sculpture, that not there alone
Had Polycletus, but e'en nature's self
Been shamed. The angel (who came down to earth
With tidings of the peace so many years
Wept for in vain, that oped the heavenly gates
From their long interdict) before us seem'd,
In a sweet act, so sculptured to the life,
He look'd no silent image. One had sworn
He had said " Hail!" for she was imaged there,
By whom the key did open to God's love;
And in her act as sensibly imprest
That word, "Behold the handmaid of the Lord,"
As figure seal'd on wax. "Fix not thy mind
On one place only," said the guide beloved,
Who had me near him on that part where lies
The heart of man. My sight forthwith I turn'd,
And mark'd, behind the virgin mother's form,
Upon that side where he that moved me stood,
Another story graven on the rock.

 I past athwart the bard, and drew me near,
That it might stand more aptly for my view.
There, in the self-same marble, were engraved
The cart and kine, drawing the sacred ark,
That from unbidden office awes mankind.
Before it came much people; and the whole
Parted in seven quires. One sense cried "Nay,"
Another, "Yes, they sing." Like doubt arose
Betwixt the eye and smell, from the curl'd fume
Of incense breathing up the well-wrought toil.
Preceding the blest vessel, onward came,
With light dance leaping, girt in humble guise,
Israel's sweet harper: in that hap he seem'd

Less, and yet more, than kingly. Opposite,
At a great palace, from the lattice forth
Look'd Michol, like a lady full of scorn
And sorrow. To behold the tablet next,
Which, at the back of Michol, whitely shone,
I moved me. There, was storied on the rock
The exalted glory of the Roman prince,
Whose mighty worth moved Gregory to earn
His mighty conquest, Trajan the Emperor.
A widow at his bridle stood, attired
In tears and mourning. Round about them troop'd
Full throng of knights; and overhead in gold
The eagles floated, struggling with the wind.
The wretch appear'd amid all these to say:
"Grant vengeance, Sire! for, woe beshrew this heart,
My son is murder'd." He replying seem'd:
"Wait now till I return." And she, as one
Made hasty by her grief: "O Sire! if thou
Dost not return?"—"Where I am, who then is,
May right thee."—"What to thee is other's good,
If thou neglect thy own?"—"Now comfort thee;"
At length he answers. "It beseemeth well
My duty be perform'd, ere I move hence:
So justice wills; and pity bids me stay."

  He, whose ken nothing new surveys, produced
That visible speaking, new to us and strange,
The like not found on earth. Fondly I gazed
Upon those patterns of meek humbleness,
Shapes yet more precious for their artist's sake;
When "Lo!" the Poet whisper'd, "where this way
(But slack their pace) a multitude advance.
These to the lofty steps shall guide us on."

  Mine eyes, though bent on view of novel sights,
Their loved allurement, were not slow to turn.

THE VISION.

    Reader! I would not that amazed thou miss
Of thy good purpose, hearing how just God
Decrees our debts be cancel'd. Ponder not
The form of suffering. Think on what succeeds:
Think that, at worst, beyond the mighty doom
It cannot pass. "Instructor!" I began,
"What I see hither tending, bears no trace
Of human semblance, nor of aught beside
That my foil'd sight can guess." He answering thus:
"So curb'd to earth, beneath their heavy terms
Of torment stoop they, that mine eye at first
Struggled as thine. But look intently thither;
And disentangle with thy labouring view,
What, underneath those stones, approacheth: now,
E'en now, mayst thou discern the pangs of each."

    Christians and proud! O poor and wretched ones!
That, feeble in the mind's eye, lean your trust
Upon unstaid perverseness: know ye not
That we are worms, yet made at last to form
The winged insect, imp'd with angel plumes,
That to heaven's justice unobstructed soars?
Why buoy ye up aloft your unfledged souls?
Abortive then and shapeless ye remain,
Like the untimely embryon of a worm.

    As, to support incumbent floor or roof,
For corbel, is a figure sometimes seen,
That crumples up its knees unto its breast;
With the feign'd posture, stirring ruth unfeign'd
In the beholder's fancy; so I saw
These fashion'd, when I noted well their guise.

    Each, as his back was laden, came indeed
Or more or less contracted; and it seem'd
As he, who show'd most patience in his look,
Wailing exclaim'd: "I can endure no more."

CANTO XI.

ARGUMENT.

After a prayer uttered by the spirits who were spoken of in the last Canto, Virgil inquires the way upwards, and is answered by one, who declares himself to have been Omberto, son of the Count of Santafiore. Next our Poet distinguishes Oderigi, the illuminator, who discourses on the vanity of worldly fame, and points out to him the soul of Provenzano Salvani.

"O THOU Almighty Father! who dost make
The heavens thy dwelling, not in bounds confined,
But that, with love intenser, there thou view'st
Thy primal effluence; hallow'd be thy name:
Join, each created being, to extol
Thy might; for worthy humblest thanks and praise
Is thy blest Spirit. May thy kingdom's peace
Come unto us; for we, unless it come,
With all our striving, thither tend in vain.
As, of their will, the angels unto thee
Tender meet sacrifice, circling thy throne
With loud hosannas; so of theirs be done
By saintly men on earth. Grant us, this day,
Our daily manna, without which he roams
Through this rough desert retrograde, who most
Toils to advance his steps. As we to each
Pardon the evil done us, pardon thou
Benign, and of our merit take no count.
'Gainst the old adversary, prove thou not
Our virtue, easily subdued; but free
From his incitements, and defeat his wiles.
This last petition, dearest Lord! is made
Not for ourselves; since that were needless now:
But for their sakes who after us remain."

Thus for themselves and us good speed imploring,
Those spirits went beneath a weight like that
We sometimes feel in dreams; all, sore beset,
But with unequal anguish; wearied all;
Round the first circuit; purging as they go
The world's gross darkness off. In our behoof
If their vows still be offer'd, what can here
For them be vow'd and done by such, whose wills
Have root of goodness in them? Well beseems
That we should help them wash away the stains
They carried hence; that so, made pure and light,
They may spring upward to the starry spheres.

"Ah! so may mercy-temper'd justice rid
Your burdens speedily; that ye have power
To stretch your wing, which e'en to your desire
Shall lift you; as ye show us on which hand
Toward the ladder leads the shortest way.
And if there be more passages than one,
Instruct us of that easiest to ascend:
For this man, who comes with me, and bears yet
The charge of fleshy raiment Adam left him,
Despite his better will, but slowly mounts."
From whom the answer came unto these words,
Which my guide spake, appear'd not; but 'twas said,
"Along the bank to rightward come with us;
And ye shall find a pass that mocks not toil
Of living man to climb: and were it not
That I am hinder'd by the rock, wherewith
This arrogant neck is tamed, whence needs I stoop
My visage to the ground; him, who yet lives,
Whose name thou speak'st not, him I fain would view;
To mark if e'er I knew him, and to crave
His pity for the fardel that I bear.
I was of Latium; of a Tuscan born,

A mighty one; Aldobrandesco's name,
My sire's, I know not if ye e'er have heard.
My old blood and forefathers' gallant deeds
Made me so haughty, that I clean forgot
The common mother; and to such excess
Wax'd in my scorn of all men, that I fell,
Fell therefore; by what fate, Sienna's sons,
Each child in Campagnatico, can tell.
I am Omberto: not me, only, pride
Hath injured, but my kindred all involved
In mischief with her. Here my lot ordains
Under this weight to groan, till I appease
God's angry justice, since I did it not
Amongst the living, here amongst the dead."

 Listening I bent my visage down: and one
(Not he who spake) twisted beneath the weight
That urged him, saw me, knew me straight, and call'd;
Holding his eyes with difficultly fix'd
Intent upon me, stooping as I went
Companion of their way. "O!" I exclaim'd,
"Art thou not Oderigi? art not thou
Agobbio's glory, glory of that art
Which they of Paris call the limner's skill?"

 "Brother!" said he, "with tints, that gayer smile,
Bolognian Franco's pencil lines the leaves.
His all the honour now; my light obscured.
In truth, I had not been thus courteous to him
The whilst I lived, through eagerness of zeal
For that pre-eminence my heart was bent on.
Here, of such pride, the forfeiture is paid.
Nor were I even here, if, able still
To sin, I had not turn'd me unto God.
O powers of man! how vain your glory, nipt
E'en in its height of verdure, if an age

Less bright succeed not. Cimabue thought
To lord it over painting's field; and now
The cry is Giotto's, and his name eclipsed.
Thus hath one Guido from the other snatch'd
The letter'd prize: and he, perhaps, is born,
Who shall drive either from their nest. The noise
Of worldly fame is but a blast of wind,
That blows from diverse points, and shifts its name,
Shifting the point it blows from. Shalt thou more
Live in the mouths of mankind, if thy flesh
Part shrivel'd from thee, than if thou hadst died
Before the coral and the pap were left;
Or e'er some thousand years have past? and that
Is, to eternity compared, a space
Briefer than is the twinkling of an eye
To the heaven's slowest orb. He there, who treads
So leisurely before me, far and wide
Through Tuscany resounded once; and now
Is in Sienna scarce with whispers named:
There was he sovereign, when destruction caught
The maddening rage of Florence, in that day
Proud as she now is loathsome. Your renown
Is as the herb, whose hue doth come and go;
And his might withers it, by whom it sprang
Crude from the lap of earth." I thus to him:
"True are thy sayings: to my heart they breathe
The kindly spirit of meekness, and allay
What tumours rankle there. But who is he,
Of whom thou spakest but now?" "This," he replied,
"Is Provenzano. He is here, because
He reach'd with grasp presumptuous at the sway
Of all Sienna. Thus he still hath gone,
Thus goeth never-resting, since he died.
Such is the acquittance render'd back of him,

Who, in the mortal life, too much hath dared."
I then: "If soul, that to life's verge delays
Repentance, linger in that lower space,
Nor hither mount (unless good prayers befriend),
Or ever time, long as it lived, be past;
How chanced admittance was vouchsafed to him?"

"When at his glory's topmost height," said he,
"Respect of dignity all cast aside,
Freely he fix'd him on Sienna's plain,
A suitor to redeem his suffering friend,
Who languish'd in the prison-house of Charles;
Nor, for his sake, refused through every vein
To tremble. More I will not say; and dark,
I know, my words are; but thy neighbours soon
Shall help thee to a comment on the text.
This is the work, that from these limits freed him."

CANTO XII.

ARGUMENT.

Dante being desired by Virgil to look down on the ground which they are treading, observes that it is wrought over with imagery exhibiting various instances of pride recorded in history and fable. They leave the first cornice, and are ushered to the next by an angel who points out the way.

WITH equal pace, as oxen in the yoke,
I, with that laden spirit, journey'd on,
Long as the mild instructor suffer'd me;
But, when he bade me quit him, and proceed
(For "Here," said he, "behoves with sail and oars
Each man, as best he may, push on his bark"),
Upright, as one disposed for speed, I raised
My body, still in thought submissive bow'd.
  I now my leader's track not loth pursued;
And each had shown how light we fared along,
When thus he warned me: "Bend thine eyesight down:
For thou, to ease the way, shalt find it good
To ruminate the bed beneath thy feet."
  As, in memorial of the buried, drawn
Upon earth-level tombs, the sculptured form
Of what was once, appears (at sight whereof
Tears often stream forth, by remembrance waked,
Whose sacred stings the piteous often feel),
So saw I there, but with more curious skill
Of portraiture o'erwrought, whate'er of space
From forth the mountain stretches. On one part
Him I beheld, above all creatures erst
Created noblest, lightening fall from heaven:
On the other side, with bolt celestial pierced,
Briareus; cumbering earth he lay, through dint
Of mortal ice-stroke. The Thymbræan god,
With Mars, I saw, and Pallas, round their sire,

Arm'd still, and gazing on the giants' limbs
Strewn o'er the ethereal field. Nimrod I saw:
At foot of the stupendous work he stood,
As if bewilder'd, looking on the crowd
Leagued in his proud attempt on Sennaar's plain.

 O Niobe! in what a trance of woe
Thee I beheld, upon that highway drawn,
Seven sons on either side thee slain. O Saul!
How ghastly didst thou look, on thine own sword
Expiring, in Gilboa, from that hour
Ne'er visited with rain from heaven, or dew.

 O fond Arachne! thee I also saw,
Half spider now, in anguish, crawling up
The unfinish'd web thou weaved'st to thy bane.

 O Rehoboam! here thy shape doth seem
Louring no more defiance; but fear-smote,
With none to chase him, in his chariot whirl'd.

 Was shown beside upon the solid floor
How dear Alcmæon forced his mother rate
That ornament, in evil hour received:
How, in the temple, on Sennacherib fell
His sons, and how a corpse they left him there.
Was shown the scath, and cruel mangling made
By Tomyris on Cyrus, when she cried,
"Blood thou didst thirst for: take thy fill of blood."
Was shown how routed in the battle fled
The Assyrians, Holofernes slain, and e'en
The relics of the carnage. Troy I mark'd
In ashes and in caverns. Oh! how fallen,
How abject, Ilion, was thy semblance there.

 What master of the pencil or the style
Had traced the shades and lines, that might have made
The subtlest workman wonder? Dead, the dead;
The living seem'd alive: with clearer view,

His eye beheld not, who beheld the truth,
Than mine what I did tread on, while I went
Low bending. Now swell out, and with stiff necks
Pass on, ye sons of Eve! vale not your looks,
Lest they descry the evil of your path.

    I noted not (so busied was my thought)
How much we now had circled of the mount;
And of his course yet more the sun had spent;
When he, who with still wakeful caution went,
Admonish'd: "Raise thou up thy head: for know
Time is not now for slow suspense. Behold,
That way, an angel hasting towards us. Lo,
Where duly the sixth handmaid doth return
From service on the day. Wear thou, in look
And gesture, seemly grace of reverent awe;
That gladly he may forward us aloft.
Consider that this day ne'er dawns again."

    Time's loss he had so often warn'd me 'gainst,
I could not miss the scope at which he aim'd.

    The goodly shape approach'd us, snowy white
In vesture, and with visage casting streams
Of tremulous lustre like the matin star.
His arms he open'd, then his wings; and spake:
"Onward! the steps, behold, are near; and now
The ascent is without difficulty gain'd."

    A scanty few are they, who, when they hear
Such tidings, hasten. O ye race of men!
Though born to soar, why suffer ye a wind
So slight to baffle ye? He led us on
Where the rock parted; here, against my front,
Did beat his wings; then promised I should fare
In safety on my way. As to ascend
That steep, upon whose brow the chapel stands
(O'er Rubaconte, looking lordly down

P. P.—18.   With equal pace, as oxen in the yoke,
I, with that laden spirit, journey'd on,
Long as the mild instructor suffer'd me.

Canto XII., lines 1–3.

O fond Arachne! thee I also saw,
Half spider now, in anguish, crawling up
The unfinish'd web thou weaved'st to thy bane.

Canto XII., lines 39-41.

E'en thus the blind and poor,
Near the confessionals, to crave an alms,
Stand, each his head upon his fellow's sunk.

Canto XIII., lines 55-57.

"Who then, amongst us here aloft,
Hath brought thee, if thou weenest to return?"

Canto XIII., lines 129, 130.

On the well-guided city), up the right
The impetuous rise is broken by the steps
Carved in that old and simple age, when still
The registry and label rested safe;
Thus is the acclivity relieved, which here,
Precipitous, from the other circuit falls:
But, on each hand, the tall cliff presses close.

    As, entering, there we turn'd, voices, in strain
Ineffable, sang: "Blessed are the poor
In spirit." Ah! how far unlike to these
The straits of hell: here songs to usher us,
There shrieks of woe. We climb the holy stairs:
And lighter to myself by far I seem'd
Than on the plain before; whence thus I spake:
"Say, master, of what heavy thing have I
Been lighten'd; that scarce aught the sense of toil
Affects me journeying?" He in few replied:
"When sin's broad characters, that yet remain
Upon thy temples, though well nigh effaced,
Shall be, as one is, all clean razed out;
Then shall thy feet by heartiness of will
Be so o'ercome, they not alone shall feel
No sense of labour, but delight much more
Shall wait them, urged along their upward way."

    Then like to one, upon whose head is placed
Somewhat he deems not of, but from the becks
Of others, as they pass him by; his hand
Lends therefore help to assure him, searches, finds,
And well performs such office as the eye
Wants power to execute; so stretching forth
The fingers of my right hand, did I find
Six only of the letters, which his sword,
Who bare the keys, had traced upon my brow.
The leader, as he mark'd mine action, smiled.

CANTO XIII.

ARGUMENT.

They gain the second cornice, where the sin of envy is purged; and having proceeded a little to the right, they hear voices uttered by invisible spirits recounting famous examples of charity, and next behold the shades, or souls, of the envious clad in sackcloth, and having their eyes sewed up with an iron thread. Amongst these Danto finds Sapia, a Siennese lady, from whom he learns the cause of her being there.

WE reach'd the summit of the scale, and stood
  Upon the second buttress of that mount
  Which healeth him who climbs. A cornice there,
Like to the former, girdles round the hill;
Save that its arch, with sweep less ample, bends.
  Shadow, nor image there, is seen: all smooth
The rampart and the path, reflecting nought
But the rock's sullen hue. "If here we wait,
For some to question," said the bard, "I fear
Our choice may haply meet too long delay."
  Then fixedly upon the sun his eyes
He fasten'd; made his right the central point
From whence to move; and turn'd the left aside.
"O pleasant light, my confidence and hope!
Conduct us thou," he cried, "on this new way,
Where now I venture; leading to the bourn
We seek. The universal world to thee
Owes warmth and lustre. If no other cause
Forbid, thy beams should ever be our guide."
  Far, as is measured for a mile on earth,
In brief space had we journey'd; such prompt will
Impell'd: and towards us flying, now were heard
Spirits invisible, who courteously
Unto love's table bade the welcome guest.
The voice that first flew by, call'd forth aloud,
"They have no wine," so on behind us past,

PURGATORY.—CANTO XIII.

Those sounds reiterating, nor yet lost
In the faint distance, when another came
Crying, "I am Orestes," and alike
Wing'd its fleet way. "O father!" I exclaim'd,
"What tongues are these?" and as I question'd, lo!
A third exclaiming, "Love ye those have wrong'd you."

"This circuit," said my teacher, "knots the scourge
For envy; and the cords are therefore drawn
By charity's correcting hand. The curb
Is of a harsher sound; as thou shalt hear
(If I deem rightly) ere thou reach the pass,
Where pardon sets them free. But fix thine eyes
Intently through the air; and thou shalt see
A multitude before thee seated, each
Along the shelving grot." Then more than erst
I oped mine eyes; before me view'd; and saw
Shadows with garments dark as was the rock;
And when we pass'd a little forth, I heard
A crying, "Blessed Mary! pray for us,
Michael and Peter! all ye saintly host!"

I do not think there walks on earth this day
Man so remorseless, that he had not yearn'd
With pity at the sight that next I saw.
Mine eyes a load of sorrow teem'd, when now
I stood so near them, that their semblances
Came clearly to my view. Of sackcloth vile
Their covering seem'd; and, on his shoulder, one
Did stay another, leaning; and all lean'd
Against the cliff. E'en thus the blind and poor,
Near the confessionals, to crave an alms,
Stand, each his head upon his fellow's sunk;
So most to stir compassion, not by sound
Of words alone, but that which moves not less,
The sight of misery. And as never beam

Of noon-day visiteth the eyeless man,
E'en so was heaven a niggard unto these
Of his fair light: for through the orbs of all,
A thread of wire, impiercing, knits them up,
As for the taming of a haggard hawk.

    It were a wrong, methought, to pass and look
On others, yet myself the while unseen.
To my sage counsel therefore did I turn.
He knew the meaning of the mute appeal,
Nor waited for my questioning, but said:
"Speak, and be brief, be subtile in thy words."

    On that part of the cornice, whence no rim
Engarlands its steep fall, did Virgil come;
On the other side me were the spirits, their cheeks
Bathing devout with penitential tears,
That through the dread impalement forced a way.

    I turn'd me to them, and "O shades!" said I,
"Assured that to your eyes unveil'd shall shine
The lofty light, sole object of your wish,
So may heaven's grace clear whatsoe'er of foam
Floats turbid on the conscience, that thenceforth
The stream of mind roll limpid from its source;
As ye declare (for so shall ye impart
A boon I dearly prize) if any soul
Of Latium dwell among ye: and perchance
That soul may profit, if I learn so much."

    "My brother! we are, each one, citizens
Of one true city. Any, thou wouldst say,
Who lived a stranger in Italia's land."

    So heard I answering, as appear'd, a voice,
That onward came some space from whence I stood.

    A spirit I noted, in whose look was mark'd
Expectance. Ask ye how? The chin was raised
As in one reft of sight. "Spirit," said I,

"Who for thy rise art tutoring (if thou be
That which didst answer to me), or by place,
Or name, disclose thyself, that I may know thee."

"I was," it answer'd, "of Sienna: here
I cleanse away with these the evil life,
Soliciting with tears that He, who is,
Vouchsafe him to us. Though Sapia named,
In sapience I excell'd not; gladder far
Of other's hurt, than of the good befel me.
That thou mayst own I now deceive thee not
Hear, if my folly were not as I speak it.
When now my years sloped waning down the arch,
It so bechanced, my fellow-citizens
Near Colle met their enemies in the field;
And I pray'd God to grant what He had will'd.
There were they vanquish'd, and betook themselves
Unto the bitter passages of flight.
I mark'd the hunt; and waxing out of bounds
In gladness, lifted up my shameless brow,
And, like the merlin cheated by a gleam,
Cried, 'It is over. Heaven! I fear thee not.'
Upon my verge of life I wish'd for peace
With God; nor yet repentance had supplied
What I did lack of duty, were it not
The hermit Piero, touch'd with charity,
In his devout oraisons thought on me.
But who art thou that question'st of our state,
Who go'st, as I believe, with lids unclosed,
And breathest in thy talk?"—"Mine eyes," said I,
"May yet be here ta'en from me; but not long:
For they have not offended grievously
With envious glances. But the woe beneath
Urges my soul with more exceeding dread.
That nether load already weighs me down."

She thus: "Who then, amongst us here aloft,
Hath brought thee, if thou weenest to return?"
  "He," answered I, "who standeth mute beside me.
I live: of me ask therefore, chosen spirit!
If thou desire I yonder yet should move
For thee my mortal feet."—"Oh!" she replied,
"This is so strange a thing, it is great sign
That God doth love thee. Therefore with thy prayer
Sometime assist me: and, by that I crave,
Which most thou covetest, that if thy feet
E'er tread on Tuscan soil, thou save my fame
Amongst my kindred. Them shalt thou behold
With that vain multitude, who set their hope
On Telamone's haven; there to fail
Confounded, more than when the fancied stream
They sought, of Dian call'd: but they, who lead
Their navies, more than ruin'd hopes shall mourn."

CANTO XIV.

ARGUMENT.

Our Poet on this second cornice finds also the souls of Guido del Duca of Brettinoro, and Rinieri da Calboli of Romagna; the latter of whom, hearing that he comes from the banks of the Arno, inveighs against the degeneracy of all those who dwell in the cities visited by that stream; and the former, in like manner, against the inhabitants of Romagna. On leaving these, our Poets hear voices recording noted instances of envy,

"SAY, who is he around our mountain winds,
  Or ever death has pruned his wings for flight;
  That opes his eyes, and covers them at will?"
"I know not who he is, but know thus much;
He comes not singly. Do thou ask of him,
For thou art nearer to him; and take heed,
Accost him gently, so that he may speak."
  Thus on the right two spirits, bending each
Toward the other, talk'd of me; then both
Addressing me, their faces backward lean'd,
And thus the one began: "O soul, who yet
Pent in the body, tendest towards the sky!
For charity, we pray thee, comfort us;
Recounting whence thou comest, and who thou art:
For thou dost make us, at the favour shown thee,
Marvel, as at a thing that ne'er hath been."
  "There stretches through the midst of Tuscany,"
I straight began, "a brooklet, whose well-head
Springs up in Falterona; with his race
Not satisfied, when he some hundred miles
Hath measured. From his banks bring I this frame.
To tell you who I am were words mis-spent:
For yet my name scarce sounds on rumour's lip."
  "If well I do incorporate with my thought
The meaning of thy speech," said he, who first
Address'd me, "thou dost speak of Arno's wave."

THE VISION.

    To whom the other: "Why hath he conceal'd
The title of that river, as a man
Doth of some horrible thing?" The spirit, who
Thereof was question'd, did acquit him thus:
"I know not: but 'tis fitting well the name
Should perish of that vale; for from the source,
Where teems so plenteously the Alpine steep
Maim'd of Pelorus, (that doth scarcely pass
Beyond that limit,) even to the point
Where unto ocean is restored what heaven
Drains from the exhaustless store for all earth's streams.
Throughout the space is virtue worried down,
As 'twere a snake, by all, for mortal foe;
Or through disastrous influence on the place,
Or else distortion of misguided wills
That custom goads to evil: whence in those,
The dwellers in that miserable vale,
Nature is transform'd, it seems as they
Had shared of Circe's feeding. 'Midst brute swine,
Worthier of acorns than of other food
Created for man's use, he shapeth first
His obscure way; then, sloping onward, finds
Curs, snarlers more in spite than power, from whom
He turns with scorn aside: still journeying down,
By how much more the curst and luckless foss
Swells out to largeness, e'en so much it finds
Dogs turning into wolves. Descending still
Through yet more hollow eddies, next he meets
A race of foxes, so replete with craft,
They do not fear that skill can master it.
Nor will I cease because my words are heard
By other ears than thine. It shall be well
For this man, if he keep in memory
What from no erring spirit I reveal.

Lo! I behold thy grandson, that becomes
A hunter of those wolves, upon the shore
Of the fierce stream; and cows them all with dread.
Their flesh, yet living, sets he up to sale,
Then, like an aged beast, to slaughter dooms,
Many of life he reaves, himself of worth
And goodly estimation. Smear'd with gore,
Mark how he issues from the rueful wood;
Leaving such havoc, that in thousand years
It spreads not to prime lustihood again."

As one, who tidings hears of woe to come,
Changes his looks perturb'd, from whate'er part
The peril grasp him; so beheld I change
That spirit, who had turn'd to listen; struck
With sadness, soon as he had caught the word.

His visage, and the other's speech, did raise
Desire in me to know the names of both;
Whereof, with meek entreaty, I inquired.

The shade, who late address'd me, thus resumed:
"Thy wish imports, that I vouchsafe to do
For thy sake what thou wilt not do for mine.
But, since God's will is that so largely shine
His grace in thee, I will be liberal too.
Guido of Duca know then that I am.
Envy so parch'd my blood, that had I seen
A fellow-man made joyous, thou hadst mark'd
A livid paleness overspread my cheek.
Such harvest reap I of the seed I sow'd.
O man! why place thy heart where there doth need
Exclusion of participants in good?
This is Rinieri's spirit; this, the boast
And honour of the house of Calboli;
Where of his worth no heritage remains.
Nor his the only blood, that hath been stript

THE VISION.

('Twixt Po, the mount, the Reno, and the shore)
Of all that truth or fancy asks for bliss:
But, in those limits, such a growth has sprung
Of rank and venom'd roots, as long would mock
Slow culture's toil. Where is good Lizio? where
Manardi, Traversaro, and Carpigna?
O bastard slips of old Romagna's line!
When in Bologna the low artisan,
And in Faenza yon Bernardin sprouts,
A gentle cyon from ignoble stem.
Wonder not, Tuscan, if thou see me weep,
When I recall to mind those once loved names,
Guido of Prata, and of Azzo him
That dwelt with us; Tignoso and his troop,
With Traversaro's house and Anastagio's
(Each race disherited); and beside these,
The ladies and the knights, the toils and ease,
That witch'd us into love and courtesy,
Where now such malice reigns in recreant hearts.
O Brettinoro! wherefore tarriest still,
Since forth of thee thy family hath gone,
And many, hating evil, join'd their steps?
Well doeth he, that bids his lineage cease.
Bagnacavallo; Castracaro ill,
And Conio worse, who care to propagate
A race of Counties from such blood as theirs.
Well shall ye also do, Pagani, then
When from amongst you hies your demon child;
Not so, howe'er, that thenceforth there remain
True proof of what ye were. O Hugolin,
Thou sprung of Fantolini's line! thy name
Is safe; since more is look'd for after thee
To cloud its lustre, warping from thy stock.
But, Tuscan! go thy ways; for now I take

Far more delight in weeping, than in words.
Such pity for your sakes hath wrung my heart."

    We knew those gentle spirits, at parting, heard
Our steps. Their silence therefore, of our way,
Assured us. Soon as we had quitted them,
Advancing onward, lo! a voice, that seem'd
Like volley'd lightning, when it rives the air,
Met us, and shouted, "Whosoever finds
Will slay me;" then fled from us, as the bolt
Lanced sudden from a downward-rushing cloud.
When it had given short truce unto our hearing,
Behold the other with a crash as loud
As the quick-following thunder: "Mark in me
Aglauros, turn'd to rock." I, at the sound
Retreating, drew more closely to my guide.

    Now in mute stillness rested all the air;
And thus he spake: "There was the galling bit,
Which should keep man within his boundary.
But your old enemy so baits the hook,
He drags you eager to him. Hence nor curb
Avails you, nor reclaiming call. Heaven calls,
And, round about you wheeling, courts your gaze
With everlasting beauties. Yet your eye
Turns with fond doting still upon the earth.
Therefore He smites you who discerneth all."

CANTO XV.

ARGUMENT.

An angel invites them to ascend the next steep. On their way Dante suggests certain doubts, which are resolved by Virgil; and, when they reach the third cornice, where the sin of anger is purged, our Poet, in a kind of waking dream, beholds remarkable instances of patience; and soon after they are enveloped in a dense fog.

AS much as 'twixt the third hour's close and dawn,
    Appeareth of heaven's sphere, that ever whirls
    As restless as an infant in his play;
So much appear'd remaining to the sun
Of his slope journey towards the western goal.
    Evening was there, and here the noon of night;
And full upon our forehead smote the beams.
For round the mountain, circling, so our path
Had led us, that toward the sun-set now
Direct we journey'd; when I felt a weight
Of more exceeding splendour than before,
Press on my front. The cause unknown, amaze
Possess'd me! and both hands against my brows
Lifting, I interposed them, as a screen,
That of its gorgeous superflux of light
Clips the diminish'd orb. As when the ray,
Striking on water or the surface clear
Of mirror, leaps unto the opposite part,
Ascending at a glance, e'en as it fell, .
And as much differs from the stone, that falls
Through equal space (so practic skill hath shown);
Thus, with refracted light, before me seem'd
The ground there smitten: whence, in sudden haste,
My sight recoil'd. "What is this, sire beloved!
'Gainst which I strive to shield the sight in vain?"
Cried I, "and which toward us moving seems?"

"Marvel not, if the family of heaven,"
He answer'd, "yet with dazzling radiance dim
Thy sense. It is a messenger who comes,
Inviting man's ascent. Such sights ere long,
Not grievous, shall impart to thee delight,
As thy perception is by nature wrought
Up to their pitch." The blessed angel, soon
As we had reach'd him, hail'd us with glad voice:
"Here enter on a ladder far less steep
Than ye have yet encounter'd." We forthwith
Ascending, heard behind us chanted sweet
"Blessed the merciful," and "Happy thou,
That conquer'st." Lonely each, my guide and I,
Pursued our upward way; and as we went,
Some profit from his words I hoped to win,
And thus of him inquiring, framed my speech:
"What meant Romagna's spirit, when he spake
Of bliss exclusive, with no partner shared?"

    He straight replied: "No wonder, since he knows
What sorrow waits on his own worst defect,
If he chide others, that they less may mourn.
Because ye point your wishes at a mark,
Where, by communion of possessors, part
Is lessen'd, envy bloweth up men's sighs.
No fear of that might touch ye, if the love
Of higher sphere exalted your desire.
For there, by how much more they call it *ours*,
So much propriety of each in good
Increases more, and heighten'd charity
Wraps that fair cloister in a brighter flame."

    "Now lack I satisfaction more," said I,
"Than if thou hadst been silent at the first;
And doubt more gathers on my labouring thought.
How can it chance, that good distributed,

The many, that possess it, makes more rich,
Than if 'twere shared by few?" He answering thus:
"Thy mind, reverting still to things of earth,
Strikes darkness from true light. The highest good
Unlimited, ineffable, doth so speed
To love, as beam to lucid body darts,
Giving as much of ardour as it finds.
The sempiternal effluence streams abroad,
Spreading, wherever charity extends.
So that the more aspirants to that bliss
Are multiplied, more good is there to love,
And more is loved; as mirrors, that reflect,
Each unto other, propagated light.
If these my words avail not to allay
Thy thirsting, Beatrice thou shalt see,
Who of this want, and of all else thou hast,
Shall rid thee to the full. Provide but thou,
That from thy temples may be soon erased,
E'en as the two already, those five scars,
That, when they pain thee worst, then kindliest heal."

"Thou," I had said, "content'st me;" when I saw
The other round was gain'd, and wondering eyes
Did keep me mute. There suddenly I seem'd
By an ecstatic vision wrapt away;
And in a temple saw, methought, a crowd
Of many persons; and at the entrance stood
A dame, whose sweet demeanour did express
A mother's love, who said, "Child! why hast thou
Dealt with us thus? Behold thy sire and I
Sorrowing have sought thee;" and so held her peace;
And straight the vision fled. A female next
Appear'd before me, down whose visage coursed
Those waters, that grief forces out from one
By deep resentment stung, who seem'd to say:

"If thou, Pisistratus, be lord indeed
Over this city, named with such debate
Of adverse gods, and whence each science sparkles,
Avenge thee of those arms, whose bold embrace
Hath clasped our daughter;" and to her, meseem'd,
Benign and meek, with visage undisturb'd,
Her sovran spake: "How shall we those requite
Who wish us evil, if we thus condemn
The man that loves us?" After that I saw
A multitude, in fury burning, slay
With stones a stripling youth, and shout amain
"Destroy, destroy;" and him I saw, who bow'd
Heavy with death unto the ground, yet made
His eyes, unfolded upward, gates to heaven,
Praying forgiveness of the Almighty Sire,
Amidst that cruel conflict, on his foes,
With looks that win compassion to their aim.

Soon as my spirit, from her airy flight
Returning, sought again the things whose truth
Depends not on her shaping, I observed
She had not roved to falsehood in her dreams.

Meanwhile the leader, who might see I moved
As one who struggles to shake off his sleep,
Exclaim'd: "What ails thee, that thou canst not hold
Thy footing firm; but more than half a league
Hast travel'd with closed eyes and tottering gait,
Like to a man by wine or sleep o'ercharged?"

"Beloved father! so thou deign," said I,
"To listen, I will tell thee what appear'd
Before me, when so fail'd my sinking steps,"

He thus: "Not if thy countenance were mask'd
With hundred vizards, could a thought of thine,
How small soe'er, elude me. What thou saw'st
Was shown, that freely thou mightst ope thy heart

THE VISION.

To the waters of peace, that flow diffused
From their eternal fountain. I not ask'd,
What ails thee? for such cause as he doth, who
Looks only with that eye, which sees no more,
When spiritless the body lies; but ask'd,
To give fresh vigour to thy foot. Such goads,
The slow and loitering need; that they be found
Not wanting, when their hour of watch returns."

   So on we journey'd, through the evening sky
Gazing intent, far onward as our eyes,
With level view, could stretch against the bright
Vespertine ray: and lo! by slow degrees
Gathering, a fog made towards us, dark as night.
There was no room for 'scaping; and that mist
Bereft us, both of sight and the pure air.

After that I saw
A multitude, in fury burning, slay
With stones a stripling youth, and shout amain
"Destroy, destroy."

Canto XV., lines 103–106.

"Now who art thou, that through our smoke dost cleave,
And speak'st of us, as thou thyself e'en yet
Dividedst time by calends?"

Canto XVI., lines 23–25.

"Long as 'tis lawful for me, shall my steps
Follow on thine; and since the cloudy smoke
Forbids the seeing, hearing in its stead
Shall keep us join'd."

Canto XVI., lines 32-35.

But not long
Slumber'd; for suddenly a multitude,
The steep already turning from behind,
Rush'd on.

Canto XVIII., lines 87-90.

CANTO XVI.

ARGUMENT.

As they proceed through the mist, they hear the voices of spirits praying. Marco Lombardo, one of these, points out to Dante the error of such as impute our actions to necessity; explains to him that man is endued with free will; and shows that much of human depravity results from the undue mixture of spiritual and temporal authority in rulers.

HELL'S dunnest gloom, or night unlustrous, dark,
Of every planet 'reft, and pall'd in clouds,
Did never spread before the sight a veil
In thickness like that fog, nor to the sense
So palpable and gross. Entering its shade,
Mine eyes endured not with unclosed lids;
Which marking, near me drew the faithful guide,
Offering me his shoulder for a stay.

As the blind man behind his leader walks,
Lest he should err, or stumble unawares
On what might harm him or perhaps destroy;
I journey'd through that bitter air and foul,
Still listening to my escort's warning voice,
"Look that from me thou part not." Straight I heard
Voices, and each one seem'd to pray for peace,
And for compassion, to the Lamb of God
That taketh sins away. Their prelude still
Was "Agnus Dei;" and through all the choir,
One voice, one measure ran, that perfect seem'd
The concord of their song. "Are these I hear
Spirits, O master?" I exclaim'd; and he,
"Thou aim'st aright: these loose the bonds of wrath."

"Now who art thou, that through our smoke dost cleave,
And speak'st of us, as thou thyself e'en yet
Dividedst time by calends?" So one voice
Bespake me; whence my master said, "Reply;
And ask, if upward hence the passage lead."

"O being! who doth make thee pure, to stand
Beautiful once more in thy Maker's sight;
Along with me: and thou shalt hear and wonder."
Thus I, whereto the spirit answering spake:
"Long as 'tis lawful for me, shall my steps
Follow on thine; and since the cloudy smoke
Forbids the seeing, hearing in its stead
Shall keep us join'd." I then forthwith began:
"Yet in my mortal swathing, I ascend
To higher regions; and am hither come
Thorough the fearful agony of hell.
And, if so largely God hath doled his grace,
That, clean beside all modern precedent,
He wills me to behold his kingly state;
From me conceal not who thou wast, ere death
Had loosed thee; but instruct me: and instruct
If rightly to the pass I tend; thy words
The way directing, as a safe escort."
"I was of Lombardy, and Marco call'd:
Not inexperienced of the world, that worth
I still affected, from which all have turn'd
The nerveless bow aside. Thy course tends right
Unto the summit;" and, replying thus,
He added, "I beseech thee pray for me,
When thou shalt come aloft." And I to him:
"Accept my faith for pledge I will perform
What thou requirest. Yet one doubt remains,
That wrings me sorely, if I solve it not.
Singly before it urged me, doubled now
By thine opinion, when I couple that
With one elsewhere declared; each strengthening other.
The world indeed is even so forlorn
Of all good, as thou speak'st it, and so swarms
With every evil. Yet, beseech thee, point

The cause out to me, that myself may see,
And unto others show it: for in heaven
One places it, and one on earth below."

Then heaving forth a deep and audible sigh,
"Brother!" he thus began, "the world is blind;
And thou in truth comest from it. Ye, who live,
Do so each cause refer to heaven above,
E'en as its motion, of necessity,
Drew with it all that moves. If this were so,
Free choice in you were none; nor justice would
There should be joy for virtue, woe for ill.
Your movements have their primal bent from heaven;
Not all: yet said I all; what then ensues?
Light have ye still to follow evil or good,
And of the will free power, which, if it stand
Firm and unwearied in Heaven's first essay,
Conquers at last, so it be cherished well,
Triumphant over all. To mightier force,
To better nature subject, ye abide
Free, not constrain'd by that which forms in you
The reasoning mind uninfluenced of the stars.
If then the present race of mankind err,
Seek in yourselves the cause, and find it there.
Herein thou shalt confess me no false spy.

"Forth from his plastic hand, who charm'd beholds
Her image ere she yet exist, the soul
Comes like a babe, that wantons sportively,
Weeping and laughing in its wayward moods;
As artless, and as ignorant of aught,
Save that her Maker being one who dwells
With gladness ever, willingly she turns
To whate'er yields her joy. Of some slight good
The flavour soon she tastes; and, snared by that,
With fondness she pursues it; if no guide

Recal, no rein direct her wandering course.
Hence it behoved, the law should be a curb;
A sovereign hence behoved, whose piercing view
Might mark at least the fortress and main tower
Of the true city. Laws indeed there are:
But who is he observes them? None; not he,
Who goes before, the shepherd of the flock,
Who chews the cud but doth not cleave the hoof.
Therefore the multitude, who see their guide
Strike at the very good they covet most,
Feed there and look no further. Thus the cause
Is not corrupted nature in yourselves,
But ill-conducting, that hath turn'd the world
To evil. Rome, that turn'd it unto good,
Was wont to boast two suns, whose several beams
Cast light on either way, the world's and God's.
One since hath quench'd the other; and the sword
Is grafted on the crook; and, so conjoin'd,
Each must perforce decline to worse, unawed
By fear of other. If thou doubt me, mark
The blade: each herb is judged of by its seed.
That land, through which Adice and the Po
Their waters roll, was once the residence
Of courtesy and valour, ere the day
That frown'd on Frederick; now secure may pass
Those limits, whosoe'er hath left, for shame,
To talk with good men, or come near their haunts.
Three aged ones are still found there, in whom
The old time chides the new: these deem it long
Ere God restore them to a better world:
The good Gherardo; of Palazzo he,
Conrad; and Guido of Castello, named
In Gallic phrase more fitly the plain Lombard.
On this at last conclude. The church of Rome,

Mixing two governments that ill assort,
Hath miss'd her footing, fallen into the mire,
And there herself and burden much defiled."

"O Marco!" I replied, "thine arguments
Convince me: and the cause I now discern,
Why of the heritage no portion came
To Levi's offspring. But resolve me this:
Who that Gherardo is, that as thou say'st
Is left a sample of the perish'd race,
And for rebuke to this untoward age?"

"Either thy words," said he, "deceive, or else
Are meant to try me; that thou, speaking Tuscan,
Appear'st not to have heard of good Gherardo;
The sole addition that, by which I know him;
Unless I borrow'd from his daughter Gaia
Another name to grace him. God be with you.
I bear you company no more. Behold
The dawn with white ray glimmering through the mist.
I must away—the angel comes—ere he
Appear." He said, and would not hear me more.

CANTO XVII.

ARGUMENT.

The Poet issues from that thick vapour; and soon after his fancy represents to him in lively portraiture some noted examples of anger. This imagination is dissipated by the appearance of an angel, who marshals them onward to the fourth cornice, on which the sin of gloominess or indifference is purged; and here Virgil shows him that this vice proceeds from a defect of love, and that all love can be only of two sorts, either natural, or of the soul; of which sorts the former is always right, but the latter may err either in respect of object or of degree.

CALL to remembrance, reader, if thou e'er
    Hast on an Alpine height been ta'en by cloud,
    Through which thou saw'st no better than the mole
Doth through opacous membrane; then, whene'er
The watery vapours dense began to melt
Into thin air, how faintly the sun's sphere
Seem'd wading through them: so thy nimble thought
May image, how at first I rebeheld
The sun, that bedward now his couch o'erhung.
    Thus, with my leader's feet still equaling pace
From forth that cloud I came, when now expired
The parting beams from off the nether shores.
    O quick and forgetive power! that sometimes dost
So rob us of ourselves, we take no mark
Though round about us thousand trumpets clang;
What moves thee, if the senses stir not? Light
Moves thee from heaven, spontaneous, self-inform'd;
Or, likelier, gliding down with swift illapse
By will divine. Portray'd before me came
The traces of her dire impiety,
Whose form was changed into the bird, that most
Delights itself in song: and here my mind
Was inwardly so wrapt, it gave no place
To aught that ask'd admittance from without.

Next shower'd into my fantasy a shape
As of one crucified, whose visage spake
Fell rancour, malice deep, wherein he died;
And round him Ahasuerus the great king;
Esther his bride; and Mordecai the just,
Blameless in word and deed. As of itself
That unsubstantial coinage of the brain
Burst, like a bubble, when the water fails
That fed it; in my vision straight uprose
A damsel weeping loud, and cried, "O queen!
O mother! wherefore has intemperate ire
Driven thee to loathe thy being? Not to lose
Lavinia, desperate thou hast slain thyself.
Now hast thou lost me. I am she, whose tears
Mourn, ere I fall, a mother's timeless end."

    E'en as a sleep breaks off, if suddenly
New radiance strike upon the closed lids,
The broken slumber quivering ere it dies;
Thus, from before me, sunk that imagery,
Vanishing, soon as on my face there struck
The light, outshining far our earthly beam.
As round I turn'd me to survey what place
I had arrived at, "Here ye mount:" exclaim'd
A voice, that other purpose left me none
Save will so eager to behold who spake,
I could not chuse but gaze. As 'fore the sun,
That weighs our vision down, and veils his form
In light transcendent, thus my virtue fail'd
Unequal. "This is Spirit from above,
Who marshals us our upward way, unsought;
And in his own light shrouds him. As a man
Doth for himself, so now is done for us.
For whoso waits imploring, yet sees need
Of his prompt aidance, sets himself prepared

For blunt denial, ere the suit be made.
Refuse we not to lend a ready foot
At such inviting: haste we to ascend,
Before it darken: for we may not then,
Till morn again return." So spake my guide;
And to one ladder both address'd our steps;
And the first stair approaching, I perceived
Near me as 'twere the waving of a wing,
That fann'd my face, and whisper'd: "Blessed they,
The peacemakers: they know not evil wrath."

    Now to such height above our heads were raised
The last beams, follow'd close by hooded night,
That many a star on all sides through the gloom
Shone out. "Why partest from me, O my strength?"
So with myself I communed; for I felt
My o'ertoil'd sinews slacken. We had reach'd
The summit, and were fix'd like to a bark
Arrived at land. And waiting a short space,
If aught should meet mine ear in that new round,
Then to my guide I turn'd, and said: "Loved sire!
Declare what guilt is on this circle purged.
If our feet rest, no need thy speech should pause."

    He thus to me: "The love of good, whate'er
Wanted of just proportion, here fulfils.
Here plies afresh the oar, that loiter'd ill.
But that thou mayst yet clearlier understand,
Give ear unto my words; and thou shalt cull
Some fruit may please thee well, from this delay.

    "Creator, nor created being, e'er,
My son," he thus began, "was without love,
Or natural, or the free spirit's growth.
Thou hast not that to learn. The natural still
Is without error: but the other swerves,
If on ill object bent, or through excess

Of vigour, or defect. While e'er it seeks
The primal blessings, or with measure due
The inferior, no delight, that flows from it,
Partakes of ill. But let it warp to evil,
Or with more ardour than behoves, or less,
Pursue the good; the thing created then
Works 'gainst its Maker. Hence thou must infer,
That love is germin of each virtue in ye,
And of each act no less, that merits pain.
Now since it may not be, but love intend
The welfare mainly of the thing it loves,
All from self-hatred are secure; and since
No being can be thought to exist apart,
And independent of the first, a bar
Of equal force restrains from hating that.

"Grant the distinction just; and it remains
The evil must be another's, which is loved.
Three ways such love is gender'd in your clay.
There is who hopes (his neighbour's worth deprest)
Pre-eminence himself; and covets hence,
For his own greatness, that another fall.
There is who so much fears the loss of power,
Fame, favour, glory (should his fellow mount
Above him), and so sickens at the thought,
He loves their opposite: and there is he,
Whom wrong or insult seems to gall and shame,
That he doth thirst for vengeance; and such needs
Must dote on other's evil. Here beneath,
This threefold love is mourn'd. Of the other sort
Be now instructed; that which follows good,
But with disorder'd and irregular course.

"All indistinctly apprehend a bliss,
On which the soul may rest; the hearts of all
Yearn after it; and to that wished bourn

All therefore strive to tend. If ye behold,
Or seek it, with a love remiss and lax:
This cornice, after just repenting, lays
Its penal torment on ye. Other good
There is, where man finds not his happiness:
It is not true fruition; not that blest
Essence, of every good the branch and root
The love too lavishly bestow'd on this,
Along three circles over us, is mourn'd.
Account of that division tripartite
Expect not, fitter for thine own research."

CANTO XVIII.

ARGUMENT.

Virgil discourses further concerning the nature of love. Then a multitude of spirits rush by; two of whom, in van of the rest, record instances of zeal and fervent affection, and another, who was abbot of San Zeno in Verona, declares himself to Virgil and Dante; and lastly follow other spirits, shouting forth memorable examples of the sin for which they suffer. The Poet, pursuing his meditations, falls into a dreamy slumber,

THE teacher ended, and his high discourse
Concluding, earnest in my looks inquired
If I appear'd content; and I, whom still
Unsated thirst to hear him urged, was mute,
Mute outwardly, yet inwardly I said:
"Perchance my too much questioning offends."
But he, true father, mark'd the secret wish
By diffidence restrain'd; and, speaking, gave
Me boldness thus to speak: "Master! my sight
Gathers so lively virtue from thy beams,
That all, thy words convey, distinct is seen.
Wherefore I pray thee, father, whom this heart
Holds dearest, thou wouldst deign by proof t' unfold
That love, from which, as from their source, thou bring'st
All good deeds and their opposite." He then:
"To what I now disclose be thy clear ken
Directed; and thou plainly shalt behold
How much those blind have err'd, who make themselves
The guides of men. The soul, created apt
To love, moves versatile which way soe'er
Aught pleasing prompts her, soon as she is waked
By pleasure into act. Of substance true
Your apprehension forms its counterfeit;
And, in you the ideal shape presenting,
Attacks the soul's regard. If she, thus drawn,
Incline toward it; love is that inclining,

And a new nature knit by pleasure in ye.
Then, as the fire points up, and mounting seeks
His birth-place and his lasting seat, e'en thus
Enters the captive soul into desire,
Which is a spiritual motion, that ne'er rests
Before enjoyment of the thing it loves,
Enough to show thee, how the truth from those
Is hidden, who aver all love a thing
Praise-worthy in itself; although perhaps
Its matter seem still good. Yet if the wax
Be good, it follows not the impression must."
   "What love is," I return'd, "thy words, O guide!
And my own docile mind, reveal. Yet thence
New doubts have sprung. For, from without, if love
Be offer'd to us, and the spirit knows
No other footing; tend she right or wrong,
Is no desert of hers." He answering thus:
"What reason here discovers, I have power
To show thee: that which lies beyond, expect
From Beatrice, faith not reason's task.
Spirit, substantial form, with matter join'd,
Not in confusion mix'd, hath in itself
Specific virtue of that union born,
Which is not felt except it work, nor proved
But through effect, as vegetable life
By the green leaf. From whence his intellect
Deduced its primal notices of things,
Man therefore knows not, or his appetites
Their first affections; such in you, as zeal
In bees to gather honey; at the first,
Volition, meriting nor blame nor praise.
But o'er each lower faculty supreme,
That, as she list, are summon'd to her bar,
Ye have that virtue in you, whose just voice

Uttereth counsel, and whose word should keep
The threshold of assent. Here is the source,
Whence cause of merit in you is derived;
E'en as the affections, good or ill, she takes,
Or severs, winnow'd as the chaff. Those men,
Who, reasoning, went to depth profoundest, mark'd
That innate freedom; and were thence induced
To leave their moral teaching to the world.
Grant then, that from necessity arise
All love that glows within you; to dismiss
Or harbour it, the power is in yourselves.
Remember, Beatrice, in her style,
Denominates free choice by eminence
The noble virtue; if in talk with thee
She touch upon that theme." The moon, well nigh
To midnight hour belated, made the stars
Appear to wink and fade; and her broad disk
Seem'd like a crag on fire, as up the vault
That course she journey'd, which the sun then warms;
When they of Rome behold him at his set
Betwixt Sardinia and the Corsic isle.
And now the weight, that hung upon my thought,
Was lighten'd by the aid of that clear spirit,
Who raiseth Andes above Mantua's name.
I therefore, when my questions had obtain'd
Solution plain and ample, stood as one
Musing in dreamy slumber; but not long
Slumber'd; for suddenly a multitude,
The steep already turning from behind,
Rush'd on. With fury and like random rout,
As echoing on their shores at midnight heard
Ismenus and Asopus, for his Thebes
If Bacchus' help were needed; so came these
Tumultuous, curving each his rapid step,

By eagerness impell'd of holy love.
    Soon they o'ertook us; with such swiftness moved
The mighty crowd. Two spirits at their head
Cried, weeping, "Blessed Mary sought with haste
The hilly region. Cæsar, to subdue
Ilerda, darted in Marseilles his sting,
And flew to Spain."—"Oh, tarry not: away!"
The others shouted; "let not time be lost
Through slackness of affection. Hearty zeal
To serve reanimates celestial grace."
    "O ye! in whom intenser fervency
Haply supplies, where lukewarm erst ye fail'd,
Slow or neglectful, to absolve your part
Of good and virtuous; this man, who yet lives
(Credit my tale, though strange), desires to ascend,
So morning rise to light us. Therefore say
Which hand leads nearest to the rifted rock."
    So spake my guide; to whom a shade return'd:
"Come after us, and thou shalt find the cleft.
We may not linger: such resistless will
Speeds our unwearied course. Vouchsafe us then
Thy pardon, if our duty seem to thee
Discourteous rudeness. In Verona I
Was abbot of San Zeno, when the hand
Of Barbarossa grasp'd Imperial sway,
That name ne'er utter'd without tears in Milan.
And there is he, hath one foot in his grave,
Who for that monastery ere long shall weep,
Ruing his power misused: for that his son,
Of body ill compact, and worse in mind,
And born in evil, he hath set in place
Of its true pastor." Whether more he spake,
Or here was mute, I know not: he had sped
E'en now so far beyond us. Yet thus much

I heard, and in remembrance treasured it.
    He then, who never fail'd me at my need,
Cried, "Hither turn. Lo! two with sharp remorse
Chiding their sin." In rear of all the troop
These shouted: "First they died, to whom the sea
Open'd, or ever Jordan saw his heirs:
And they, who with Æneas to the end
Endured not suffering, for their portion chose
Life without glory." Soon as they had fled
Past reach of sight, new thought within me rose
By others follow'd fast, and each unlike
Its fellow: till led on from thought to thought,
And pleasured with the fleeting train, mine eye
Was closed, and meditation changed to dream.

CANTO XIX.

ARGUMENT.

The Poet, after describing his dream, relates how, at the summoning of an angel, he ascends with Virgil to the fifth cornice, where the sin of avarice is cleansed, and where he finds Pope Adrian V.

IT was the hour, when of diurnal heat
   No reliques chafe the cold beams of the moon,
   O'erpower'd by earth, or planetary sway
Of Saturn; and the geomancer sees
His Greater Fortune up the east ascend,
Where grey dawn checkers first the shadowy cone;
When, 'fore me in my dream, a woman's shape
There came, with lips that stammer'd, eyes aslant,
Distorted feet, hands maim'd, and colour pale.
   I look'd upon her: and, as sunshine cheers
Limbs numb'd by nightly cold, e'en thus my look
Unloosed her tongue; next, in brief space, her form
Decrepit raised erect, and faded face
With love's own hue illumed. Recovering speech,
She forthwith, warbling, such a strain began,
That I, how loth soe'er, could scarce have held
Attention from the song. "I," thus she sang,
"I am the Syren, she, whom mariners
On the wide sea are wilder'd when they hear:
Such fulness of delight the listener feels.
I, from his course, Ulysses by my lay
Enchanted drew. Whoe'er frequents me once,
Parts seldom: so I charm him, and his heart
Contented knows no void." Or ere her mouth
Was closed, to shame her, at my side appear'd
A dame of semblance holy. With stern voice

"What aileth thee, that still thou look'st to earth?"
Began my leader; while the angelic shape
A little over us his station took.

Canto XIX., lines 51–53.

"Up," he exclaim'd, "brother! upon thy feet
Arise: err not: thy fellow servant I,
(Thine and all others,) of one Sovran Power.

Canto XIX., lines 131–133.

With wary steps and slow
We pass'd; and I attentive to the shades,
Whom piteously I heard lament and wail.

Canto XX., lines 17-19.

And who
Are those twain spirits, that escort thee there?
Be it not said thou scorn'st to talk with me.

Canto XXIII., line 47-49.

She utter'd: "Say, O Virgil! who is this?"
Which hearing, he approach'd, with eyes still bent
Toward that goodly presence: the other seized her,
And, her robes tearing, open'd her before,
And show'd the belly to me, whence a smell,
Exhaling loathsome, waked me. Round I turn'd
Mine eyes: and thus the teacher: "At the least
Three times my voice hath call'd thee. Rise, begone.
Let us the opening find where thou mayst pass."

    I straightway rose. Now day, pour'd down from high,
Fill'd all the circuits of the sacred mount;
And, as we journey'd, on our shoulder smote
The early ray. I follow'd, stooping low
My forehead, as a man, o'ercharged with thought,
Who bends him to the likeness of an arch
That midway spans the flood; when thus I heard,
"Come, enter here," in tone so soft and mild,
As never met the ear on mortal strand.

    With swan-like wings dispred and pointing up,
Who thus had spoken marshal'd us along,
Where, each side of the solid masonry,
The sloping walls retired; then moved his plumes,
And fanning us, affirm'd that those, who mourn,
Are blessed, for that comfort shall be theirs.

    "What aileth thee, that still thou look'st to earth?"
Began my leader; while the angelic shape
A little over us his station took.

    "New vision," I replied, "hath raised in me
Surmisings strange and anxious doubts, whereon
My soul intent allows no other thought
Or room, or entrance."—"Hast thou seen," said he,
"That old enchantress, her, whose wiles alone
The spirits o'er us weep for? Hast thou seen
How man may free him of her bonds? Enough.

Let thy heels spurn the earth; and thy raised ken
Fix on the lure, which heaven's eternal King
Whirls in the rolling spheres." As on his feet
The falcon first looks down, then to the sky
Turns, and forth stretches eager for the food,
That wooes him thither; so the call I heard:
So onward, far as the dividing rock
Gave way, I journey'd, till the plain was reach'd.

On the fifth circle when I stood at large,
A race appear'd before me, on the ground
All downward lying prone and weeping sore.
"My soul hath cleaved to the dust," I heard
With sighs so deep, they well nigh choked the words.

"O ye elect of God! whose penal woes
Both hope and justice mitigate, direct
Towards the steep rising our uncertain way."

"If ye approach secure from this our doom,
Prostration, and would urge your course with speed,
See that ye still to rightward keep the brink."

So them the bard besought; and such the words,
Beyond us some short space, in answer came.

I noted what remain'd yet hidden from them:
Thence to my liege's eyes mine eyes I bent,
And he, forthwith interpreting their suit,
Beckon'd his glad assent. Free then to act
As pleased me, I drew near, and took my stand
Over that shade whose words I late had mark'd,
And, "Spirit!" I said, "in whom repentant tears
Mature that blessed hour when thou with God
Shalt find acceptance, for a while suspend
For me that mightier care. Say who thou wast;
Why thus ye grovel on your bellies prone;
And if, in aught, ye wish my service there,
Whence living I am come." He answering spake:

"The cause why Heaven our back toward his cope
Reverses, shalt thou know: but me know first,
The successor of Peter, and the name
And title of my lineage, from that stream
That 'twixt Chiaveri and Siestri draws
His limpid waters through the lowly glen.
A month and little more by proof I learnt,
With what a weight that robe of sovereignty
Upon his shoulder rests, who from the mire
Would guard it; that each other fardel seems
But feathers in the balance. Late, alas!
Was my conversion: but, when I became
Rome's pastor, I discern'd at once the dream
And cozenage of life; saw that the heart
Rested not there, and yet no prouder height
Lured on the climber: wherefore, of that life
Nor more enamour'd, in my bosom love
Of purer being kindled. For till then
I was a soul in misery, alienate
From God, and covetous of all earthly things;
Now, as thou seest, here punish'd for my doting.
Such cleansing from the taint of avarice,
Do spirits, converted, need. This mount inflicts
No direr penalty. E'en as our eyes
Fasten'd below, nor e'er to loftier clime
Were lifted; thus hath justice level'd us,
Here on the earth. As avarice quench'd our love
Of good, without which is no working; thus
Here justice holds us prison'd, hand and foot
Chain'd down and bound, while heaven's just Lord shall please,
So long to tarry, motionless, outstretch'd."

    My knees I stoop'd, and would have spoke; but he,
Ere my beginning, by his ear perceived
I did him reverence; and "What cause," said he,

"Hath bow'd thee thus?"—"Compunction," I rejoin'd,
"And inward awe of your high dignity."
    "Up," he exclaim'd, "brother! upon thy feet
Arise; err not: thy fellow servant I
(Thine and all others'), of one Sovran Power.
If thou hast ever mark'd those holy sounds
Of gospel truth, 'nor shall be given in marriage,'
Thou mayst discern the reasons of my speech.
Go thy ways now; and linger here no more.
Thy tarrying is a let unto the tears,
With which I hasten that whereof thou spakest.
I have on earth a kinswoman; her name
Alagia, worthy in herself, so ill
Example of our house corrupt her not:
And she is all remaineth of me there."

CANTO XX.

ARGUMENT.

Among those on the fifth cornice, Hugh Capet records illustrious examples of voluntary poverty and of bounty; then tells who himself is, and speaks of his descendants on the French throne; and, lastly, adds some noted instances of avarice. When he has ended, the mountain shakes, and all the spirits sing "Glory to God."

ILL strives the will, 'gainst will more wise that strives:
   His pleasure therefore to mine own preferr'd,
   I drew the sponge yet thirsty from the wave.
   Onward I moved: he also onward moved,
Who led me, coasting still, wherever place
Along the rock was vacant; as a man
Walks near the battlements on narrow wall.
For those on the other part, who drop by drop
Wring out their all-infecting malady,
Too closely press the verge. Accurst be thou,
Inveterate wolf! whose gorge ingluts more prey
Than every beast beside, yet is not fill'd;
So bottomless thy maw.—Ye spheres of heaven!
To whom there are, as seems, who attribute
All change in mortal state, when is the day
Of his appearing, for whom fate reserves
To chase her hence?—With wary steps and slow
We pass'd; and I attentive to the shades,
Whom piteously I heard lament and wail;
And, 'midst the wailing, one before us heard
Cry out, "O blessed Virgin!" as a dame
In the sharp pangs of childbed; and "How poor
Thou wast," it added, "witness that low roof
Where thou didst lay thy sacred burden down.
O good Fabricius! thou didst virtue chuse
With poverty, before great wealth with vice."
   The words so pleased me, that desire to know

The spirit, from whose lip they seem'd to come,
Did draw me onward. Yet it spake the gift
Of Nicholas, which on the maidens he
Bounteous bestow'd, to save their youthful prime
Unblemish'd. "Spirit! who dost speak of deeds
So worthy, tell me who thou wast," I said,
"And why thou dost with single voice renew
Memorial of such praise. That boon vouchsafed
Haply shall meet reward; if I return
To finish the short pilgrimage of life,
Still speeding to its close on restless wing."

"I," answer'd he, "will tell thee; not for help,
Which thence I look for; but that in thyself
Grace so exceeding shines, before thy time
Of mortal dissolution. I was root
Of that ill plant whose shade such poison sheds
O'er all the Christian land, that seldom thence
Good fruit is gather'd. Vengeance soon should come,
Had Ghent and Douay, Lille and Bruges power;
And vengeance I of heaven's great Judge implore.
Hugh Capet was I hight; from me descend
The Philips and the Louis, of whom France
Newly is govern'd: born of one, who plied
The slaughterer's trade at Paris. When the race
Of ancient kings had vanish'd (all save one
Wrapt up in sable weeds) within my gripe
I found the reins of empire, and such powers
Of new acquirement, with full store of friends,
That soon the widow'd circlet of the crown
Was girt upon the temples of my son,
He, from whose bones the anointed race begins.
Till the great dower of Provence had removed
The stains, that yet obscured our lowly blood,
Its sway indeed was narrow; but howe'er

It wrought no evil: there, with force and lies,
Began its rapine: after, for amends,
Poitou it seized, Navarre and Gascony.
To Italy cames Charles; and for amends,
Young Conradine, an innocent victim, slew;
And sent the angelic teacher back to heaven,
Still for amends. I see the time at hand,
That forth from France invites another Charles
To make himself and kindred better known.
Unarm'd he issues, saving with that lance,
Which the arch-traitor tilted with; and that
He carries with so home a thrust, as rives
The bowels of poor Florence. No increase
Of territory hence, but sin and shame
Shall be his guerdon; and so much the more
As he more lightly deems of such foul wrong.
I see the other (who a prisoner late
Had stept on shore) exposing to the mart
His daughter, whom he bargains for, as do
The Corsairs for their slaves. O avarice!
What canst thou more, who hast subdued our blood
So wholly to thyself, they feel no care
Of their own flesh? To hide with direr guilt
Past ill and future, lo! the flower-de-luce
Enters Alagna; in his Vicar Christ
Himself a captive, and his mockery
Acted again. Lo! to his holy lip
The vinegar and gall once more applied;
And he 'twixt living robbers doom'd to bleed.
Lo! the new Pilate, of whose cruelty
Such violence cannot fill the measure up,
With no decree to sanction, pushes on
Into the temple his yet eager sails.

"O sovran Master! when shall I rejoice

To see the vengeance, which thy wrath, well-pleased,
In secret silence broods?—While daylight lasts,
So long what thou didst hear of her, sole spouse
Of the Great Spirit, and on which thou turn'dst
To me for comment, is the general theme
Of all our prayers: but, when it darkens, then
A different strain we utter: then record
Pygmalion, whom his gluttonous thirst of gold
Made traitor, robber, parricide: the woes
Of Midas, which his greedy wish ensued,
Mark'd for derision to all future times:
And the fond Achan, how he stole the prey,
That yet he seems by Joshua's ire pursued.
Sapphira with her husband next we blame;
And praise the forefeet, that with furious ramp
Spurn'd Heliodorus. All the mountain round
Rings with the infamy of Thracia's king,
Who slew his Phrygian charge: and last a shout
Ascends: 'Declare, O Crassus! for thou know'st,
The flavour of thy gold.' The voice of each
Now high, now low, as each his impulse prompts,
Is led through man a pitch, acute or grave.
Therefore, not singly, I erewhile rehearsed
That blessedness we tell of in the day:
But near me, none, beside, his accent raised."

 From him we now had parted, and essay'd
With utmost efforts to surmount the way;
When I did feel, as nodding to its fall,
The mountain tremble; whence an icy chill
Seized on me, as on one to death convey'd.
So shook not Delos, when Latona there
Couch'd to bring forth the twin-born eyes of heaven.

 Forthwith from every side a shout arose
So vehement, that suddenly my guide

Drew near, and cried: "Doubt not, while I conduct thee."
"Glory!" all shouted (such the sounds mine ear
Gather'd from those, who near me swell'd the sounds),
"Glory in the highest be to God." We stood
Immovably suspended, like to those,
The shepherds, who first heard in Bethlehem's field
That song: till ceased the trembling, and the song
Was ended: then our hallow'd path resumed,
Eying the prostrate shadows, who renew'd
Their custom'd mourning. Never in my breast
Did ignorance so struggle with desire
Of knowledge, if my memory do not err,
As in that moment; nor through haste dared I
To question, nor myself could aught discern.
So on I fared, in thoughtfulness and dread.

CANTO XXI.

ARGUMENT.

The two Poets are overtaken by the spirit of Statius, who, being cleansed, is on his way to Paradise, and who explains the cause of the mountain shaking, and of the hymn; his joy at beholding Virgil.

THE natural thirst, ne'er quench'd but from the well
 Whereof the woman of Samaria craved
 Excited; haste, along the cumber'd path,
After my guide, impell'd; and pity moved
My bosom for the 'vengeful doom though just.
When lo! even as Luke relates, that Christ
Appear'd unto the two upon their way,
New-risen from his vaulted grave; to us
A shade appear'd, and after us approach'd,
Contemplating the crowd beneath its feet.
We were not ware of it; so first it spake,
Saying, "God give you peace, my brethren!" then
Sudden we turn'd: and Virgil such salute,
As fitted that kind greeting, gave; and cried:
"Peace in the blessed council be thy lot,
Awarded by that righteous court which me
To everlasting banishment exiles."
 "How!" he exclaim'd, nor from his speed meanwhile
Desisting: "If that ye be spirits whom God
Vouchsafes not room above; who up the height
Has been thus far your guide?" To whom the bard:
"If thou observe the tokens, which this man,
Traced by the finger of the angel, bears;
'Tis plain that in the kingdom of the just
He needs must share. But sithence she, whose wheel

Spins day and night, for him not yet had drawn
That yarn, which on the fatal distaff piled,
Clotho apportions to each wight that breathes;
His soul, that sister is to mine and thine,
Not of herself could mount; for not like ours
Her ken: whence I, from forth the ample gulf
Of hell, was ta'en, to lead him, and will lead
Far as my lore avails. But, if thou know,
Instruct us for what cause, the mount erewhile
Thus shook, and trembled: wherefore all at once
Seem'd shouting, even from his wave-wash'd foot."

    That questioning so tallied with my wish,
The thirst did feel abatement of its edge
E'en from expectance. He forthwith replied:
"In its devotion, nought irregular
This mount can witness, or by punctual rule
Unsanction'd; here from every change exempt,
Other than that, which heaven in itself
Doth of itself receive, no influence
Can reach us. Tempest none, shower, hail, or snow,
Hoar frost, or dewy moistness, higher falls
Than that brief scale of threefold steps: thick clouds,
Nor scudding rack, are ever seen: swift glance
Ne'er lightens; nor Thaumantian Iris gleams,
That yonder often shifts on each side heaven.
Vapour adust doth never mount above
The highest of the trinal stairs, whereon
Peter's vicegerent stands. Lower perchance,
With various motion rock'd, trembles the soil:
But here, through wind in earth's deep hollow pent,
I know not how, yet never trembled: then
Trembles, when any spirit feels itself
So purified, that it may rise, or move
For rising; and such loud acclaim ensues.

Purification, by the will alone,
Is proved, that free to change society
Seizes the soul rejoicing in her will.
Desire of bliss is present from the first;
But strong propension hinders, to that wish
By the just ordinance of heaven opposed;
Propension now as eager to fulfil
The allotted torment, as erewhile to sin.
And I, who in this punishment had lain
Five hundred years and more, but now have felt
Free wish for happier clime. Therefore thou felt'st
The mountain tremble; and the spirits devout
Heard'st, over all his limits, utter praise
To that liege Lord, whom I entreat their joy
To hasten." Thus he spake: and, since the draught
Is grateful ever as the thirst is keen,
No words may speak my fulness of content.

"Now," said the instructor sage, "I see the net
That takes ye here: and how the toils are loosed;
Why rocks the mountain, and why ye rejoice.
Vouchsafe, that from thy lips I next may learn
Who on the earth thou wast; and wherefore here,
So many an age, were prostrate."—"In that time,
When the good Titus, with Heaven's King to help,
Avenged those piteous gashes, whence the blood
By Judas sold did issue; with the name
Most lasting and most honour'd, there, was I
Abundantly renown'd," the shade replied,
"Not yet with faith endued. So passing sweet
My vocal spirit; from Tolosa, Rome
To herself drew me, where I merited
A myrtle garland to inwreathe my brow.
Statius they name me still. Of Thebes I sang.
And next of great Achilles; but i' the way

Fell with the second burthen. Of my flame
Those sparkles were the seeds, which I derived
From the bright fountain of celestial fire
That feeds unnumber'd lamps; the song I mean
Which sounds Æneas' wanderings: that the breast
I hung at; that the nurse, from whom my veins
Drank inspiration: whose authority
Was ever sacred with me. To have lived
Co-eval with the Mantuan, I would bide
The revolution of another sun
Beyond my stated years in banishment."

 The Mantuan, when he heard him, turn'd to me;
And holding silence, by his countenance
Enjoin'd me silence: but the power, which wills,
Bears not supreme control: laughter and tears
Follow so closely on the passion prompts them,
They wait not for the motions of the will
In natures most sincere. I did but smile,
As one who winks; and thereupon the shade
Broke off, and peer'd into mine eyes, where best
Our looks interpret. "So to good event
Mayst thou conduct such great emprize," he cried,
"Say, why across thy visage beam'd, but now,
The lightning of a smile." On either part
Now am I straiten'd; one conjures me speak,
The other to silence binds me: whence a sigh
I utter, and the sigh is heard. "Speak on,"
The teacher cried: "and do not fear to speak;
But tell him what so earnestly he asks."
Whereon I thus: "Perchance, O ancient spirit!
Thou marvel'st at my smiling. There is room
For yet more wonder. He, who guides my ken
On high, he is that Mantuan, led by whom
Thou didst presume of men and gods to sing.

If other cause thou deem'dst for which I smiled,
Leave it as not the true one: and believe
Those words, thou spakest of him, indeed the cause."
    Now down he bent to embrace my teacher's feet;
But he forbade him: "Brother! do it not:
Thou art a shadow, and behold'st a shade."
He, rising, answer'd thus: "Now hast thou proved
The force and ardour of the love I bear thee,
When I forget we are but things of air,
And, as a substance, treat an empty shade."

CANTO XXII.

ARGUMENT.

Dante, Virgil, and Statius mount to the sixth cornice, where the sin of gluttony is cleansed, the two Latin Poets discoursing by the way. Turning to the right, they find a tree hung with sweet-smelling fruit, and watered by a shower that issues from the rock. Voices are heard to proceed from among the leaves, recording examples of temperance.

NOW we had left the angel, who had turn'd
To the sixth circle our ascending step;
One gash from off my forehead razed; while they,
Whose wishes tend to justice, shouted forth,
"Blessed!" and ended with "I thirst:" and I,
More nimble than along the other straits,
So journey'd, that, without the sense of toil,
I follow'd upward the swift-footed shades;
When Virgil thus began: "Let its pure flame
From virtue flow, and love can never fail
To warm another's bosom, so the light
Shine manifestly forth. Hence, from that hour,
When, 'mongst us in the purlieus of the deep,
Came down the spirit of Aquinum's bard,
Who told of thine affection, my good will
Hath been for thee of quality as strong
As ever link'd itself to one not seen.
Therefore these stairs will now seem short to me.
But tell me: and, if too secure, I loose
The rein with a friend's licence, as a friend
Forgive me, and speak now as with a friend:
How chanced it covetous desire could find
Place in that bosom, 'midst such ample store
Of wisdom, as thy zeal had treasured there?"

First somewhat moved to laughter by his words,
Statius replied: "Each syllable of thine
Is a dear pledge of love. Things oft appear,
That minister false matter to our doubts,
When their true causes are removed from sight.
Thy question doth assure me, thou believest
I was on earth a covetous man; perhaps
Because thou found'st me in that circle placed.
Know then I was too wide of avarice:
And e'en for that excess, thousands of moons
Have wax'd and waned upon my sufferings.
And were it not that I with heedful care
Noted, where thou exclaim'st as if in ire
With human nature, 'Why, thou cursed thirst
Of gold! dost not with juster measure guide
The appetite of mortals?' I had met
The fierce encounter of the voluble rock.
Then was I ware that, with too ample wing,
The hands may haste to lavishment; and turn'd,
As from my other evil, so from this,
In penitence. How many from their grave
Shall with shorn locks arise, who living, ay,
And at life's last extreme, of this offence,
Through ignorance, did not repent! And know,
The fault, which lies direct from any sin
In level opposition, here, with that,
Wastes its green rankness on one common heap.
Therefore, if I have been with those, who wail
Their avarice, to cleanse me; through reverse
Of their transgression, such hath been my lot."
  To whom the sovran of the pastoral song:
"While thou didst sing that cruel warfare waged
By the twin sorrow of Jocasta's womb,
From thy discourse with Clio there, it seems

As faith had not been thine; without the which,
Good deeds suffice not. And if so, what sun
Rose on thee, or what candle pierced the dark,
That thou didst after see to hoise the sail,
And follow where the fisherman had led?"

    He answering thus: "By thee conducted first,
I enter'd the Parnassian grots, and quaff'd
Of the clear spring: illumined first by thee,
Open'd mine eyes to God. Thou didst, as one,
Who, journeying through the darkness, bears a light
Behind, that profits not himself, but makes
His followers wise, when thou exclaimedst, 'Lo!
A renovated world, Justice return'd,
Times of primeval innocence restored,
And a new race descended from above.'
Poet and Christian both to thee I owed.
That thou mayst mark more clearly what I trace,
My hand shall stretch forth to inform the lines
With livelier colouring. Soon o'er all the world,
By messengers from heaven, the true belief
Teem'd now prolific; and that word of thine,
Accordant, to the new instructors chimed.
Induced by which agreement, I was wont
Resort to them: and soon their sanctity
So won upon me, that, Domitian's rage
Pursuing them, I mix'd my tears with theirs,
And, while on earth I stay'd, still succour'd them;
And their most righteous customs made me scorn
All sects besides. Before I led the Greeks,
In tuneful fiction, to the streams of Thebes,
I was baptised: but secretly, through fear,
Remain'd a Christian, and conform'd long time
To Pagan rites. Four centuries and more,
I, for that lukewarmness, was fain to pace

Round the fourth circle. Thou then, who hast raised
The covering which did hide such blessing from me,
Whilst much of this ascent is yet to climb,
Say, if thou know, where our old Terence bides,
Cæcilius, Plautus, Varro: if condemn'd
They dwell, and in what province of the deep."
"These," said my guide, "with Persius and myself,
And others many more, are with that Greek,
Of mortals, the most cherish'd by the nine,
In the first ward of darkness. There, oft-times,
We of that mount hold converse, on whose top
For aye our nurses live. We have the bard
Of Pella, and the Teian, Agatho,
Simonides, and many a Grecian else
Ingarlanded with laurel. Of thy train,
Antigone is there, Deiphile,
Argia, and as sorrowful as erst
Ismene, and who show'd Langia's wave:
Deidamia with her sisters there,
And blind Tiresias' daughter, and the bride
Sea-born of Peleus." Either poet now
Was silent; and no longer by the ascent
Or the steep walls obstructed, round them cast
Inquiring eyes. Four handmaids of the day
Had finish'd now their office, and the fifth
Was at the chariot-beam, directing still
Its flamy point aloof; when thus my guide:
"Methinks, it well behoves us to the brink
Bend the right shoulder, circuiting the mount,
As we have ever used." So custom there
Was usher to the road; the which we chose
Less doubtful, as that worthy shade complied.

  They on before me went: I sole pursued,
Listening their speech, that to my thoughts convey'd

Mysterious lessons of sweet poesy.
But soon they ceased; for midway of the road
A tree we found, with goodly fruitage hung,
And pleasant to the smell: and as a fir,
Upward from bough to bough, less ample spreads;
So downward this less ample spread; that none,
Methinks, aloft may climb. Upon the side,
That closed our path, a liquid crystal fell
From the steep rock, and through the sprays above
Stream'd showering. With associate step the bards
Drew near the plant; and, from amidst the leaves,
A voice was heard: "Ye shall be chary of me;"
And after added: "Mary took more thought
For joy and honour of the nuptial feast,
Than for herself, who answers now for you.
The women of old Rome were satisfied
With water for their beverage. Daniel fed
On pulse, and wisdom gain'd. The primal age
Was beautiful as gold: and hunger then
Made acorns tasteful; thirst, each rivulet
Run nectar. Honey and locusts were the food,
Whereon the Baptist in the wilderness
Fed, and that eminence of glory reach'd
And greatness, which the Evangelist records."

CANTO XXIII.

ARGUMENT.

They are overtaken by the spirit of Forese, who had been a friend of our Poet's on earth, and who now inveighs bitterly against the immodest dress of their countrywomen at Florence.

ON the green leaf mine eyes were fix'd, like his
Who throws away his days in idle chase
Of the diminutive birds, when thus I heard
The more than father warn me: "Son! our time
Asks thriftier using. Linger not: away."
    Thereat my face and steps at once I turn'd
Toward the sages, by whose converse cheer'd
I journey'd on, and felt no toil: and lo!
A sound of weeping, and a song: "My lips,
O Lord!" and these so mingled, it gave birth
To pleasure and to pain. "O Sire beloved!
Say what is this I hear." Thus I inquired.
    "Spirits," said he, "who, as they go, perchance,
Their debt of duty pay." As on their road
The thoughtful pilgrims, overtaking some
Not known unto them, turn to them, and look,
But stay not; thus, approaching from behind
With speedier motion, eyed us, as they pass'd,
A crowd of spirits, silent and devout.
The eyes of each were dark and hollow; pale
Their visage, and so lean withal, the bones
Stood staring through the skin. I do not think
Thus dry and meagre Erisicthon show'd,
When pinch'd by sharp-set famine to the quick.
    "Lo!" to myself I mused, "the race, who lost
Jerusalem, when Mary with dire beak
Prey'd on her child." The sockets seem'd as rings,

From which the gems were dropt. Who reads the name
Of man upon his forehead, there the M
Had traced most plainly. Who would deem, that scent
Of water and an apple could have proved
Powerful to generate such pining want,
Not knowing how it wrought? While now I stood,
Wondering what thus could waste them (for the cause
Of their gaunt hollowness and scaly rind
Appear'd not), lo! a spirit turn'd his eyes
In their deep-sunken cells, and fasten'd them
On me, then cried with vehemence aloud:
"What grace is this vouchsafed me?" By his looks
I ne'er had recognized him: but the voice
Brought to my knowledge what his cheer conceal'd.
Remembrance of his altered lineaments
Was kindled from that spark: and I agnized
The visage of Forese. "Ah! respect
This wan and leprous-wither'd skin," thus he
Suppliant implored, "this macerated flesh.
Speak to me truly of thyself. And who
Are those twain spirits, that escort thee there?
Be it not said thou scorn'st to talk with me."

"That face of thine," I answer'd him, "which dead
I once bewail'd, disposes me not less
For weeping, when I see it thus transform'd.
Say then, by Heaven, what blasts ye thus? The whilst
I wonder, ask not speech from me: unapt
Is he to speak, whom other will employs."

He thus: "The water and the plant, we pass'd,
With power are gifted, by the eternal will
Infused; the which so pines me. Every spirit,
Whose song bewails his gluttony indulged
Too grossly, here in hunger and in thirst
Is purified. The odour, which the fruit,

And spray that showers upon the verdure, breathe,
Inflames us with desire to feed and drink.
Nor once alone encompassing our route,
We come to add fresh fuel to the pain:
Pain, said I? solace rather: for that will,
To the tree, leads us, by which Christ was led
To call on Eli, joyful, when he paid
Our ransom from his vein." I answering thus:
"Forese! from that day, in which the world
For better life thou changedst, not five years
Have circled. If the power of sinning more
Were first concluded in thee, ere thou knew'st
That kindly grief which re-espouses us
To God, how hither art thou come so soon?
I thought to find thee lower, there, where time
Is recompense for time. He straight replied:
"To drink up the sweet wormwood of affliction
I have been brought thus early, by the tears
Stream'd down my Nella's cheeks. Her prayers devout,
Her sighs have drawn me from the coast, where oft
Expectance lingers; and have set me free
From the other circles. In the sight of God
So much the dearer is my widow prized,
She whom I loved so fondly, as she ranks
More singly eminent for virtuous deeds.
The tract, most barbarous of Sardinia's isle,
Hath dames more chaste, and modester by far,
Than that wherein I left her. O sweet brother!
What wouldst thou have me say? A time to come
Stands full within my view, to which this hour
Shall not be counted of an ancient date,
When from the pulpit shall be loudly warn'd
The unblushing dames of Florence, lest they bare
Unkerchief'd bosoms to the common gaze.

What savage women hath the world e'er seen,
What Saracens, for whom there needed scourge
Of spiritual or other discipline,
To force them walk with covering on their limbs?
But did they see, the shameless ones, what Heaven
Wafts on swift wing toward them while I speak,
Their mouths were oped for howling: they shall taste
Of sorrow (unless foresight cheat me here)
Or e'er the cheek of him be clothed with down,
Who is now rock'd with lullaby asleep.
Ah! now, my brother, hide thyself no more:
Thou seest how not I alone, but all,
Gaze, where thou veil'st the intercepted sun."

 Whence I replied: "If thou recall to mind
What we were once together, even yet
Remembrance of those days may grieve thee sore.
That I forsook that life, was due to him
Who there precedes me, some few evenings past,
When she was round, who shines with sister lamp
To his that glisters yonder," and I show'd
The sun. "'Tis he, who through profoundest night
Of the true dead has brought me, with this flesh
As true, that follows. From that gloom the aid
Of his sure comfort drew me on to climb,
And, climbing, wind along this mountain-steep,
Which rectifies in you whate'er the world
Made crooked and depraved. I have his word,
That he will bear me company as far
As till I come where Beatrice dwells:
But there must leave me. Virgil is that spirit,
Who thus hath promised," and I pointed to him;
"The other is that shade, for whom so late
Your realm, as he arose, exulting, shook
Through every pendent cliff and rocky bound."

CANTO XXIV.

ARGUMENT.

Forese points out several others by name who are here, like himself, purifying themselves from the vice of gluttony; and amongst the rest, Buonaggiunta of Lucca, with whom our Poet converses. Forese then predicts the violent end of Dante's political enemy, Corso Donati; and when he has quitted them, the Poet, in company with Statius and Virgil, arrives at another tree, from whence issue voices that record ancient examples of gluttony; and proceeding forwards, they are directed by an angel which way to ascend to the next cornice of the mountain.

OUR journey was not slacken'd by our talk,
Nor yet our talk by journeying. Still we spake,
And urged our travel stoutly, like a ship
When the wind sits astern. The shadowy forms,
That seem'd things dead and dead again, drew in
At their deep-delved orbs rare wonder of me,
Perceiving I had life; and I my words
Continued, and thus spake: "He journeys up
Perhaps more tardily than else he would,
For others' sake. But tell me, if thou know'st
Where is Piccarda? Tell me, if I see
Any of mark, among this multitude
Who eye me thus."—"My sister (she for whom,
'Twixt beautiful and good, I cannot say
Which name was fitter) wears e'en now her crown,
And triumphs in Olympus." Saying this,
He added: "Since spare diet hath so worn
Our semblance out, 'tis lawful here to name
Each one. This," and his finger then he raised,
"Is Buonaggiunta,—Buonaggiunta, he
Of Lucca: and that face beyond him, pierced
Unto a leaner fineness than the rest,
Had keeping of the church; he was of Tours,
And purges by wan abstinence away
Bolsena's eels and cups of muscadel."

The shadowy forms,
That seem'd things dead and dead again, drew in
At their deep-delved orbs rare wonder of me,
Perceiving I had life.

Canto XXIV., lines 4-7.

P. P.—31. At length, as undeceived, they went their way:
And we approach the tree, whom vows and tears
Sue to in vain; the mighty tree.

Canto XXIV., lines 112–114.

He show'd me many others, one by one:
And all, as they were named, seem'd well content;
For no dark gesture I discern'd in any.
I saw, through hunger, Ubaldino grind
His teeth on emptiness; and Boniface,
That waved the crozier o'er a numerous flock:
I saw the Marquis, who had time erewhile
To swill at Forli with less drought; yet so,
Was one ne'er sated. I howe'er, like him
That, gazing 'midst a crowd, singles out one,
So singled him of Lucca; for methought
Was none amongst them took such note of me.
Somewhat I heard him whisper of Gentucca:
The sound was indistinct, and murmur'd there,
Where justice, that so strips them, fix'd her sting.

"Spirit!" said I, "it seems as thou wouldst fain
Speak with me. Let me hear thee. Mutual wish
To converse prompts, which let us both indulge."

He, answering, straight began: "Woman is born,
Whose brow no wimple shades yet, that shall make
My city please thee, blame it as they may.
Go then with this forewarning. If aught false
My whisper too implied, the event shall tell.
But say, if of a truth I see the man
Of that new lay the inventor, which begins
With 'Ladies, ye that con the lore of love.'"

To whom I thus: "Count of me but as one,
Who am the scribe of love; that, when he breathes,
Take up my pen, and, as he dictates, write."

"Brother!" said he, "the hindrance, which once held
The notary, with Guittone and myself,
Short of that new and sweeter style I hear,
Is now disclosed: I see how ye your plumes
Stretch, as the inditer guides them; which, no question,

Ours did not. He that seeks a grace beyond,
Sees not the distance parts one style from other."
And, as contented, here he held his peace.

    Like as the birds, that winter near the Nile,
In squared regiment direct their course,
Then stretch themselves in file for speedier flight;
Thus all the tribe of spirits, as they turn'd
Their visage, faster fled, nimble alike
Through leanness and desire. And as a man,
Tired with the motion of a trotting steed,
Slacks pace, and stays behind his company,
Till his o'erbreathed lungs keep temperate time;
E'en so Forese let that holy crew
Proceed, behind them lingering at my side,
And saying: "When shall I again behold thee?"

    "How long my life may last," said I, "I know not:
This know, how soon soever I return,
My wishes will before me have arrived:
Sithence the place, where I am set to live,
Is, day by day, more scoop'd of all its good;
And dismal ruin seems to threaten it."

    "Go now," he cried: "lo! he, whose guilt is most,
Passes before my vision, dragg'd at heels
Of an infuriate beast. Toward the vale,
Where guilt hath no redemption, on it speeds,
Each step increasing swiftness on the last;
Until a blow it strikes, that leaveth him
A corse most vilely shatter'd. No long space
Those wheels have yet to roll" (therewith his eyes
Look'd up to heaven), "ere thou shalt plainly see
That which my words may not more plainly tell.
I quit thee: time is precious here: I lose
Too much, thus measuring my pace with thine."

    As from a troop of well rank'd chivalry,

PURGATORY.—CANTO XXIV.

One knight, more enterprising than the rest,
Pricks forth at gallop, eager to display
His prowess in the first encounter proved;
So parted he from us, with lengthen'd strides;
And left me on the way with those twain spirits,
Who were such mighty marshals of the world.

When he beyond us had so fled, mine eyes
No nearer reach'd him, than my thought his words;
The branches of another fruit, thick hung,
And blooming fresh, appear'd. E'en as our steps
Turn'd thither: not far off, it rose to view.
Beneath it were a multitude, that raised
Their hands, and shouted forth I know not what
Unto the boughs; like greedy and fond brats,
That beg, and answer none obtain from him,
Of whom they beg; but more to draw them on,
He, at arm's length, the object of their wish
Above them holds aloft, and hides it not.

At length, as undeceived, they went their way:
And we approach the tree, whom vows and tears
Sue to in vain; the mighty tree. "Pass on,
And come not near. Stands higher up the wood,
Whereof Eve tasted: and from it was ta'en
This plant." Such sounds from mid'st the thickets came.
Whence I, with either bard, close to the side
That rose, pass'd forth beyond. "Remember," next
We heard, "those unblest creatures of the clouds,
How they their twyfold bosoms, overgorged,
Opposed in fight to Theseus: call to mind
The Hebrews, how, effeminate, they stoop'd
To ease their thirst; whence Gideon's ranks were thinn'd,
As he to Madian march'd adown the hills."

Thus near one border coasting, still we heard
The sins of gluttony, with woe erewhile

Reguerdon'd. Then along the lonely path,
Once more at large, full thousand paces on
We travel'd, each contemplative and mute.

"Why pensive journey so ye three alone?"
Thus suddenly a voice exclaim'd: whereat
I shook, as doth a scared and paltry beast;
Then raised my head, to look from whence it came.

Was ne'er, in furnace, glass, or metal, seen
So bright and glowing red, as was the shape
I now beheld. "If ye desire to mount,"
He cried; "here must ye turn. This way he goes
Who goes in quest of peace." His countenance
Had dazzled me; and to my guides I faced
Backward, like one who walks as sound directs.

As when, to harbinger the dawn, springs up
On freshen'd wing the air of May, and breathes
Of fragrance, all impregn'd with herb and flowers;
E'en such a wind I felt upon my front
Blow gently, and the moving of a wing
Perceived, that, moving, shed ambrosial smell;
And then a voice: "Blessed are they, whom grace
Doth so illume, that appetite in them
Exhaleth no inordinate desire,
Still hungering as the rule of temperance wills."

CANTO XXV.

ARGUMENT.

Virgil and Statius resolve some doubts that have arisen in the mind of Dante from what he had just seen. They all arrive on the seventh and last cornice, where the sin of incontinence is purged in fire; and the spirits of those suffering therein are heard to record illustrious instances of chastity.

IT was an hour, when he who climbs, had need
   To walk uncrippled: for the sun had now
   To Taurus the meridian circle left,
And to the Scorpion left the night. As one,
That makes no pause, but presses on his road,
Whate'er betide him, if some urgent need
Impel; so enter'd we upon our way,
One before other; for, but singly, none
That steep and narrow scale admits to climb.

   E'en as the young stork lifteth up his wing
Through wish to fly, yet ventures not to quit
The nest, and drops it; so in me desire
Of questioning my guide arose, and fell,
Arriving even to the act that marks
A man prepared for speech. Him all our haste
Restrain'd not; but thus spake the sire beloved:
"Fear not to speed the shaft, that on thy lip
Stands trembling for its flight." Encouraged thus,
I straight began: "How there can leanness come,
Where is no want of nourishment to feed?"

   "If thou," he answer'd, "hadst remember'd thee,
How Meleager with the wasting brand
Wasted alike, by equal fires consumed;
This would not trouble thee: and hadst thou thought,

How in the mirror your reflected form
With mimic motion vibrates; what now seems
Hard, had appear'd no harder than the pulp
Of summer-fruit mature. But that thy will
In certainty may find its full repose,
Lo Statius here! on him I call, and pray
That he would now be healer of thy wound."

"If, in thy presence, I unfold to him
The secrets of heaven's vengeance, let me plead
Thine own injunction to exculpate me."
So Statius answer'd, and forthwith began:
"Attend my words, O son, and in thy mind
Receive them; so shall they be light to clear
The doubt thou offer'st. Blood, concocted well,
Which by the thirsty veins is ne'er imbibed,
And rests as food superfluous, to be ta'en
From the replenish'd table, in the heart
Derives effectual virtue, that informs
The several human limbs, as being that
Which passes through the veins itself to make them.
Yet more concocted it descends, where shame
Forbids to mention: and from thence distils
In natural vessels on another's blood.
There each unite together; one disposed
To endure, to act the other, through that power
Derived from whence it came; and being met,
It 'gins to work, coagulating first:
Then vivifies what its own substance made
Consist. With animation now indued,
The active virtue (differing from a plant
No further, than that this is on the way,
And at its limit that) continues yet
To operate, that now it moves, and feels,
As sea-sponge clinging to the rock: and there

PURGATORY.—CANTO XXV.

Assumes the organic powers its seed convey'd.
This is the moment, son! at which the virtue,
That from the generating heart proceeds,
Is pliant and expansive; for each limb
Is in the heart by forgeful nature plann'd.
How babe of animal becomes, remains
For thy considering. At this point, more wise,
Than thou, has err'd, making the soul disjoin'd
From passive intellect, because he saw
No organ for the latter's use assign'd.

"Open thy bosom to the truth that comes.
Know, soon as in the embryo, to the brain
Articulation is complete, then turns
The primal Mover with a smile of joy
On such great work of nature; and imbreathes
New spirit replete with virtue, that what here
Active it finds, to its own substance draws:
And forms an individual soul, that lives,
And feels, and bends reflective on itself.
And that thou less mayst marvel at the word,
Mark the sun's heat; how that to wine doth change,
Mix'd with the moisture filter'd through the vine.

"When Lachesis hath spun the thread, the soul
Takes with her both the human and divine,
Memory, intèlligence, and will, in act
Far keener than before; the other powers
Inactive all and mute. No pause allow'd,
In wondrous sort self-moving, to one strand
Of those, where the departed roam, she falls:
Here learns her destined path. Soon as the place
Receives her, round the plastic virtue beams,
Distinct as in the living limbs before:
And as the air, when saturate with showers,
The causal beam refracting, decks itself

With many a hue; so here the ambient air
Weareth that form, which influence of the soul
Imprints on it: and like the flame, that where
The fire moves, thither follows; so, henceforth,
The new form on the spirit follows still:
Hence hath it semblance, and is shadow call'd,
With each sense, even to the sight, endued:
Hence speech is ours, hence laughter, tears, and sighs,
Which thou mayst oft have witness'd on the mount.
The obedient shadow fails not to present
Whatever varying passion moves within us.
And this the cause of what thou marvel'st at."

    Now the last flexure of our way we reach'd;
And to the right hand turning other care
Awaits us. Here the rocky precipice
Hurls forth redundant flames: and from the rim
A blast up-blown, with forcible rebuff
Driveth them back, sequester'd from its bound.

    Behoved us, one by one, along the side,
That border'd on the void, to pass; and I
Fear'd on one hand the fire, on the other fear'd
Headlong to fall: when thus the instructor warn'd;
"Strict rein must in this place direct the eyes.
A little swerving and the way is lost."

    Then from the bosom of the burning mass,
"O God of mercy!" heard I sung, and felt
No less desire to turn. And when I saw
Spirits along the flame proceeding, I
Between their footsteps and mine own was fain
To share by turns my view. At the hymn's close
They shouted loud, "I do not know a man;"
Then in low voice again took up the strain;
Which once more ended, "To the wood," they cried,
"Ran Dian, and drave forth Callisto stung

P. P.—32.

                                      Here the rocky precipice
Hurls forth redundant flames; and from the rim
A blast up-blown, with forcible rebuff
Driveth them back, sequester'd from its bound.

Canto XXV., lines 107- 110.

Then from the bosom of the burning mass,
"O God of mercy!" heard I sung, and felt
No less desire to turn.

Canto XXV., lines 117–119.

And when I saw
Spirits along the flame proceeding, I
Between their footsteps and mine own was fain
To share by turns my view.

Canto XXV., lines 119-122.

A lady young and beautiful, I dream'd,
Was passing o'er a lea; and, as she came,
Methought I saw her ever and anon
Bending to cull the flowers.

Canto XXVII., lines 97-100.

With Cytherea's poison:" then return'd
Unto their song; then many a pair extoll'd,
Who lived in virtue chastely and the bands
Of wedded love. Nor from that task, I ween,
Surcease they; whilesoe'er the scorching fire
Enclasps them. Of such skill appliance needs,
To medicine the wound that healeth last.

CANTO XXVI.

ARGUMENT.

The spirits wonder at seeing the shadow cast by the body of Dante on the flame as he passes it. This moves one of them to address him. It proves to be Guido Guinicelli, the Italian poet, who points out to him the spirit of Arnault Daniel, the Provençal, with whom he also speaks.

WHILE singly thus along the rim we walk'd,.
Oft the good master warn'd me: "Look thou well.
Avail it that I caution thee." The sun
Now all the western clime irradiate changed
From azure tinct to white; and, as I pass'd,
My passing shadow made the umber'd flame
Burn ruddier. At so strange a sight I mark'd
That many a spirit marvel'd on his way.
    This bred occasion first to speak of me.
"He seems," said they, "no insubstantial frame:"
Then, to obtain what certainty they might,
Stretch'd towards me, careful not to overpass
The burning pale. "O thou! who followest
The others, haply not more slow than they,
But moved by reverence; answer me, who burn
In thirst and fire: nor I alone, but these
All for thine answer do more thirst, than doth
Indian or Æthiop for the cooling stream.
Tell us, how is it that thou makest thyself
A wall against the sun, as thou not yet
Into the inextricable toils of death
Hadst enter'd?" Thus spake one: and I had straight
Declared me, if attention had not turn'd
To new appearance. Meeting these, there came,

Midway the burning path, a crowd, on whom
Earnestly gazing, from each part I view
The shadows all press forward, severally
Each snatch a hasty kiss, and then away.
E'en so the emmets, 'mid their dusky troops,
Peer closely one at other, to spy out
Their mutual road perchance, and how they thrive.

   That friendly greeting parted, ere dispatch
Of the first onward step, from either tribe
Loud clamour rises: those, who newly come,
Shout "Sodom and Gomorrah!" these, "The cow
Pasiphae enter'd, that the beast she woo'd
Might rush unto her luxury." Then as cranes,
That part towards the Riphæan mountains fly,
Part towards the Lybic sands, these to avoid
The ice, and those the sun; so hasteth off
One crowd, advances the other; and resume
Their first song, weeping, and their several shout.

   Again drew near my side the very same,
Who had erewhile besought me; and their looks
Mark'd eagerness to listen. I, who twice
Their will had noted, spake: "O spirits! secure,
Whene'er the time may be, of peaceful end;
My limbs, nor crude, nor in mature old age,
Have I left yonder: here they bear me, fed
With blood, and sinew-strung. That I no more
May live in blindness, hence I tend aloft.
There is a dame on high, who wins for us
This grace, by which my mortal through your realm
I bear. But may your utmost wish soon meet
Such full fruition, that the orb of Heaven,
Fullest of love, and of most ample space,
Receive you: as ye tell (upon my page
Henceforth to stand recorded) who ye are;

And what this multitude, that at your backs
Have past behind us." As one, mountain-bred,
Rugged and clownish, if some city's walls
He chance to enter, round him stares agape,
Confounded and struck dumb; e'en such appear'd
Each spirit. But when rid of that amaze
(Not long the inmate of a noble heart),
He, who before had question'd, thus resumed:
"O blessed! who, for death preparing, takest
Experience of our limits, in thy bark;
Their crime, who not with us proceed, was that
For which, as he did triumph, Cæsar heard
The shout of 'queen,' to taunt him. Hence their cry
Of 'Sodom,' as they parted; to rebuke
Themselves, and aid the burning by their shame.
Our sinning was Hermaphrodite: but we,
Because the law of human kind we broke,
Following like beasts our vile concupiscence,
Hence parting from them, to our own disgrace
Record the name of her, by whom the beast
In bestial tire was acted. Now our deeds
Thou know'st, and how we sinn'd. If thou by name
Wouldst haply know us, time permits not now
To tell so much, nor can I. Of myself
Learn what thou wishest. Guinicelli I;
Who having truly sorrow'd ere my last,
Already cleanse me." With such pious joy,
As the two sons upon their mother gazed
From sad Lycurgus rescued; such my joy
(Save that I more repress'd it) when I heard
From his own lips the name of him pronounced,
Who was a father to me, and to those
My betters, who have ever used the sweet
And pleasant rhymes of love. So nought I heard,

PURGATORY.—CANTO XXVI.

Nor spake; but long time thoughtfully I went
Gazing on him; and, only for the fire,
Approach'd not nearer. When my eyes were fed
By looking on him; with such solemn pledge,
As forces credence, I devoted me
Unto his service wholly. In reply
He thus bespake me: "What from thee I hear
Is graved so deeply on my mind, the waves
Of Lethe shall not wash it off, nor make
A whit less lively. But as now thy oath
Has seal'd the truth, declare what cause impels
That love, which both thy looks and speech bewray."

"Those dulcet lays," I answer'd; "which, as long
As of our tongue the beauty does not fade,
Shall make us love the very ink that traced them."

"Brother!" he cried, and pointed at the shade
Before him, "there is one, whose mother speech
Doth owe to him a fairer ornament.
He in love ditties, and the tales of prose,
Without a rival stands; and lets the fools
Talk on, who think the songster of Limoges
O'ertops him. Rumour and the popular voice
They look to, more than truth; and so confirm
Opinion, ere by art or reason taught.
Thus many of the elder time cried up
Guittone, giving him the prize, till truth
By strength of numbers vanquish'd. If thou own
So ample privilege, as to have gain'd
Free entrance to the cloister, whereof Christ
Is Abbot of the college; say to him
One paternoster for me, far as needs
For dwellers in this world, where power to sin
No longer tempts us." Haply to make way
For one that follow'd next, when that was said,

He vanish'd through the fire, as through the wave
A fish, that glances diving to the deep.
    I, to the spirit he had shown me, drew
A little onward, and besought his name,
For which my heart, I said, kept gracious room.
He frankly thus began: "Thy courtesy
So wins on me, I have nor power nor will
To hide me. I am Arnault; and with songs,
Sorely waymenting for my folly past,
Thorough this ford of fire I wade, and see
The day, I hope for, smiling in my view.
I pray ye by the worth that guides ye up
Unto the summit of the scale, in time
Remember ye my sufferings." With such words
He disappear'd in the refining flame.

CANTO XXVII.

ARGUMENT.

An angel sends them forward through the fire to the last ascent, which leads to the terrestrial Paradise, situated on the summit of the mountain. They have not proceeded many steps on their way upward, when the fall of night hinders them from going further; and our Poet, who has lain down with Virgil and Statius to rest, beholds in a dream two females, figuring the active and contemplative life. With the return of morning, they reach the height; and here Virgil gives Dante full liberty to use his own pleasure and judgment in the choice of his way, till he shall meet with Beatrice.

NOW was the sun so station'd, as when first
His early radiance quivers on the heights,
Where stream'd his Maker's blood; while Libra hangs
Above Hesperian Ebro; and new fires,
Meridian, flash on Ganges' yellow tide.
So day was sinking, when the angel of God
Appear'd before us. Joy was in his mien.
Forth of the flame he stood upon the brink;
And with a voice, whose lively clearness far
Surpass'd our human, "Blessed are the pure
In heart," he sang: then near him as we came,
"Go ye not further, holy spirits!" he cried,
"Ere the fire pierce you: enter in; and list
Attentive to the song ye hear from thence."
I, when I heard his saying, was as one
Laid in the grave. My hands together clasp'd,
And upward stretching, on the fire I look'd;
And busy fancy conjured up the forms
Erewhile beheld alive consumed in flames.
The escorting spirits turn'd with gentle looks
Toward me; and the Mantuan spake: "My son,
Here torment thou mayst feel, but canst not death.
Remember thee, remember thee, if I

Safe e'en on Geryon brought thee; now I come
More near to God, wilt thou not trust me now?
Of this be sure; though in its womb that flame
A thousand years contain'd thee, from thy head
No hair should perish. If thou doubt my truth,
Approach; and with thy hands thy vesture's hem
Stretch forth, and for thyself confirm belief.
Lay now all fear, oh! lay all fear aside.
Turn hither, and come onward undismay'd."

 I still, though conscience urged, no step advanced.
 When still he saw me fix'd and obstinate,
Somewhat disturb'd he cried: "Mark now, my son,
From Beatrice thou art by this wall
Divided." As at Thisbe's name the eye
Of Pyramus was open'd (when life ebb'd
Fast from his veins), and took one parting glance,
While vermeil dyed the mulberry; thus I turn'd
To my sage guide, relenting, when I heard
The name that springs for ever in my breast.

 He shook his forehead; and, "How long," he said,
"Linger we now?" then smiled, as one would smile
Upon a child that eyes the fruit and yields.
Into the fire before me then he walk'd;
And Statius, who erewhile no little space
Had parted us, he pray'd to come behind.

 I would have cast me into molten glass
To cool me, when I enter'd; so intense
Raged the conflagrant mass. The sire beloved,
To comfort me, as he proceeded, still
Of Beatrice talk'd. "Her eyes," saith he,
"E'en now I seem to view." From the other side
A voice, that sang, did guide us; and the voice
Following, with heedful ear, we issued forth,
There where the path led upward. "Come," we heard,

"Come, blessed of my Father." Such the sounds,
That hail'd us from within a light, which shone
So radiant, I could not endure the view.
"The sun," it added, "hastes: and evening comes.
Delay not: ere the western sky is hung
With blackness, strive ye for the pass." Our way
Upright within the rock arose, and faced
Such part of heaven, that from before my steps
The beams were shrouded of the sinking sun.

    Nor many stairs were overpast when now
By fading of the shadow we perceived
The sun behind us couch'd; and ere one face
Of darkness o'er its measureless expanse
Involved the horizon, and the night her lot
Held individual, each of us had made
A stair his pallet; not that will, but power,
Had fail'd us, by the nature of that mount
Forbidden further travel. As the goats,
That late have skipt and wanton'd rapidly
Upon the craggy cliffs, ere they had ta'en
Their supper on the herb, now silent lie
And ruminate beneath the umbrage brown,
While noon-day rages; and the goatherd leans
Upon his staff, and leaning watches them:
And as the swain, that lodges out all night
In quiet by his flock, lest beast of prey
Disperse them: even so all three abode,
I as a goat, and as the shepherds they,
Close pent on either side by shelving rock.

    A little glimpse of sky was seen above;
Yet by that little I beheld the stars,
In magnitude and lustre shining forth
With more than wonted glory. As I lay,
Gazing on them, and in that fit of musing,

THE VISION.

Sleep overcame me, sleep, that bringeth oft
Tidings of future hap. About the hour,
As I believe, when Venus from the east
First lighten'd on the mountain, she whose orb
Seems alway glowing with the fire of love,
A lady young and beautiful, I dream'd,
Was passing o'er a lea; and, as she came,
Methought I saw her ever and anon
Bending to cull the flowers; and thus she sang:
"Know ye, whoever of my name would ask,
That I am Leah: for my brow to weave
A garland, these fair hands unwearied ply.
To please me at the crystal mirror, here
I deck me. But my sister Rachel, she
Before her glass abides the livelong day,
Her radiant eyes beholding, charm'd no less,
Than I with this delightful task. Her joy
In contemplation, as in labour mine."
  And now as glimmering dawn appear'd, that breaks
More welcome to the pilgrim still, as he
Sojourns less distant on his homeward way,
Darkness from all sides fled, and with it fled
My slumber; whence I rose, and saw my guide
Already risen. "That delicious fruit,
Which through so many a branch the zealous care
Of mortals roams in quest of, shall this day
Appease thy hunger." Such the words I heard
From Virgil's lip; and never greeting heard,
So pleasant as the sounds. Within me straight
Desire so grew upon desire to mount,
Thenceforward at each step I felt the wings
Increasing for my flight. When we had run
O'er all the ladder to its topmost round,
As there we stood, on me the Mantuan fix'd

His eyes, and thus he spake: "Both fires, my son,
The temporal and eternal, thou hast seen;
And art arrived, where of itself my ken
No further reaches. I, with skill and art,
Thus far have drawn thee. Now thy pleasure take
For guide. Thou hast o'ercome the steeper way,
O'ercome the straiter. Lo! the sun, that darts
His beam upon thy forehead: lo! the herb,
The arborets and flowers, which of itself
This land pours forth profuse. Till those bright eyes
With gladness come, which, weeping, made me haste
To succor thee, thou mayst or seat thee down,
Or wander where thou wilt. Expect no more
Sanction of warning voice or sign from me,
Free of thy own arbitrement to chuse,
Discreet, judicious. To distrust thy sense
Were henceforth error. I invest thee then
With crown and mitre, sovereign o'er thyself."

CANTO XXVIII.

ARGUMENT.

Dante wanders through the forest of the terrestrial Paradise, till he is stopped by a stream, on the other side of which he beholds a fair lady, culling flowers. He speaks to her; and she, in reply, explains to him certain things touching the nature of that place, and tells that the water, which flows between them, is here called Lethe, and in another place has the name of Eunoe.

THROUGH that celestial forest, whose thick shade
With lively greenness the new-springing day
Attemper'd, eager now to roam, and search
Its limits round, forthwith I left the bank;
Along the champain leisurely my way
Pursuing, o'er the ground, that on all sides
Delicious odour breathed. A pleasant air,
That intermitted never, never veer'd,
Smote on my temples, gently, as a wind
Of softest influence: at which the sprays,
Obedient all, lean'd trembling to that part
Where first the holy mountain casts his shade;
Yet were not so disorder'd, but that still
Upon their top the feather'd quiristers
Applied their wonted art, and with full joy
Welcomed those hours of prime, and warbled shrill
Amid the leaves, that to their jocund lays
Kept tenour; even as from branch to branch,
Along the piny forests on the shore
Of Chiassi, rolls the gathering melody,
When Eolus hath from his cavern loosed
The dripping south. Already had my steps,
Though slow, so far into that ancient wood
Transported me, I could not ken the place

Where I had entered; when, behold! my path
When bounded by a rill, which, to the left,
With little rippling waters bent the grass
That issued from its brink. On earth no wave,
How clean soe'er, that would not seem to have
Some mixture in itself, compared with this,
Transpicuous clear; yet darkly on it roll'd,
Darkly beneath perpetual gloom, which ne'er
Admits or sun or moon-light there to shine.

    My feet advanced not; but my wondering eyes
Pass'd onward, o'er the streamlet, to survey
The tender may-bloom, flushed through many a hue,
In prodigal variety: and, there,
As object, rising suddenly to view,
That from our bosom every thought beside
With the rare marvel chases, I beheld
A lady all alone, who, singing, went,
And culling flower from flower, wherewith her way
Was all o'er painted. "Lady beautiful!
Thou, who (if looks, that use to speak the heart,
Are worthy of our trust) with love's own beam
Dost warm thee," thus to her my speech I framed;
"Ah! please thee hither towards the streamlet bend
Thy steps so near, that I may list thy song.
Beholding thee and this fair place, methinks,
I call to mind where wander'd and how look'd
Proserpine, in that season, when her child
The mother lost, and she the bloomy spring."

    As when a lady, turning in the dance,
Doth foot it featly, and advances scarce
One step before the other to the ground;
Over the yellow and vermilion flowers
Thus turn'd she at my suit, most maiden-like,
Valing her sober eyes; and came so near,

That I distinctly caught the dulcet sound.
Arriving where the limpid waters now
Laved the green swerd, her eyes she deign'd to raise,
That shot such splendour on me, as I ween
Ne'er glanced from Cytherea's, when her son
Had sped his keenest weapon to her heart.
Upon the opposite bank she stood and smiled;
As through her graceful fingers shifted still
The intermingling dyes, which without seed
That lofty land unbosoms. By the stream
Three paces only were we sunder'd: yet,
The Hellespont, where Xerxes pass'd it o'er
(A curb for ever to the pride of man),
Was by Leander not more hateful held
For floating, with inhospitable wave,
'Twixt Sestus and Abydos, than by me
That flood, because it gave no passage thence.

    "Strangers ye come; and haply in this place,
That cradled human nature in her birth,
Wondering, ye not without suspicion view
My smiles: but that sweet strain of psalmody,
'Thou, Lord! hast made me glad,' will give ye light,
Which may uncloud your minds. And thou, who stand'st
The foremost, and didst make thy suit to me,
Say if aught else thou wish to hear: for I
Came prompt to answer every doubt of thine."

    She spake; and I replied: "I know not how
To reconcile this wave, and rustling sound
Of forest leaves, with what I late have heard
Of opposite report." She answering thus:
"I will unfold the cause, whence that proceeds,
Which makes thee wonder; and so purge the cloud
That hath enwrapt thee. The First Good, whose joy
Is only in himself, created man,

For happiness; and gave this goodly place,
His pledge and earnest of eternal peace.
Favour'd thus highly, through his own defect
He fell; and here made short sojourn; he fell,
And, for the bitterness of sorrow, changed
Laughter unblamed and ever-new delight.
That vapours none, exhaled from earth beneath,
Or from the waters (which, wherever heat
Attracts them, follow), might ascend thus far
To vex man's peaceful state, this mountain rose
So high toward the heaven, nor fears the rage
Of elements contending; from that part
Exempted, where the gate his limit bars.
Because the circumambient air, throughout,
With its first impulse circles still, unless
Aught interpose to check or thwart its course;
Upon the summit, which on every side
To visitation of the impassive air
Is open, doth that motion strike, and makes
Beneath its sway the umbrageous wood resound:
And in the shaken plant such power resides,
That it impregnates with its efficacy
The voyaging breeze, upon whose subtle plume
That, wafted, flies abroad; and the other land,
Receiving (as 'tis worthy in itself,
Or in the clime that warms it), doth conceive;
And from its womb produces many a tree
Of various virtue. This when thou hast heard,
The marvel ceases, if in yonder earth
Some plant, without apparent seed, be found
To fix its fibrous stem. And further learn,
That with prolific foison of all seeds
This holy plain is fill'd, and in itself
Bears fruit that ne'er was pluck'd on other soil.

"The water, thou behold'st, springs not from vein,
Restored by vapour, that the cold converts;
As stream that intermittently repairs
And spends his pulse of life; but issues forth
From fountain, solid, undecaying, sure:
And, by the will omnific, full supply
Feeds whatsoe'er on either side it pours;
On this, devolved with power to take away
Remembrance of offence; on that, to bring
Remembrance back of every good deed done.
From whence its name of Lethe on this part;
On the other, Eunoe: both of which must first
Be tasted, ere it work; the last exceeding
All flavours else. Albeit thy thirst may now
Be well contented, if I here break off,
No more revealing; yet a corollary
I freely give beside: nor deem my words
Less grateful to thee, if they somewhat pass
The stretch of promise. They, whose verse of yore
The golden age recorded and its bliss,
On the Parnassian mountain, of this place
Perhaps had dream'd. Here was man guiltless; here
Perpetual spring, and every fruit; and this
The far-famed nectar." Turning to the bards,
When she had ceased, I noted in their looks
A smile at her conclusion; then my face
Again directed to the lovely dame.

Already had my steps,
Though slow, so far into that ancient wood
Transported me, I could not ken the place
Where I had enter'd.

Canto XXVIII., lines 22-25.

Beneath a sky
So beautiful, came four and twenty elders,
By two and two, with flower-de-luces crown'd.

Canto XXIX., lines 80-82.

P. P.—38.   The one so ruddy, that her form had scarce
            Been known within a furnace of clear flame;
            The next did look, as if the flesh and bones
            Were emerald; snow new-fallen seem'd the third.
                            Canto XXIX., lines 118-121.

A virgin in my view appear'd, beneath
Green mantle, robed in hue of living flame.

Canto XXX., lines 32, 33.

CANTO XXIX.

ARGUMENT.

The lady, who in a following canto is called Matilda, moves along the side of the stream in a contrary direction to the current, and Dante keeps equal pace with her on the opposite bank. A marvellous sight, preceded by music, appears in view.

SINGING, as if enamour'd, she resumed
And closed the song, with "Blessed they whose sins
Are cover'd." Like the wood-nymphs then, that tripp'd
Singly across the sylvan shadows; one
Eager to view, and one to escape the sun;
So moved she on, against the current, up
The verdant rivage. I, her mincing step
Observing, with as tardy step pursued.

Between us not an hundred paces trod,
The bank, on each side bending equally,
Gave me to face the orient. Nor our way
Far onward brought us, when to me at once
She turn'd, and cried: "My brother! look, and hearken."
And lo! a sudden lustre ran across
Through the great forest on all parts, so bright,
I doubted whether lightning were abroad;
But that, expiring ever in the spleen
That doth unfold it, and this during still,
And waxing still in splendour, made me question
What it might be: and a sweet melody
Ran through the luminous air. Then did I chide,
With warrantable zeal, the hardihood
Of our first parent; for that there, where earth
Stood in obedience to the heavens, she only,
Woman, the creature of an hour, endured not

Restraint of any veil, which had she borne
Devoutly, joys, ineffable as these,
Had from the first, and long time since, been mine.

 While, through that wilderness of primy sweets
That never fade, suspense I walk'd, and yet
Expectant of beatitude more high;
Before us, like a blazing fire, the air
Under the green boughs glow'd; and, for a song,
Distinct the sound of melody was heard.

 O ye thrice holy virgins! for your sakes
If e'er I suffer'd hunger, cold, and watching,
Occasion calls on me to crave your bounty.
Now through my breast let Helicon his stream
Pour copious, and Urania with her choir
Arise to aid me; while the verse unfolds
Things, that do almost mock the grasp of thought.

 Onward a space, what seem'd seven trees of gold
The intervening distance to mine eye
Falsely presented; but, when I was come
So near them, that no lineament was lost
Of those, with which a doubtful object, seen
Remotely, plays on the misdeeming sense;
Then did the faculty, that ministers
Discourse to reason, these for tapers of gold
Distinguish; and i' the singing trace the sound
"Hosanna." Above, their beauteous garniture
Flamed with more ample lustre, than the moon
Through cloudless sky at midnight, in her noon.

 I turn'd me, full of wonder, to my guide;
And he did answer with a countenance
Charged with no less amazement: whence my view
Reverted to those lofty things, which came
So slowly moving towards us, that the bride
Would have outstript them on her bridal day.

The lady call'd aloud: "Why thus yet burns
Affection in thee for these living lights,
And dost not look on that which follows them?"

I straightway mark'd a tribe behind them walk,
As if attendant on their leaders, clothed
With raiment of such whiteness, as on earth
Was never. On my left, the watery gleam
Borrow'd, and gave me back, when there I look'd,
As in a mirror, my left side portray'd.

When I had chosen on the river's edge
Such station, that the distance of the stream
Alone did separate me; there I stay'd
My steps for clearer prospect, and beheld
The flames go onward, leaving, as they went,
The air behind them painted as with trail
Of liveliest pencils; so distinct were mark'd
All those seven listed colours, whence the sun
Maketh his bow, and Cynthia her zone.
These streaming gonfalons did flow beyond
My vision; and ten paces, as I guess,
Parted the outermost. Beneath a sky
So beautiful, came four and twenty elders,
By two and two, with flower-de-luces crown'd.
All sang one song: "Blessed be thou among
The daughters of Adam! and thy loveliness
Blessed for ever!" After that the flowers,
And the fresh herblets, on the opposite brink,
Were free from that elected race; as light
In heaven doth second light, came after them
Four animals, each crown'd with verdurous leaf.
With six wings each was plumed; the plumage full
Of eyes; and the eyes of Argus would be such,
Were they endued with life. Reader! more rhymes
I will not waste in shadowing forth their form:

For other need so straitens, that in this
I may not give my bounty room. But read
Ezekiel; for he paints them, from the north
How he beheld them come by Chebar's flood,
In whirlwind, cloud, and fire; and even such
As thou shalt find them character'd by him,
Here were they; save as to the pennons: there,
From him departing, John accords with me.

    The space, surrounded by the four, enclosed
A car triumphal: on two wheels it came,
Drawn at a Gryphon's neck; and he above
Stretch'd either wing uplifted, 'tween the midst
And the three listed hues, on each side, three;
So that the wings did cleave or injure none;
And out of sight they rose. The members, far
As he was bird, were golden: white the rest,
With vermeil intervein'd. So beautiful
A car, in Rome, ne'er graced Augustus' pomp,
Or Africanus'; e'en the sun's itself
Were poor to this; that chariot of the sun,
Erroneous, which in blazing ruin fell
At Tellus' prayer devout, by the just doom
Mysterious of all-seeing Jove. Three nymphs,
At the right wheel, came circling in smooth dance:
The one so ruddy, that her form had scarce
Been known within a furnace of clear flame;
The next did look, as if the flesh and bones
Were emerald; snow new-fallen seem'd the third.
Now seem'd the white to lead, the ruddy now;
And from her song who led, the others took
Their measure, swift or slow. At the other wheel,
A band quaternion, each in purple clad,
Advanced with festal step, as, of them, one
The rest conducted; one, upon whose front

PURGATORY.—CANTO XXIX.

Three eyes were seen. In rear of all this group,
Two old men I beheld, dissimilar
In raiment, but in port and gesture like,
Solid and mainly grave; of whom, the one
Did show himself some favour'd counsellor
Of the great Coan, him, whom nature made
To serve the costliest creature of her tribe:
His fellow mark'd an opposite intent;
Bearing a sword, whose glitterance and keen edge,
E'en as I view'd it with the flood between,
Appall'd me. Next, four others I beheld
Of humble seeming: and, behind them all,
One single old man, sleeping as he came,
With a shrewd visage. And these seven, each
Like the first troop were habited; but wore
No braid of lilies on their temples wreathed.
Rather, with roses and each vermeil flower,
A sight, but little distant, might have sworn,
That they were all on fire above their brow.

Whenas the car was o'er against me, straight
Was heard a thundering, at whose voice it seem'd
The chosen multitude were stay'd; for there,
With the first ensigns, made they solemn halt.

CANTO XXX.

ARGUMENT.

Beatrice descends from heaven, and rebukes the poet.

SOON as that polar light, fair ornament
   Of the first heaven, which hath never known
   Setting nor rising, nor the shadowy veil
Of other cloud than sin, to duty there
Each way convoying, as that lower doth
The steersman to his port, stood firmly fixed;
Forthwith the saintly tribe, who in the van
Between the Gryphon and its radiance came,
Did turn them to the car, as to their rest:
And one, as if commission'd from above,
In holy chant thrice shouted forth aloud
"Come, spouse! from Libanus:" and all the rest
Took up the song.—At the last audit, so
The blest shall rise, from forth his cavern each
Uplifting lightly his new-vested flesh;
As, on the sacred litter, at the voice
Authoritative of that elder, sprang
A hundred ministers and messengers
Of life eternal. "Blessed thou, who comest!"
And, "Oh!" they cried, "from full hands scatter ye
Unwithering lilies:" and, so saying, cast
Flowers over head and round them on all sides.
   I have beheld, ere now, at break of day,
The eastern clime all roseate; and the sky
Opposed, one deep and beautiful serene;
And the sun's face so shaded, and with mists

PURGATORY.—CANTO XXX.

Attemper'd, at his rising, that the eye
Long while endured the sight: thus, in a cloud
Of flowers, that from those hands angelic rose,
And down within and outside of the car
Fell showering, in white veil with olive wreathed,
A virgin in my view appear'd, beneath
Green mantle, robed in hue of living flame:
And o'er my spirit, that so long a time
Had from her presence felt no shuddering dread,
Albeit mine eyes discern'd her not, there moved
A hidden virtue from her, at whose touch
The power of ancient love was strong within me.

No sooner on my vision streaming, smote
The heavenly influence, which, years past, and e'en
In childhood, thrill'd me, than towards Virgil I
Turn'd me to leftward: panting, like a babe,
That flees for refuge to his mother's breast,
If aught have terrified or work'd him woe:
And would have cried, "There is no dram of blood,
That doth not quiver in me. The old flame
Throws out clear tokens of reviving fire."
But Virgil had bereaved us of himself;
Virgil, my best-loved father; Virgil, he
To whom I gave me up for safety: nor
All our prime mother lost, avail'd to save
My undew'd cheeks from blur of soiling tears.

"Dante! weep not that Virgil leaves thee; nay,
Weep thou not yet: behoves thee feel the edge
Of other sword; and thou shalt weep for that."

As to the prow or stern, some admiral
Paces the deck, inspiriting his crew,
When 'mid the sail-yards all hands ply aloof;
Thus, on the left side of the car, I saw
(Turning me at the sound of mine own name,

Which here I am compell'd to register)
The virgin station'd, who before appear'd
Veil'd in that festive shower angelical.

    Towards me, across the stream, she bent her eyes;
Though from her brow the veil descending, bound
With foliage of Minerva, suffer'd not
That I beheld her clearly: then with act
Full royal, still insulting o'er her thrall,
Added, as one who, speaking, keepeth back
The bitterest saying, to conclude the speech:
"Observe me well. I am, in sooth, I am
Beatrice. What! and hast thou deign'd at last
Approach the mountain? Knewest not, O man!
Thy happiness is here?" Down fell mine eyes
On the clear fount; but there, myself espying,
Recoil'd, and sought the greenswerd; such a weight
Of shame was on my forehead. With a mien
Of that stern majesty, which doth surround
A mother's presence to her awe-struck child,
She look'd; a flavour of such bitterness
Was mingled in her pity. There her words
Brake off; and suddenly the angels sang,
"In thee, O gracious Lord! my hope hath been:"
But went no further than, "Thou, Lord! hast set
My feet in ample room." As snow, that lies,
Amidst the living rafters on the back
Of Italy, congeal'd, when drifted high
And closely piled by rough Sclavonian blasts;
Breathe but the land whereon no shadow falls,
And straightway melting it distils away,
Like a fire-wasted taper: thus was I,
Without a sigh or tear, or ever these
Did sing, that, with the chiming of heaven's sphere,
Still in their warbling chime: but when the strain

Of dulcet symphony express'd for me
Their soft compassion, more than could the words,
"Virgin! why so consumest him?" then, the ice,
Congeal'd about my bosom, turn'd itself
To spirit and water; and with anguish forth
Gush'd, through the lips and eyelids, from the heart.

    Upon the chariot's same edge still she stood,
Immovable; and thus address'd her words
To those bright semblances with pity touch'd:
"Ye in the eternal day your vigils keep;
So that nor night nor slumber, with close stealth,
Conveys from you a single step, in all
The goings on of time: thence, with more heed
I shape mine answer, for his ear intended,
Who there stands weeping; that the sorrow now
May equal the transgression. Not alone
Through operation of the mighty orbs,
That mark each seed to some predestined aim,
As with aspect or fortunate or ill
The constellations meet; but through benign
Largess of heavenly graces, which rain down
From such a height as mocks our vision, this man
Was, in the freshness of his being, such,
So gifted virtually, that in him
All better habits wondrously had thrived.
The more of kindly strength is in the soil,
So much doth evil seed and lack of culture
Mar it the more, and make it run to wildness.
These looks sometime upheld him; for I show'd
My youthful eyes, and led him by their light
In upright walking. Soon as I had reach'd
The threshold of my second age, and changed
My mortal for immortal; then he left me,
And gave himself to others. When from flesh

THE VISION.

To spirit I had risen, and increase
Of beauty and of virtue circled me,
I was less dear to him, and valued less.
His steps were turn'd into deceitful ways,
Following false images of good, that make
No promise perfect. Nor avail'd me aught
To sue for inspirations, with the which,
I, both in dreams of night, and otherwise,
Did call him back; of them, so little reck'd him.
Such depth he fell, that all device was short
Of his preserving, save that he should view
The children of perdition. To this end
I visited the purlieus of the dead:
And one, who hath conducted him thus high,
Received my supplications urged with weeping.
It were a breaking of God's high decree,
If Lethe should be past, and such food tasted,
Without the cost of some repentant tear."

CANTO XXXI.

ARGUMENT.

Beatrice continues her reprehension of Dante, who confesses his error, and falls to the ground. Coming to himself again, he is by Matilda drawn through the waters of Lethe, and presented first to the four virgins who figure the cardinal virtues; these in their turn lead him to the Gryphon, a symbol of our Saviour; and the three virgins representing the evangelical virtues intercede for him with Beatrice, that she would display to him her second beauty.

"O THOU!" her words she thus without delay
   Resuming, turn'd their point on me, to whom
   They, with but lateral edge, seem'd harsh before:
"Say thou, who stand'st beyond the holy stream,
If this be true. A charge, so grievous, needs,
Thine own avowal." On my faculty
Such strange amazement hung, the voice expired
Imperfect, ere its organs gave it birth.
   A little space refraining, then she spake:
"What dost thou muse on? Answer me. The wave
On thy remembrances of evil yet
Hath done no injury." A mingled sense
Of fear and of confusion, from my lips
Did such a "Yea" produce, as needed help
Of vision to interpret. As when breaks,
In act to be discharged, a cross-bow bent
Beyond its pitch, both nerve and bow o'erstretch'd;
The flagging weapon feebly hits the mark:
Thus, tears and sighs forth gushing, did I burst,
Beneath the heavy load: and thus my voice
Was slacken'd on its way. She straight began:
"When my desire invited thee to love
The good, which sets a bound to our aspirings;

What bar of thwarting foss or linked chain
Did meet thee, that thou so shouldst quit the hope
Of further progress? or what bait of ease,
Or promise of allurement, led thee on
Elsewhere, that thou elsewhere shouldst rather wait?"
    A bitter sigh I drew, then scarce found voice
To answer; hardly to these sounds my lips
Gave utterance, wailing: "Thy fair looks withdrawn,
Things present, with deceitful pleasures, turn'd
My steps aside." She answering spake: "Hadst thou
Been silent, or denied what thou avow'st,
Thou hadst not hid thy sin the more; such eye
Observes it. But whene'er the sinner's cheek
Breaks forth into the precious-streaming tears
Of self-accusing, in our court the wheel
Of justice doth run counter to the edge.
Howe'er, thou mayst profit by thy shame
For errors past, and that henceforth more strength
May arm thee, when thou hear'st the Syren-voice;
Lay thou aside the motive to this grief,
And lend attentive ear, while I unfold
How opposite a way my buried flesh
Should have impell'd thee. Never didst thou spy,
In art or nature, aught so passing sweet,
As were the limbs that in their beauteous frame
Enclosed me, and are scatter'd now in dust.
If sweetest thing thus fail'd thee with my death,
What, afterward, of mortal, should thy wish
Have tempted? When thou first hadst felt the dart
Of perishable things, in my departing
For better realms, thy wing thou shouldst have pruned
To follow me; and never stoop'd again,
To 'bide a second blow, for a slight girl,
Or other gaud as transient and as vain.

The beauteous dame, her arms expanding, clasp'd
My temples, and immerged me where 'twas fit
The waves should drench me.

Canto XXXI., lines 100–102.

P. P.—41.

At her side,
As 'twere that none might bear her off, I saw
A giant stand; and ever and anon
They mingled kisses.

Canto XXXII., lines 148–151.

The new and inexperienced bird awaits,
Twice it may be, or thrice, the fowler's aim;
But in the sight of one whose plumes are full,
In vain the net is spread, the arrow wing'd."

  I stood, as children silent and ashamed
Stand, listening, with their eyes upon the earth,
Acknowledging their fault, and self-condemn'd.
And she resumed: "If, but to hear, thus pains thee;
Raise thou thy beard, and lo! what sight shall do."

  With less reluctance yields a sturdy holm,
Rent from its fibres by a blast, that blows
From off the pole, or from Iarbas' land,
Than I at her behest my visage raised:
And thus the face denoting by the beard,
I mark'd the secret sting her words convey'd.

  No sooner lifted I mine aspect up,
Than I perceived those primal creatures cease
Their flowery sprinkling; and mine eyes beheld
(Yet unassured and wavering in their view)
Beatrice; she, who towards the mystic shape,
That joins two natures in one form, had turn'd:
And, even under shadow of her veil,
And parted by the verdant rill that flow'd
Between, in loveliness she seem'd as much
Her former self surpassing, as on earth
All others she surpass'd. Remorseful goads
Shot sudden through me. Each thing else, the more
Its love had late beguiled me, now the more
Was loathsome. On my heart so keenly smote
The bitter consciousness, that on the ground
O'erpower'd I fell: and what my state was then,
She knows, who was the cause. When now my strength
Flow'd back, returning outward from the heart,
The lady, whom alone I first had seen,

I found above me. "Loose me not," she cried:
"Loose not thy hold:" and lo! had dragg'd me high
As to my neck into the stream; while she,
Still as she drew me after, swept along
Swift as a shuttle, bounding o'er the wave.

   The blessed shore approaching, then was heard
So sweetly, "Tu asperges me," that I
May not remember, much less tell the sound.

   The beateous dame, her arms expanding, clasp'd
My temples, and immerged me where 'twas fit
The wave should drench me: and, thence raising up,
Within the fourfold dance of lovely nymphs
Presented me so laved; and with their arm
They each did cover me. "Here are we nymphs,
And in the heaven are stars. Or ever earth
Was visited of Beatrice, we,
Appointed for her handmaids, tended on her.
We to her eyes will lead thee: but the light
Of gladness, that is in them, well to scan,
Those yonder three, of deeper ken than ours,
Thy sight shall quicken." Thus began their song:
And then they led me to the Gryphon's breast,
Where, turn'd toward us, Beatrice stood.
"Spare not thy vision. We have station'd thee
Before the emeralds, whence love, erewhile,
Hath drawn his weapons on thee." As they spake,
A thousand fervent wishes riveted
Mine eyes upon her beaming eyes, that stood,
Still fix'd toward the Gryphon, motionless.
As the sun strikes a mirror, even thus
Within those orbs the twyfold being shone;
For ever varying, in one figure now
Reflected, now in other. Reader! muse
How wondrous in my sight it seem'd, to mark

A thing, albeit stedfast in itself,
Yet in its imaged semblance mutable.

    Full of amaze, and joyous, while my soul
Fed on the viand, whereof still desire
Grows with satiety; the other three,
With gesture that declared a loftier line,
Advanced: to their own carol, on they came
Dancing, in festive ring angelical.

    "Turn, Beatrice!" was their song: "Oh! turn
Thy saintly sight on this thy faithful one,
Who, to behold thee, many a wearisome pace
Hath measured. Gracious at our prayer, vouchsafe
Unveil to him thy cheeks: that he may mark
Thy second beauty, now conceal'd." O splendour!
O sacred light eternal! who is he,
So pale with musing in Pierian shades,
Or with that fount so lavishly imbued,
Whose spirit should not fail him in the essay
To represent thee such as thou didst seem,
When under cope of the still-chiming heaven
Thou gavest to open air thy charms reveal'd?

CANTO XXXII.

ARGUMENT.

Dante is warned not to gaze too fixedly on Beatrice. The procession moves on, accompanied by Matilda, Statius, and Dante, till they reach an exceeding lofty tree, where divers strange chances befall.

MINE eyes with such an eager coveting
   Were bent to rid them of their ten years' thirst,
   No other sense was waking: and e'en they
Were fenced on either side from heed of aught;
So tangled, in its custom'd toils, that smile
Of saintly brightness drew me to itself:
When forcibly, toward the left, my sight
The sacred virgins turn'd; for from their lips
I heard the warning sounds: "Too fix'd a gaze!"
   Awhile my vision labour'd; as when late
Upon the o'erstrain'd eyes the sun hath smote:
But soon, to lesser object, as the view
Was now recover'd (lesser in respect
To that excess of sensible, whence late
I had perforce been sunder'd), on their right
I mark'd that glorious army wheel, and turn,
Against the sun and sevenfold lights, their front.
As when, their bucklers for protection raised,
A well-ranged troop, with portly banners curl'd,
Wheel circling, ere the whole can change their ground;
E'en thus the goodly regiment of heaven,
Proceeding, all did pass us ere the car
Had sloped his beam. Attendant at the wheels
The damsels turn'd; and on the Gryphon moved
The sacred burden, with a pace so smooth,

No feather on him trembled. The fair dame,
Who through the wave had drawn me, companied
By Statius and myself, pursued the wheel,
Whose orbit, rolling, mark'd a lesser arch.

    Through the high wood, now void (the more her blame,
Who by the serpent was beguiled), I pass'd,
With step in cadence to the harmony
Angelic. Onward had we moved, as far,
Perchance, as arrow at three several flights
Full wing'd had sped, when from her station down
Descended Beatrice. With one voice
All murmur'd "Adam;" circling next a plant
Despoil'd of flowers and leaf, on every bough.
Its tresses, spreading more as more they rose,
Were such, as 'midst their forest wilds, for height,
The Indians might have gazed at. "Blessed thou,
Gryphon! whose beak hath never pluck'd that tree
Pleasant to taste: for hence the appetite
Was warp'd to evil." Round the stately trunk
Thus shouted forth the rest, to whom return'd
The animal twice-gender'd: "Yea! for so
The generation of the just are saved."
And turning to the chariot-pole, to foot
He drew it of the widow'd branch, and bound
There, left unto the stock whereon it grew.

    As when large floods of radiance from above
Stream, with that radiance mingled, which ascends
Next after setting of the scaly sign,
Our plants then burgein, and each wears anew
His wonted colours, ere the sun have yoked
Beneath another star his flamy steeds;
Thus putting forth a hue more faint than rose,
And deeper than the violet, was renew'd
The plant, erewhile in all its branches bare.

THE VISION.

Unearthly was the hymn, which then arose.
I understood it not, nor to the end
Endured the harmony. Had I the skill
To pencil forth how closed the unpitying eyes
Slumbering, when Syrinx warbled (eyes that paid
So dearly for their watching), then, like painter,
That with a model paints, I might design
The manner of my falling into sleep.
But feign who will the slumber cunningly,
I pass it by to when I waked; and tell,
How suddenly a flash of splendour rent
The curtain of my sleep, and one cries out,
"Arise: what dost thou?" As the chosen three,
On Tabor's mount, admitted to behold
The blossoming of that fair tree, whose fruit
Is coveted of angels, and doth make
Perpetual feast in heaven; to themselves
Returning, at the word whence deeper sleeps
Were broken, they their tribe diminish'd saw;
Both Moses and Elias gone, and changed
The stole their master wore; thus to myself
Returning, over me beheld I stand
The piteous one, who, cross the stream, had brought
My steps. "And where," all doubting, I exclaim'd,
"Is Beatrice?"—"See her," she replied,
"Beneath the fresh leaf, seated on its root.
Behold the associate choir, that circles her.
The others, with a melody more sweet
And more profound, journeying to higher realms,
Upon the Gryphon tend." If there her words
Were closed, I know not; but mine eyes had now
Ta'en view of her, by whom all other thoughts
Were barr'd admittance. On the very ground
Alone she sat, as she had there been left

A guard upon the wain, which I beheld
Bound to the twyform beast. The seven nymphs
Did make themselves a cloister round about her;
And, in their hands, upheld those lights secure
From blast septentrion and the gusty south.

"A little while thou shalt be forester here;
And citizen shalt be, for ever with me,
Of that true Rome, wherein Christ dwells a Roman.
To profit the misguided world, keep now
Thine eyes upon the car; and what thou seest,
Take heed thou write, returning to that place."

Thus Beatrice: at whose feet inclined
Devout, at her behest, my thought and eyes,
I, as she bade, directed. Never fire,
With so swift motion, forth a stormy cloud
Leap'd downward from the welkin's furthest bound,
As I beheld the bird of Jove descend
Down through the tree; and, as he rush'd, the rind
Disparting crush beneath him; buds much more,
And leaflets. On the car, with all his might
He struck; whence, staggering, like a ship it reel'd,
At random driven, to starboard now, o'ercome,
And now to larboard, by the vaulting waves.

Next, springing up into the chariot's womb,
A fox I saw, with hunger seeming pined
Of all good food. But, for his ugly sins
The saintly maid rebuking him, away
Scampering he turn'd, fast as his hide-bound corpse
Would bear him. Next, from whence before he came,
I saw the eagle dart into the hull
O' the car, and leave it with his feathers lined:
And then a voice, like that which issues forth
From heart with sorrow rived, did issue forth
From heaven, and, "O poor bark of mine!" it cried,

THE VISION.

"How badly art thou freighted." Then it seem'd
That the earth open'd, between either wheel;
And I beheld a dragon issue thence,
That through the chariot fix'd his forkèd train;
And like a wasp, that draggeth back the sting,
So drawing forth his baleful train, he dragg'd
Part of the bottom forth; and went his way,
Exulting. What remain'd, as lively turf
With green herb, so did clothe itself with plumes,
Which haply had, with purpose chaste and kind,
Been offer'd; and therewith were closed the wheels,
Both one and other, and the beam, so quickly,
A sigh were not breathed sooner. Thus transform'd,
The holy structure, through its several parts,
Did put forth heads; three on the beam, and one
On every side: the first like oxen horn'd;
But with a single horn upon their front,
The four. Like monster, sight hath never seen.
O'er it methought there sat, secure as rock
On mountain's lofty top, a shameless whore,
Whose ken roved loosely round her. At her side,
As 'twere that none might bear her off, I saw
A giant stand; and ever and anon
They mingled kisses. But, her lustful eyes
Chancing on me to wander, that fell minion
Scourged her from head to foot all o'er; then full
Of jealousy, and fierce with rage, unloosed
The monster, and dragg'd on, so far across
The forest, that from me its shades alone
Shielded the harlot and the new-form'd brute.

Were further space allow'd
Then, Reader! might I sing, though but in part,
That beverage, with whose sweetness I had ne'er
Been sated.

Canto XXXIII., lines 134-137.

CANTO XXXIII.

ARGUMENT.

After a hymn sung, Beatrice leaves the tree, and takes with her the seven virgins, Matilda, Statius, and Dante. She then darkly predicts to our Poets some future events. Lastly, the whole band arrive at the fountain, from whence the two streams, Lethe and Eunoe, separating, flow different ways; and Matilda, at the desire of Beatrice, causes our Poet to drink of the latter stream.

"THE heathen, Lord! are come:" responsive thus,
The trinal now, and now the virgin band
Quaternion, their sweet psalmody began,
Weeping; and Beatrice listen'd, sad
And sighing, to the song, in such a mood,
That Mary, as she stood beside the cross,
Was scarce more changed. But when they gave her place
To speak, then, risen upright on her feet,
She, with a colour glowing bright as fire,
Did answer: "Yet a little while, and ye
Shall see me not; and, my beloved sisters!
Again a little while, and ye shall see me."

Before her then she marshal'd all the seven;
And, beckoning only, motion'd me, the dame,
And that remaining sage, to follow her.

So on she pass'd; and had not set, I ween,
Her tenth step to the ground, when, with mine eyes,
Her eyes encounter'd; and, with visage mild,
"So mend thy pace," she cried, "that if my words
Address thee, thou mayst still be aptly placed
To hear them." Soon as duly to her side
I now had hasten'd: "Brother!" she began,
"Why makest thou no attempt at questioning,

As thus we walk together?" Like to those
Who, speaking with too reverent an awe
Before their betters, draw not forth the voice
Alive unto their lips, befell me then
That I in sounds imperfect thus began:
"Lady! what I have need of, that thou know'st;
And what will suit my need." She answering thus:
"Of fearfulness and shame, I will that thou
Henceforth do rid thee; that thou speak no more,
As one who dreams. Thus far be taught of me:
The vessel which thou saw'st the serpent break,
Was, and is not: let him, who hath the blame,
Hope not to scare God's vengeance with a sop.
Without an heir for ever shall not be
That eagle, he, who left the chariot plumed,
Which monster made it first and next a prey.
Plainly I view, and therefore speak, the stars
E'en now approaching, whose conjunction, free
From all impedient and bar, brings on
A season, in the which, one sent from God
(Five hundred, five, and ten, do mark him out),
That foul one, and the accomplice of her guilt,
The giant, both, shall slay. And if perchance
My saying, dark as Themis or as Sphinx,
Fail to persuade thee (since like them it foils
The intellect with blindness), yet erelong
Events shall be the Naiads, that will solve
This knotty riddle; and no damage light
On flock or field. Take heed; and as these words
By me are utter'd, teach them even so
To those who live that life, which is a race
To death: and when thou writest them, keep in mind
Not to conceal how thou hast seen the plant,
That twice hath now been spoil'd. This whoso robs,

This whoso plucks, with blasphemy of deed
Sins against God, who for his use alone
Creating hallow'd it. For taste of this,
In pain and in desire, five thousand years
And upward, the first soul did yearn for him
Who punish'd in himself the fatal gust.

   "Thy reason slumbers, if it deem this height,
And summit thus inverted, of the plant,
Without due cause: and were not vainer thoughts,
As Elsa's numbing waters, to thy soul,
And their fond pleasures had not dyed it dark
As Pyramus the mulberry; thou hadst seen,
In such momentous circumstance alone,
God's equal justice morally implied
In the forbidden tree. But since I mark thee,
In understanding, harden'd into stone,
And, to that hardness, spotted too and stain'd,
So that thine eye is dazzled at my word;
I will, that, if not written, yet at least
Painted thou take it in thee, for the cause,
That one brings home his staff inwreathed with palm."

   I thus: "As wax by seal, that changeth not
Its impress, now is stamp'd my brain by thee.
But wherefore soars thy wish'd-for speech so high
Beyond my sight, that loses it the more,
The more it strains to reach it?"—"To the end
That thou mayst know," she answer'd straight, "the school,
That thou hast follow'd; and how far behind,
When following my discourse, its learning halts:
And mayst behold your art, from the divine
As distant, as the disagreement is
'Twixt earth and heaven's most high and rapturous orb."

   "I not remember," I replied, "that e'er
I was estranged from thee; nor for such fault

Doth conscience chide me." Smiling she return'd:
"If thou canst not remember, call to mind
How lately thou hast drunk of Lethe's wave;
And, sure as smoke doth indicate a flame,
In that forgetfulness itself conclude
Blame from thy alienated will incurr'd.
From henceforth, verily, my words shall be
As naked, as will suit them to appear
In thy unpractised view." More sparkling now,
And with retarded course, the sun possess'd
The circle of mid-day, that varies still
As the aspect varies of each several clime;
When, as one, sent in vaward of a troop
For escort, pauses, if perchance he spy
Vestige of somewhat strange and rare; so paused
The sevenfold band, arriving at the verge
Of a dun umbrage hoar, such as is seen,
Beneath green leaves and gloomy branches, oft
To overbrow a bleak and alpine cliff.
And, where they stood, before them, as it seem'd,
I, Tigris and Euphrates both, beheld
Forth from one fountain issue; and, like friends,
Linger at parting. "O enlightening beam!
O glory of our kind! beseech thee say
What water this, which, from one source derived,
Itself removes to distance from itself?"

    To such entreaty answer thus was made:
"Entreat Matilda, that she teach thee this."

    And here, as one who clears himself of blame
Imputed, the fair dame return'd: "Of me
He this and more hath learnt; and I am safe
That Lethe's water hath not hid it from him."

    And Beatrice: "Some more pressing care,
That oft the memory 'reaves, perchance hath made

His mind's eye dark. But lo, where Eunoe flows!
Lead thither; and, as thou art wont, revive
His fainting virtue." As a courteous spirit,
That proffers no excuses, but as soon
As he hath token of another's will,
Makes it his own; when she had ta'en me, thus
The lovely maiden moved her on, and call'd
To Statius, with an air most lady-like:
"Come thou with him." Were further space allow'd,
Then, reader! might I sing, though but in part,
That beverage, with whose sweetness I had ne'er
Been sated. But, since all the leaves are full,
Appointed for this second strain, mine art
With warning bridle checks me. I return'd
From the most holy wave, regenerate,
E'en as new plants renew'd with foliage new
Pure and made apt for mounting to the stars.

PARADISE.

THE VISION OF DANTE.

PARADISE.

CANTO I.

ARGUMENT.

The Poet ascends with Beatrice towards the first heaven, and is by her resolved of certain doubts which arise in his mind.

HIS glory, by whose might all things are moved,
Pierces the universe, and in one part
Sheds more resplendence, elsewhere less. In heaven,
That largeliest of his light partakes, was I,
Witness of things, which, to relate again,
Surpasseth power of him who comes from thence;
For that, so near approaching its desire,
Our intellect is to such depth absorb'd,
That memory cannot follow. Nathless all,
That in my thoughts I of that sacred realm
Could store, shall now be matter of my song.
    Benign Apollo! this last labour aid;
And make me such a vessel of thy worth,
As thy own laurel claims, of me beloved.
Thus far hath one of steep Parnassus' brows
Sufficed me; henceforth, there is need of both
For my remaining enterprise. Do thou
Enter into my bosom, and there breathe
So, as when Marsyas by thy hand was dragg'd

Forth from his limbs, unsheathed. O power divine!
If thou to me of thine impart so much,
That of that happy realm the shadow'd form
Traced in my thoughts I may set forth to view;
Thou shalt behold me of thy favour'd tree
Come to the foot, and crown myself with leaves:
For to that honour thou, and my high theme
Will fit me. If but seldom, mighty Sire!
To grace his triumph, gathers thence a wreath
Cæsar, or bard (more shame for human wills
Depraved), joy to the Delphic god must spring
From the Peneian foliage, when one breast
Is with such thirst inspired. From a small spark
Great flame hath risen: after me, perchance,
Others with better voice may pray, and gain,
From the Cyrrhæan city, answer kind.

    Through divers passages, the world's bright lamp
Rises to mortals; but through that which joins
Four circles with the threefold cross, in best
Course, and in happiest constellation set
He comes; and, to the worldly wax, best gives
Its temper and impression. Morning there,
Here eve was well nigh by such passage made;
And whiteness had o'erspread that hemisphere,
Blackness the other part; when to the left
I saw Beatrice turn'd, and on the sun
Gazing, as never eagle fix'd his ken.
As from the first a second beam is wont
To issue, and reflected upwards rise,
Even as a pilgrim bent on his return:
So of her act, that through the eyesight pass'd
Into my fancy, mine was form'd: and straight,
Beyond our mortal wont, I fix'd mine eyes
Upon the sun. Much is allow'd us there,

That here exceeds our power; thanks to the place
Made for the dwelling of the human kind.

   I suffered it not long; and yet so long,
That I beheld it bickering sparks around,
As iron that comes boiling from the fire.
And suddenly upon the day appear'd
A day new-risen; as he, who hath the power,
Had with another sun bedeck'd the sky.

   Her eyes fast fix'd on the eternal wheels,
Beatrice stood unmoved; and I with ken
Fix'd upon her, from upward gaze removed,
At her aspect, such inwardly became
As Glaucus, when he tasted of the herb
That made him peer among the ocean gods:
Words may not tell of that transhuman change;
And therefore let the example serve, though weak,
For those whom grace hath better proof in store.

   If I were only what thou didst create,
Then newly, Love! by whom the heaven is ruled;
Thou know'st, who by thy light didst bear me up.
Whenas the wheel which thou dost ever guide,
Desired Spirit! with its harmony,
Temper'd of thee and measured, charm'd mine ear,
Then seem'd to me so much of heaven to blaze
With the sun's flame, that rain or flood ne'er made
A lake so broad. The newness of the sound,
And that great light, inflamed me with desire,
Keener than e'er was felt, to know their cause.

   Whence she, who saw me, clearly as myself,
To calm my troubled mind, before I ask'd,
Open'd her lips, and gracious thus began:
"With false imagination thou thyself
Makest dull; so that thou seest not the thing,
Which thou hadst seen, had that been shaken off.

THE VISION.

Thou art not on the earth as thou believest;
For lightning, scaped from its own proper place,
Ne'er ran, as thou hast hither now return'd."
    Although divested of my first-raised doubt
By those brief words accompanied with smiles,
Yet in new doubt was I entangled more,
And said: "Already satisfied, I rest
From admiration deep; but now admire
How I above those lighter bodies rise."
    Whence, after utterance of a piteous sigh,
She towards me bent her eyes, with such a look,
As on her frenzied child a mother casts;
Then thus began: "Among themselves all things
Have order; and from hence the form, which makes
The universe resemble God. In this
The higher creatures see the printed steps
Of that eternal worth, which is the end
Whither the line is drawn. All natures lean,
In this their order, diversly: some more,
Some less approaching to their primal source.
Thus they to different havens are moved on
Through the vast sea of being, and each one
With instinct given, that bears it in its course:
This to the lunar sphere directs the fire;
This moves the hearts of mortal animals;
This the brute earth together knits, and binds.
Nor only creatures, void of intellect,
Are aim'd at by this bow; but even those,
That have intelligence and love, are pierced.
That Providence, who so well orders all,
With her own light makes ever calm the heaven,
In which the substance, that hath greatest speed,
Is turn'd: and thither now, as to our seat
Predestined, we are carried by the force

Of that strong cord, that never looses dart
But at fair aim and glad. Yet it is true,
That as, oft-times, but ill accords the form
To the design of art, through sluggishness
Or unreplying matter; so this course
Is sometimes quitted by the creature, who
Hath power, directed thus, to bend elsewhere;
As from a cloud the fire is seen to fall,
From its original impulse warp'd to earth,
By vitious fondness. Thou no more admire
Thy soaring (if I rightly deem), than lapse
Of torrent downwards from a mountain's height.
There would in thee for wonder be more cause,
If, free of hinderance, thou hadst stay'd below,
As living fire unmoved upon the earth."

So said, she turn'd toward the heaven her face.

CANTO II.

ARGUMENT.

Dante and his celestial guide enter the moon. The cause of the spots or shadows which appear in that body is explained to him.

ALL ye, who in small bark have following sail'd,
Eager to listen, on the adventurous track
Of my proud keel, that singing cuts her way,
Backward return with speed, and your own shores
Revisit; nor put out to open sea,
Where losing me, perchance ye may remain
Bewilder'd in deep maze. The way I pass,
Ne'er yet was run: Minerva breathes the gale;
Apollo guides me; and another Nine,
To my rapt sight, the arctic beams reveal.
Ye other few who have outstretch'd the neck
Timely for food of angels, on which here
They live, yet never know satiety;
Through the deep brine ye fearless may put out
Your vessel; marking well the furrow broad
Before you in the wave, that on both sides
Equal returns. Those, glorious, who pass'd o'er
To Colchos, wonder'd not as ye will do,
When they saw Jason following the plough.

The increate perpetual thirst, that draws
Toward the realm of God's own form, bore us
Swift almost as the heaven ye behold.

Beatrice upward gazed, and I on her;
And in such space as on the notch a dart
Is placed, then loosen'd flies, I saw myself
Arrived, where wonderous thing engaged my sight.

Whence she, to whom no care of mine was hid,
Turning to me, with aspect glad as fair,
Bespake me: "Gratefully direct thy mind
To God, through whom to this first star we come."

    Meseem'd as if a cloud had cover'd us,
Translucent, solid, firm, and polish'd bright,
Like adamant, which the sun's beams had smit.
Within itself the ever-during pearl
Received us; as the wave a ray of light
Receives, and rests unbroken. If I then
Was of corporeal frame, and it transcend
Our weaker thought, how one dimension thus
Another could endure, which needs must be
If body enter body; how much more
Must the desire inflame us to behold
That essence, which discovers by what means
God and our nature join'd! There will be seen
That, which we hold through faith; not shown by proof,
But in itself intelligibly plain,
E'en as the truth that man at first believes.

    I answer'd: "Lady! I with thoughts devout,
Such as I best can frame, give thanks to him,
Who hath removed me from the mortal world.
But tell, I pray thee, whence the gloomy spots
Upon this body, which below on earth
Give rise to talk of Cain in fabling quaint?"

    She somewhat smiled, then spake: "If mortals err
In their opinion, when the key of sense
Unlocks not, surely wonder's weapon keen
Ought not to pierce thee: since thou find'st, the wings
Of reason to pursue the senses' flight
Are short. But what thy own thought is, declare."

    Then I: "What various here above appears,
Is caused, I deem, by bodies dense or rare."

She then resumed: "Thou certainly wilt see
In falsehood thy belief o'erwhelm'd, if well
Thou listen to the arguments which I
Shall bring to face it. The eighth sphere displays
Numberless lights, the which, in kind and size,
May be remark'd of different aspects:
If rare or dense of that were cause alone,
One single virtue then would be in all;
Alike distributed, or more, or less.
Different virtues needs must be the fruits
Of formal principles; and these, save one,
Will by thy reasoning be destroy'd. Beside,
If rarity were of that dusk the cause,
Which thou inquirest, either in some part
That planet must throughout be void, nor fed
With its own matter; or, as bodies share
Their fat and leanness, in like manner this
Must in its volume change the leaves. The first,
If it were true, had through the sun's eclipse
Been manifested, by transparency
Of light, as through aught rare beside effused.
But this is not. Therefore remains to see
The other cause: and, if the other fall,
Erroneous so must prove what seem'd to thee.
If not from side to side this rarity
Pass through, there needs must be a limit, whence
Its contrary no further lets it pass.
And hence the beam, that from without proceeds,
Must be pour'd back; as colour comes, through glass
Reflected, which behind it lead conceals.
Now wilt thou say, that there of murkier hue,
Than, in the other part, the ray is shown,
By being thence refracted further back.
From this perplexity will free thee soon

Experience, if thereof thou trial make,
The fountain whence your arts derive their streams.
Three mirrors shalt thou take, and two remove
From thee alike; and more remote the third,
Betwixt the former pair, shall meet thine eyes:
Then turn'd toward them, cause behind thy back
A light to stand, that on the three shall shine,
And thus reflected come to thee from all.
Though that, beheld most distant, do not stretch
A space so ample, yet in brightness thou
Wilt own it equaling the rest. But now
As under snow the ground, if the warm ray
Smites it, remains dismantled of the hue
And cold, that cover'd it before; so thee,
Dismantled in thy mind, I will inform
With light so lively, that the tremulous beam
Shall quiver where it falls. Within the heaven,
Where peace divine inhabits, circles round
A body, in whose virtue lies the being
Of all that it contains. The following heaven,
That hath so many lights, this being divides,
Through different essences, from it distinct,
And yet contain'd within it. The other orbs
Their separate distinctions variously
Dispose, for their own seed and produce apt.
Thus do these organs of the world proceed,
As thou beholdest now, from step to step;
Their influences from above deriving,
And thence transmitting downwards. Mark me well;
How through this passage to the truth I ford,
The truth thou lovest; that thou henceforth, alone,
Mayst know to keep the shallows, safe, untold.

"The virtue and motion of the sacred orbs,
As mallet by the workman's hands, must needs

By blessed movers be inspired. This heaven,
Made beauteous by so many luminaries,
From the deep spirit, that moves its circling sphere,
Its image takes and impress as a seal:
And as the soul, that dwells within your dust,
Through members different, yet together form'd,
In different powers resolves itself; e'en so
The intellectual efficacy unfolds
Its goodness multiplied throughout the stars;
On its own unity revolving still.
Different virtue compact different
Makes with the precious body it enlivens,
With which it knits, as life in you is knit.
From its original nature full of joy,
The virtue mingled through the body shines,
As joy through pupil of the living eye.
From hence proceeds that which from light to light
Seems different, and not from dense or rare.
This is the formal cause, that generates,
Proportion'd to, its power, the dusk or clear."

CANTO III.

ARGUMENT.

In the moon Dante meets with Piccarda, the sister of Forese, who tells him that this planet is allotted to those who, after having made profession of chastity and a religious life, had been compelled to violate their vows; and she then points out to him the spirit of the Empress Costanza.

THAT sun, which erst with love my bosom warm'd,
Had of fair truth unveil'd the sweet aspect,
By proof of right, and of the false reproof;
And I, to own myself convinced and free
Of doubt, as much as needed, raised my head
Erect for speech. But soon a sight appear'd,
Which, so intent to mark it, held me fix'd,
That of confession I no longer thought.
  As through translucent and smooth glass, or wave
Clear and unmoved, and flowing not so deep
As that its bed is dark, the shape returns
So faint of our impictured lineaments,
That, on white forehead set, a pearl as strong
Comes to the eye; such saw I many a face,
All stretch'd to speak; from whence I straight conceived,
Delusion opposite to that, which raised,
Between the man and fountain, amorous flame.
  Sudden, as I perceived them, deeming these
Reflected semblances, to see of whom
They were, I turn'd mine eyes, and nothing saw;
Then turn'd them back, directed on the light
Of my sweet guide, who, smiling, shot forth beams
From her celestial eyes. "Wonder not thou,"
She cried, "at this my smiling, when I see

Thy childish judgment; since not yet on truth
It rests the foot, but, as it still is wont,
Makes thee fall back in unsound vacancy.
True substances are these, which thou behold'st,
Hither through failure of their vow exiled.
But speak thou with them; listen, and believe,
That the true light, which fills them with desire,
Permits not from its beams their feet to stray."
    Straight to the shadow, which for converse seem'd
Most earnest, I address'd me: and began
As one by over-eagerness perplex'd:
"O spirit, born for joy! who in the rays
Of life eternal, of that sweetness know'st
The flavour, which, not tasted, passes far
All apprehension; me it well would please,
If thou wouldst tell me of thy name, and this
Your station here." Whence she with kindness prompt,
And eyes glistering with smiles: "Our charity,
To any wish by justice introduced,
Bars not the door; no more than she above,
Who would have all her court be like herself.
I was a virgin sister in the earth:
And if thy mind observe me well, this form
With such addition graced of loveliness
Will not conceal me long; but thou wilt know
Piccarda, in the tardiest sphere thus placed,
Here 'mid these other blessed also blest.
Our hearts, whose high affections burn alone
With pleasure from the Holy Spirit conceived,
Admitted to his order, dwell in joy.
And this condition, which appears so low,
Is for this cause assign'd us, that our vows
Were, in some part, neglected and made void."
    Whence I to her replied: "Something divine

Such saw I many a face,
All stretched to speak.

Canto III., lines 14, 15.

So drew
Full more than thousand splendours towards us.

Canto V., lines 99, 100.

Beams in your countenances wonderous fair;
From former knowledge quite transmuting you.
Therefore to recollect was I so slow.
But what thou say'st hath to my memory
Given now such aid, that to retrace your forms
Is easier. Yet inform me, ye, who here
Are happy; long ye for a higher place,
More to behold, and more in love to dwell?"

    She with those other spirits gently smiled;
Then answer'd with such gladness, that she seem'd
With love's first flame to glow: "Brother! our will
Is, in composure, settled by the power
Of charity, who makes us will alone
What we possess, and nought beyond desire:
If we should wish to be exalted more,
Then must our wishes jar with the high will
Of him, who sets us here; which in these orbs
Thou wilt confess not possible, if here
To be in charity must needs befall,
And if her nature well thou contemplate.
Rather it is inherent in this state
Of blessedness, to keep ourselves within
The divine will, by which our wills with his
Are one. So that as we, from step to step,
Are placed throughout this kingdom, pleases all,
Even as our King, who in us plants his will;
And in his will is our tranquillity:
It is the mighty ocean, whither tends
Whatever it creates and nature makes."

    Then saw I clearly how each spot in heaven
Is Paradise, though with like gracious dew
The supreme virtue shower not over all.

    But as it chances, if one sort of food
Hath satiated, and of another still

THE VISION.

The appetite remains, that this is ask'd,
And thanks for that return'd; even so did I,
In word and motion, bent from her to learn
What web it was, through which she had not drawn
The shuttle to its point. She thus began:
"Exalted worth and perfectness of life
The Lady higher up inshrine in heaven,
By whose pure laws upon your nether earth
The robe and veil they wear; to that intent,
That e'en till death they may keep watch, or sleep,
With their great bridegroom, who accepts each vow,
Which to his gracious pleasure love conforms.
I from the world, to follow her, when young
Escaped; and, in her vesture mantling me,
Made promise of the way her sect enjoins.
Thereafter men, for ill than good more apt,
Forth snatch'd me from the pleasant cloister's pale.
God knows how, after that, my life was framed.
This other splendid shape, which thou behold'st
At my right side, burning with all the light
Of this our orb, what of myself I tell
May to herself apply. From her, like me
A sister, with like violence were torn
The saintly folds, that shaded her fair brows.
E'en when she to the world again was brought
In spite of her own will and better wont,
Yet not for that the bosom's inward veil
Did she renounce. This is the luminary
Of mighty Constance, who from that loud blast,
Which blew the second over Suabia's realm,
That power produced, which was the third and last."
    She ceased from further talk, and then began
"Ave Maria" singing; and with that song
Vanish'd, as heavy substance through deep wave.

Mine eye, that, far as it was capable,
Pursued her, when in dimness she was lost,
Turn'd to the mark where greater want impell'd,
And bent on Beatrice all its gaze.
But she, as lightning, beam'd upon my looks;
So that the sight sustain'd it not at first.
Whence I to question her became less prompt.

CANTO IV.

ARGUMENT.

While they still continue in the moon, Beatrice removes certain doubts which Dante had conceived respecting the place assigned to the blessed, and respecting the will absolute or conditional. He inquires whether it is possible to make satisfaction for a vow broken.

BETWEEN two kinds of food, both equally
 Remote and tempting, first a man might die
 Of hunger, ere he one could freely chuse.
E'en so would stand a lamb between the maw
Of two fierce wolves, in dread of both alike:
E'en so between two deer a dog would stand.
Wherefore, if I was silent, fault nor praise
I to myself impute; by equal doubts
Held in suspense; since of necessity
It happen'd. Silent was I, yet desire
Was painted in my looks; and thus I spake
My wish more earnestly than language could.
 As Daniel, when the haughty king he freed
From ire, that spurr'd him on to deeds unjust
And violent; so did Beatrice then.
 "Well I discern," she thus her words address'd,
"How thou art drawn by each of these desires;
So that thy anxious thought is in itself
Bound up and stifled, nor breathes freely forth.
Thou arguest: if the good intent remain,
What reason that another's violence
Should stint the measure of my fair desert?
 "Cause too thou find'st for doubt, in that it seems
That spirits to the stars, as Plato deem'd,
Return. These are the questions which thy will

Urge equally; and therefore I, the first,
Of that will treat which hath the more of gall.
Of seraphim he who is most enskied,
Moses and Samuel, and either John,
Chuse which thou wilt, nor even Mary's self,
Have not in any other heaven their seats,
Than have those spirits which so late thou saw'st;
Nor more or fewer years exist; but all
Make the first circle beauteous, diversly
Partaking of sweet life, as more or less
Afflation of eternal bliss pervades them.
Here were they shown thee, not that fate assigns
This for their sphere, but for a sign to thee
Of that celestial furthest from the height.
Thus needs, that ye may apprehend, we speak:
Since from things sensible alone ye learn
That, which, digested rightly, after turns
To intellectual. For no other cause
The Scripture, condescending graciously
To your perception, hands and feet to God
Attributes, nor so means; and holy church
Doth represent with human countenance
Gabriel, and Michael, and him who made
Tobias whole. Unlike what here thou seest,
The judgment of Timæus, who affirms
Each soul restored to its particular star;
Believing it to have been taken thence,
When nature gave it to inform her mold:
Yet to appearance his intention is
Not what his words declare: and so to shun
Derision, haply thus he hath disguised
His true opinion. If his meaning be,
That to the influencing of these orbs revert
The honour and the blame in human acts,

Perchance he doth not wholly miss the truth.
This principle, not understood aright,
Erewhile perverted well nigh all the world;
So that it fell to fabled names of Jove,
And Mercury, and Mars. That other doubt,
Which moves thee, is less harmful; for it brings
No peril of removing thee from me.

"That, to the eye of man, our justice seems
Unjust, is argument for faith, and not
For heretic declension. But, to the end
This truth may stand more clearly in your view,
I will content thee even to thy wish.

"If violence be, when that which suffers, nought
Consents to that which forceth, not for this
These spirits stood exculpate. For the will,
That wills not, still survives unquench'd, and doth,
As nature doth in fire, though violence
Wrest it a thousand times; for, if it yield
Or more or less, so far it follows force.
And thus did these, when they had power to seek
The hallow'd place again. In them, had will
Been perfect, such as once upon the bars
Held Laurence firm, or wrought in Scævola
To his own hand remorseless; to the path,
Whence they were drawn, their steps had hasten'd back,
When liberty return'd: but in too few,
Resolve, so stedfast, dwells. And by these words,
If duly weigh'd, that argument is void,
Which oft might have perplex'd thee still. But now
Another question thwarts thee, which, to solve,
Might try thy patience without better aid.
I have, no doubt, instill'd into thy mind,
That blessed spirit may not lie; since near
The source of primal truth it dwells for aye:

And thou mightst after of Piccarda learn
That Constance held affection to the veil;
So that she seems to contradict me here.
Not seldom, brother, it hath chanced for men
To do what they had gladly left undone;
Yet, to shun peril, they have done amiss:
E'en as Alcmæon, at his father's suit
Slew his own mother; so made pitiless,
Not to lose pity. On this point bethink thee,
That force and will are blended in such wise
As not to make the offence excusable.
Absolute will agrees not to the wrong;
But inasmuch as there is fear of woe
From non-compliance, it agrees. Of will
Thus absolute, Piccarda spake, and I
Of the other; so that both have truly said."

    Such was the flow of that pure rill, that well'd
From forth the fountain of all truth; and such
The rest, that to my wandering thoughts I found.

    "O thou, of primal love the prime delight,
Goddess!" I straight replied, "whose lively words
Still shed new heat and vigour through my soul;
Affection fails me to requite thy grace
With equal sum of gratitude: be his
To recompense, who sees and can reward thee.
Well I discern, that by that truth alone
Enlighten'd, beyond which no truth may roam,
Our mind can satisfy her thirst to know:
Therein she resteth, e'en as in his lair
The wild beast, soon as she hath reach'd that bound.
And she hath power to reach it; else desire
Were given to no end. And thence doth doubt
Spring, like a shoot, around the stock of truth;
And it is nature which, from height to height,

On to the summit prompts us. This invites,
This doth assure me, Lady! reverently
To ask thee of another truth, that yet
Is dark to me. I fain would know, if man
By other works well done may so supply
The failure of his vows, that in your scale
They lack not weight." I spake; and on me straight
Beatrice look'd, with eyes that shot forth sparks
Of love celestial, in such copious stream,
That, virtue sinking in me overpower'd,
I turn'd; and downward bent, confused, my sight.

CANTO V.

ARGUMENT.

The question proposed in the last canto is answered. Dante ascends with Beatrice to the planet Mercury, which is the second heaven; and here he finds a multitude of spirits, one of whom offers to satisfy him of anything he may desire to know from them.

"IF beyond earthly wont, the flame of love
Illume me, so that I o'ercome thy power
Of vision, marvel not: but learn the cause
In that perfection of the sight, which, soon
As apprehending, hasteneth on to reach
The good it apprehends. I well discern,
How in thine intellect already shines
The light eternal, which to view alone
Ne'er fails to kindle love; and if aught else
Your love seduces, 'tis but that it shows
Some ill-mark'd vestige of that primal beam.
  "This wouldst thou know: if failure of the vow
By other service may be so supplied,
As from self-question to assure the soul."
  Thus she her words, not heedless of my wish,
Began; and thus, as one who breaks not off
Discourse, continued in her saintly strain.
"Supreme of gifts, which God, creating, gave
Of his free bounty, sign most evident
Of goodness, and in his account most prized,
Was liberty of will; the boon, wherewith
All intellectual creatures, and them sole,
He hath endow'd. Hence now thou mayst infer
Of what high worth the vow, which so is framed,

That when man offers, God well-pleased accepts:
For in the compact between God and him,
This treasure, such as I describe it to thee,
He makes the victim; and of his own act.
What compensation therefore may he find?
If that, whereof thou hast oblation made,
By using well thou think'st to consecrate,
Thou wouldst of theft do charitable deed.
Thus I resolve thee of the greater point.

"But forasmuch as holy church, herein
Dispensing, seems to contradict the truth
I have discover'd to thee, yet behoves
Thou rest a little longer at the board,
Ere the crude aliment which thou hast ta'en,
Digested fitly, to nutrition turn.
Open thy mind to what I now unfold;
And give it inward keeping. Knowledge comes
Of learning well retain'd, unfruitful else.

"This sacrifice, in essence, of two things
Consisteth; one is that, whereof 'tis made;
The covenant, the other. For the last,
It ne'er is cancel'd, if not kept: and hence
I spake, erewhile, so strictly of its force.
For this it was enjoin'd the Israelites,
Though leave were given them, as thou know'st, to change,
The offering, still to offer. The other part,
The matter and the substance of the vow,
May well be such, as that, without offence,
It may for other substance be exchanged.
But, at his own discretion, none may shift
The burden on his shoulders; unreleased
By either key, the yellow and the white.
Nor deem of any change, as less than vain,
If the last bond be not within the new

Included, as the quatre in the six.
No satisfaction therefore can be paid
For what so precious in the balance weighs,
That all in counterpoise must kick the beam.
Take then no vow at random: ta'en, with faith
Preserve it; yet not bent, as Jephthah once,
Blindly to execute a rash resolve,
Whom better it had suited to exclaim,
'I have done ill,' than to redeem his pledge
By doing worse: or, not unlike to him
In folly, that great leader of the Greeks;
Whence, on the altar, Iphigenia mourn'd
Her virgin beauty, and hath since made mourn
Both wise and simple, even all, who hear
Of so fell sacrifice. Be ye more staid,
O Christians! not, like feather, by each wind
Removeable; nor think to cleanse yourselves
In every water. Either testament,
The old and new, is yours: and for your guide,
The shepherd of the church. Let this suffice
To save you. When by evil lust enticed,
Remember ye be men, not senseless beasts;
Nor let the Jew, who dwelleth in your streets,
Hold you in mockery. Be not as the lamb,
That, fickle wanton, leaves its mother's milk,
To dally with itself in idle play."

 Such were the words that Beatrice spake:
These ended, to that region, where the world
Is liveliest, full of fond desire she turn'd.

 Though mainly prompt new question to propose,
Her silence and changed look did keep me dumb.
And as the arrow, ere the cord is still,
Leapeth unto its mark; so on we sped
Into the second realm. There I beheld

THE VISION.

The dame, so joyous, enter, that the orb
Grew brighter at her smiles; and, if the star
Were moved to gladness, what then was my cheer,
Whom nature hath made apt for every change!
 As in a quiet and clear lake the fish,
If aught approach them from without, do draw
Towards it, deeming it their food; so drew
Full more than thousand splendours towards us;
And in each one was heard: "Lo! one arrived
To multiply our loves!" and as each came,
The shadow, streaming forth effulgence new,
Witness'd augmented joy. Here, Reader! think,
If thou didst miss the sequel of my tale,
To know the rest how sorely thou wouldst crave;
And thou shalt see what vehement desire
Possess'd me, soon as these had met my view,
To know their state. "O born in happy hour!
Thou, to whom grace vouchsafes, or e'er thy close
Of fleshly warfare, to behold the thrones
Of that eternal triumph; know, to us
The light communicated, which through heaven
Expatiates without bound. Therefore, if aught
Thou of our beams wouldst borrow for thine aid,
Spare not; and, of our radiance, take thy fill."
 Thus of those piteous spirits one bespake me;
And Beatrice next: "Say on; and trust
As unto gods."—"How in the light supreme
Thou harbour'st, and from thence the virtue bring'st,
That, sparkling in thine eyes, denotes thy joy,
I mark; but who thou art, am still to seek;
Or wherefore, worthy spirit! for thy lot
This sphere assign'd, that oft from mortal ken
Is veil'd by other's beams." I said; and turn'd
Toward the lustre, that with greeting kind

Erewhile had hail'd me. Forthwith, brighter far
Than erst, it wax'd: and, as himself the sun
Hides through excess of light, when his warm gaze
Hath on the mantle of thick vapours prey'd;
Within its proper ray the saintly shape
Was, through increase of gladness, thus conceal'd;
And, shrouded so in splendour, answer'd me,
E'en as the tenour of my song declares.

CANTO VI.

ARGUMENT.

The spirit, who had offered to satisfy the inquiries of Dante, declares himself to be the Emperor Justinian; and after speaking of his own actions, recounts the victories, before him, obtained under the Roman Eagle. He then informs our Poet that the soul of Romeo the pilgrim is in the same star.

"AFTER that Constantine the eagle turn'd
   Against the motions of the heaven, that roll'd
   Consenting with its course, when he of yore,
Lavinia's spouse, was leader of the flight;
A hundred years twice told and more, his seat
At Europe's extreme point, the bird of Jove
Held, near the mountains, whence he issued first;
There under shadow of his sacred plumes
Swaying the world, till through successive hands
To mine he came devolved. Cæsar I was;
And am Justinian; destined by the will
Of that prime love, whose influence I feel,
From vain excess to clear the incumber'd laws.
Or e'er that work engaged me, I did hold
In Christ one nature only; with such faith
Contented. But the blessed Agapete,
Who was chief shepherd, he with warning voice
To the true faith recall'd me. I believed
His words: and what he taught, now plainly see,
As thou in every contradiction seest
The true and false opposed. Soon as my feet
Were to the church reclaim'd, to my great task,
By inspiration of God's grace impell'd,
I gave me wholly; and consign'd mine arms

To Belisarius, with whom heaven's right hand
Was link'd in such conjointment, 'twas a sign
That I should rest. To thy first question thus
I shape mine answer, which were ended here,
But that its tendency doth prompt perforce
To some addition; that thou well mayst mark,
What reason on each side they have to plead,
By whom that holiest banner is withstood,
Both who pretend its power and who oppose.

"Beginning from that hour, when Pallas died
To give it rule, behold the valorous deeds
Have made it worthy reverence. Not unknown
To thee, how for three hundred years and more
It dwelt in Alba, up to those fell lists
Where, for its sake, were met the rival three;
Nor aught unknown to thee, which it achieved
Down from the Sabines' wrong to Lucrece' woe;
With its seven kings conquering the nations round;
Nor all it wrought, by Roman worthies borne
'Gainst Brennus and the Epirot prince, and hosts
Of single chiefs, or states in league combined
Of social warfare: hence, Torquatus stern,
And Quintius named of his neglected locks,
The Decii, and the Fabii hence acquired
Their fame, which I with duteous zeal embalm.
By it the pride of Arab hordes was quell'd,
When they, led on by Hannibal, o'erpass'd
The Alpine rocks, whence glide thy currents, Po!
Beneath its guidance, in their prime of days
Scipio and Pompey triumph'd; and that hill
Under whose summit thou didst see the light,
Rued its stern bearing. After, near the hour,
When heaven was minded that o'er all the world
His own deep calm should brood, to Cæsar's hand

Did Rome consign it; and what then it wrought
From Var unto the Rhine, saw Isere's flood,
Saw Loire and Seine, and every vale, that fills
The torrent Rhone. What after that it wrought,
When from Ravenna it came forth, and leap'd
The Rubicon, was of so bold a flight,
That tongue nor pen may follow it. Towards Spain
It wheel'd its bands, then toward Dyrrachium smote,
And on Pharsalia, with so fierce a plunge,
E'en the warm Nile was conscious to the pang;
Its natives shores Antandros, and the streams
Of Simois revisited, and there
Where Hector lies; then ill for Ptolemy
His pennons shook again; lightening, thence fell
On Juba; and the next, upon your west,
At sound of the Pompeian trump, return'd.

"What following, and in its next bearer's gripe,
It wrought, is now by Cassius and Brutus
Bark'd of in hell; and by Perugia's sons,
And Modena's, was mourn'd. Hence weepeth still
Sad Cleopatra, who, pursued by it,
Took from the adder black and sudden death.
With him it ran e'en to the Red Sea coast;
With him composed the world to such a peace,
That of his temple Janus barr'd the door.

"But all the mighty standard yet had wrought,
And was appointed to perform thereafter,
Throughout the mortal kingdom which it sway'd,
Falls in appearance dwindled and obscured,
If one with steady eye and perfect thought
On the third Cæsar look; for to his hands,
The living Justice, in whose breath I move,
Committed glory, e'en into his hands,
To execute the vengeance of its wrath.

P. P.—45.　　　　　　　　　　　　　　　　　　　　The left bank
That Rhone, when he hath mix'd with Sorga, laves,
In me its lord expected.

Canto VIII., lines 60–62.

About us thus,
Of sempiternal roses, bending, wreathed
Those garlands twain; and to the innermost
E'en thus the external answer'd.

Canto XII., lines 16-19.

"Hear now, and wonder at, what next I tell.
After with Titus it was sent to wreak
Vengeance for vengeance of the ancient sin.
And, when the Lombard tooth, with fang impure,
Did gore the bosom of the holy church,
Under its wings, victorious Charlemain
Sped to her rescue. Judge then for thyself
Of those, whom I erewhile accused to thee,
What they are, and how grievous their offending,
Who are the cause of all your ills. The one
Against the universal ensign rears
The yellow lilies; and with partial aim,
That, to himself, the other arrogates:
So that 'tis hard to see who most offends.
Be yours, ye Ghibellines, to veil your hearts
Beneath another standard: ill is this
Follow'd of him, who severs it and justice:
And let not with his Guelphs the new-crown'd Charles
Assail it; but those talons hold in dread,
Which from a lion of more lofty port
Have rent the casing. Many a time ere now
The sons have for the sire's transgression wail'd:
Nor let him trust the fond belief, that heaven
Will truck its armour for his lilied shield.

"This little star is furnish'd with good spirits,
Whose mortal lives were busied to that end,
That honour and renown might wait on them:
And, when desires thus err in their intention,
True love must needs ascend with slacker beam.
But it is part of our delight, to measure
Our wages with the merit; and admire
The close proportion. Hence doth heavenly justice
Temper so evenly affection in us,
It ne'er can warp to any wrongfulness.

Of diverse voices is sweet music made:
So in our life the different degrees
Render sweet harmony among these wheels.
  "Within the pearl, that now encloseth us,
Shines Romeo's light, whose goodly deed and fair
Met ill acceptance. But the Provençals,
That were his foes, have little cause for mirth.
Ill shapes that man his course, who makes his wrong
Of other's worth. Four daughters were there born
To Raymond Berenger; and every one
Became a queen: and this for him did Romeo,
Though of mean state and from a foreign land.
Yet envious tongues incited him to ask
A reckoning of that just one, who return'd
Twelve fold to him for ten. Aged and poor
He parted thence: and if the world did know
The heart he had, begging his life by morsels,
'Twould deem the praise it yields him scantly dealt."

CANTO VII.

ARGUMENT.

In consequence of what has been said by Justinian, who together with the other spirits have now disappeared, some doubts arise in the mind of Dante respecting the human redemption. These difficulties are fully explained by Beatrice.

"HOSANNA Sanctus Deus Sabaoth,
    Superillustrans claritate tua
    Felices ignes horum malahoth."
Thus chanting saw I turn that substance bright,
With fourfold lustre to its orb again,
Revolving; and the rest, unto their dance,
With it, moved also; and, like swiftest sparks,
In sudden distance from my sight were veil'd.

    Me doubt possess'd; and "Speak," it whisper'd me,
"Speak, speak unto thy lady; that she quench
Thy thirst with drops of sweetness." Yet blank awe,
Which lords it o'er me, even at the sound
Of Beatrice's name, did bow me down
As one in slumber held. Not long that mood
Beatrice suffer'd: she, with such a smile,
As might have made one blest amid the flames,
Beaming upon me, thus her words began:
"Thou in thy thought art pondering (as I deem,
And what I deem is truth) how just revenge
Could be with justice punish'd: from which doubt
I soon will free thee; so thou mark my words;
For they of weighty matter shall possess thee.
Through suffering not a curb upon the power
That will'd in him, to his own profiting,
That man, who was unborn, condemn'd himself;

And, in himself, all who since him have lived,
His offspring: whence, below, the human kind
Lay sick in grievous error many an age;
Until it pleased the Word of God to come
Amongst them down, to his own person joining
The nature from its Maker far estranged,
By the mere act of his eternal love.
Contemplate here the wonder I unfold.
The nature with its Maker thus conjoin'd,
Created first was blameless, pure and good;
But, through itself alone, was driven forth
From Paradise, because it had eschew'd
The way of truth and life, to evil turn'd.
Ne'er then was penalty so just as that
Inflicted by the cross, if thou regard
The nature in assumption doom'd; ne'er wrong
So great, in reference to him, who took
Such nature on him, and endured the doom.
So different effects flow'd from one act:
For by one death God and the Jews were pleased;
And heaven was open'd, though the earth did quake.
Count it not hard henceforth, when thou dost hear
That a just vengeance was, by righteous court,
Justly revenged. But yet I see thy mind,
By thought on thought arising, sore perplex'd;
And, with how vehement desire, it asks
Solution of the maze. What I have heard,
Is plain, thou sayst: but wherefore God this way
For our redemption chose, eludes my search.

"Brother! no eye of man not perfected,
Nor fully ripen'd in the flame of love,
May fathom this decree. It is a mark,
In sooth, much aim'd at, and but little kenn'd:
And I will therefore show thee why such way

Was worthiest. The celestial love, that spurns
All envying in its bounty, in itself
With such effulgence blazeth, as sends forth
All beauteous things eternal. What distils
Immediate thence, no end of being knows;
Bearing its seal immutably imprest.
Whatever thence immediate falls, is free,
Free wholly, uncontrollable by power
Of each thing new: by such conformity
More grateful to its author, whose bright beams,
Though all partake their shining, yet in those
Are liveliest, which resemble him the most.
These tokens of pre-eminence on man
Largely bestow'd, if any of them fail,
He needs must forfeit his nobility,
No longer stainless. Sin alone is that,
Which doth disfranchise him, and make unlike
To the chief good; for that its light in him
Is darken'd. And to dignity thus lost
Is no return; unless, where guilt makes void,
He for ill pleasure pay with equal pain.
Your nature, which entirely in its seed
Transgress'd, from these distinctions fell, no less
Than from its state in Paradise; nor means
Found of recovery (search all methods out
As strictly as thou may) save one of these,
The only fords were left through which to wade:
Either, that God had of his courtesy
Released him merely; or else, man himself
For his own folly by himself atoned.

"Fix now thine eye, intently as thou canst,
On the everlasting counsel; and explore,
Instructed by my words, the dread abyss.

"Man in himself had ever lack'd the means

THE VISION.

Of satisfaction, for he could not stoop
Obeying, in humility so low,
As high, he, disobeying, thought to soar:
And, for this reason, he had vainly tried,
Out of his own sufficiency, to pay
The rigid satisfaction. Then behoved
That God should by his own ways lead him back
Unto the life, from whence he fell, restored:
By both his ways, I mean, or one alone.
But since the deed is ever prized the more,
The more the doer's good intent appears;
Goodness celestial, whose broad signature
Is on the universe, of all its ways
To raise ye up, was fain to leave out none.
Nor aught so vast or so magnificent,
Either for him who gave or who received,
Between the last night and the primal day,
Was or can be. For God more bounty show'd,
Giving himself to make man capable
Of his return to life, than had the terms
Been mere and unconditional release.
And for his justice, every method else
Were all too scant, had not the Son of God
Humbled himself to put on mortal flesh.

"Now, to content thee fully, I revert;
And further in some part unfold my speech,
That thou mayst see it clearly as myself.

"I see, thou sayst, the air, the fire I see,
The earth and water, and all things of them
Compounded, to corruption turn, and soon
Dissolve. Yet these were also things create.
Because, if what were told me had been true,
They from corruption had been therefore free.

"The angels, O my brother! and this clime

Wherein thou art, impassible and pure,
I call created, even as they are
In their whole being. But the elements,
Which thou hast named, and what of them is made,
Are by created virtue inform'd: create,
Their substance; and create, the informing virtue
In these bright stars, that round them circling move.
The soul of every brute and of each plant,
The ray and motion of the sacred lights,
Draw from complexion with meet power endued.
But this our life the eternal good inspires
Immediate, and enamours of itself;
So that our wishes rest for ever here.

"And hence thou mayst by inference conclude
Our resurrection certain, if thy mind
Consider how the human flesh was framed,
When both our parents at the first were made."

CANTO VIII.

ARGUMENT.

The Poet ascends with Beatrice to the third heaven, which is the planet Venus; and here finds the soul of Charles Martel, King of Hungary, who had been Dante's friend on earth, and who now, after speaking of the realms to which he was heir, unfolds the cause why children differ in disposition from their parents.

THE world was, in its day of peril dark,
    Wont to believe the dotage of fond love,
    From the fair Cyprian deity, who rolls
In her third epicycle, shed on men
By stream of potent radiance: therefore they
Of elder time, in their old error blind,
Not her alone with sacrifice adored
And invocation, but like honours paid
To Cupid and Dione, deem'd of them
Her mother, and her son, him whom they feign'd
To sit in Dido's bosom: and from her,
Whom I have sung preluding, borrow'd they
The appellation of that star, which views
Now obvious, and now averse, the sun.
    I was not ware that I was wafted up
Into its orb; but the new loveliness,
That graced my lady, gave me ample proof
That we had enter'd there. And as in flame
A sparkle is distinct, or voice in voice
Discern'd, when one its even tenour keeps,
The other comes and goes; so in that light
I other luminaries saw, that coursed
In circling motion, rapid more or less,
As their eternal vision each impels.

PARADISE.—CANTO VIII.

Never was blast from vapour charged with cold,
Whether invisible to eye or no,
Descended with such speed, it had not seem'd
To linger in dull tardiness, compared
To those celestial lights, that towards us came,
Leaving the circuit of their joyous ring,
Conducted by the lofty seraphim.
And after them, who in the van appear'd,
Such an Hosanna sounded as hath left
Desire, ne'er since extinct in me, to hear
Renew'd the strain. Then, parting from the rest,
One near us drew, and sole began: "We all
Are ready at thy pleasure, well disposed
To do thee gentle service. We are they
To whom thou in the world erewhile didst sing;
'O ye! whose intellectual ministry
Moves the third heaven:' and in one orb we roll,
One motion, one impulse, with those who rule
Princedoms in heaven; yet are of love so full,
That to please thee 'twill be as sweet to rest."
After mine eyes had with meek reverence
Sought the celestial guide, and were by her
Assured, they turn'd again unto the light,
Who had so largely promised; and with voice
That bare the lively pressure of my zeal,
"Tell who ye are," I cried. Forthwith it grew
In size and splendour, through augmented joy;
And thus it answer'd: "A short date, below,
The world possess'd me. Had the time been more,
Much evil, that will come, had never chanced.
My gladness hides thee from me, which doth shine
Around, and shroud me, as an animal
In its own silk enswathed. Thou lovedst me well,
And hadst good cause; for had my sojourning

Been longer on the earth, the love I bare thee
Had put forth more than blossoms. The left bank,
That Rhone, when he hath mix'd with Sorga, laves,
In me its lord expected, and that horn
Of fair Ausonia, with its boroughs old,
Bari, and Croton, and Gaeta piled,
From where the Trento disembogues his waves,
With Verde mingled, to the salt-sea flood.
Already on my temples beam'd the crown,
Which gave me sovereignty over the land
By Danube wash'd, whenas he strays beyond
The limits of his German shores. The realm,
Where, on the gulf by stormy Eurus lash'd,
Betwixt Pelorus and Pachynian heights,
The beautiful Trinacria lies in gloom
(Not through Typhœus, but the vapoury cloud
Bituminous upsteam'd), *that* too did look
To have its sceptre wielded by a race
Of monarchs, sprung through me from Charles and Rodolph;
Had not ill-lording, which doth desperate make
The people ever, in Palermo raised
The shout of 'death,' re-echoed loud and long.
Had but my brother's foresight keen'd as much,
He had been warier, that the greedy want
Of Catalonia might not work his bale.
And truly need there is that he forecast,
Or other for him, lest more freight be laid
On his already over-laden bark.
Nature in him, from bounty fallen to thrift,
Would ask the guard of braver arms, than such
As only care to have their coffers fill'd."

"My liege! it doth enhance the joy thy words
Infuse into me, mighty as it is,
To think my gladness manifest to thee,

As to myself, who own it, when thou look'st
Into the source and limit of all good,
There, where thou markest that which thou dost speak,
Thence prized of me the more. Glad thou hast made me:
Now make intelligent, clearing the doubt
Thy speech hath raised in me; for much I muse,
How bitter can spring up, when sweet is sown."

  I thus inquiring; he forthwith replied:
"If I have power to show one truth, soon that
Shall face thee, which thy questioning declares
Behind thee now conceal'd. The Good, that guides
And blessed makes this realm which thou dost mount,
Ordains its providence to be the virtue
In these great bodies: nor the natures only
The all-perfect mind provides for, but with them
That which preserves them too; for nought, that lies
Within the range of that unerring bow,
But is as level with the destined aim,
As ever mark to arrow's point opposed.
Were it not thus, these heavens thou dost visit,
Would their effect so work, it would not be
Art, but destruction; and this may not chance,
If the intellectual powers, that move these stars,
Fail not, and who, first faulty made them, fail.
Wilt thou this truth more clearly evidenced?"

  To whom I thus: "It is enough: no fear,
I see, lest nature in her part should tire."

  He straight rejoin'd: "Say, were it worse for man,
If he lived not in fellowship on earth?"

  "Yea," answer'd I; "nor here a reason needs."

  "And may that be, if different estates
Grow not of different duties in your life?
Consult your teacher, and he tells you 'no.'"

  Thus did he come, deducing to this point,

And then concluded: "For this cause behoves,
The roots, from whence your operations come,
Must differ. Therefore one is Solon born;
Another, Xerxes; and Melchisedec
A third; and he a fourth, whose airy voyage
Cost him his son. In her circuitous course,
Nature, that is the seal to mortal wax,
Doth well her art, but no distinction owns
'Twixt one or other household. Hence befalls
That Esau is so wide of Jacob: hence
Quirinus of so base a father springs,
He dates from Mars his lineage. Were it not
That Providence celestial overruled,
Nature, in generation, must the path
Traced by the generator still pursue
Unswervingly. Thus place I in thy sight
That, which was late behind thee. But, in sign
Of more affection for thee, 'tis my will
Thou wear this corollary. Nature ever,
Finding discordant fortune, like all seed
Out of its proper climate, thrives but ill.
And were the world below content to mark
And work on the foundation nature lays,
It would not lack supply of excellence.
But ye perversely to religion strain
Him, who was born to gird on him the sword,
And of the fluent phraseman make your king:
Therefore your steps have wander'd from the path."

CANTO IX.

ARGUMENT.

The next spirit, who converses with our Poet in the planet Venus, is the amorous Cunizza. To her succeeds Folco, or Folques, the Provençal bard, who declares that the soul of Rahab the harlot is there also; and then, blaming the Pope for his neglect of the Holy Land, prognosticates some reverse to the Papal power.

AFTER solution of my doubt, thy Charles,
O fair Clemenza, of the treachery spake,
That must befall his seed: "Tell it not,"
Said he, "and let the destined years come round."
Nor may I tell thee more, save that the meed
Of sorrow well-deserved shall quit your wrongs.
    And now the visage of that saintly light
Was to the sun, that fills it, turn'd again,
As to the good, whose plenitude of bliss
Sufficeth all. O ye misguided souls!
Infatuate, who from such a good estrange
Your hearts, and bend your gaze on vanity,
Alas for you!—And lo! toward me, next
Another of those splendent forms approach'd,
That, by its outward brightening, testified
The will it had to pleasure me. The eyes
Of Beatrice, resting, as before,
Firmly upon me, manifested forth
Approval of my wish. "And O," I cried,
"Blest spirit! quickly be my will perform'd;
And prove thou to me, that my inmost thoughts
I can reflect on thee." Thereat the light,
That yet was new to me, from the recess,
Where it before was singing, thus began,

THE VISION.

As one who joys in kindness: "In that part
Of the depraved Italian land, which lies
Between Rialto and the fountain-springs
Of Brenta and of Piava, there doth rise,
But to no lofty eminence, a hill,
From whence erewhile a firebrand did descend,
That sorely shent the region. From one root
I and it sprang; my name on earth Cunizza:
And here I glitter, for that by its light
This star o'ercame me. Yet I nought repine,
Nor grudge myself the cause of this my lot:
Which haply vulgar hearts can scarce conceive.

"This jewel, that is next me in our heaven,
Lustrous and costly, great renown hath left,
And not to perish, ere these hundred years
Five times absolve their round. Consider thou,
If to excel be worthy man's endeavour,
When such life may attend the first. Yet they
Care not for this, the crowd that now are girt
By Adice and Tagliamento, still
Impenitent, though scourged. The hour is near
When for their stubbornness, at Padua's marsh
The water shall be changed, that laves Vicenza.
And where Cagnano meets with Sile, one
Lords it, and bears his head aloft, for whom
The web is now a-warping. Feltro too
Shall sorrow for its godless shepherd's fault,
Of so deep stain, that never, for the like,
Was Malta's bar unclosed. Too large should be
The skillet that would hold Ferrara's blood,
And wearied he, who ounce by ounce would weigh it,
The which this priest, in show of party-zeal,
Courteous will give; nor will the gift ill suit
The country's custom. We descry above

Mirrors, ye call them thrones, from which to us
Reflected shine the judgments of our God:
Whence these our sayings we avouch for good."

    She ended; and appear'd on other thoughts
Intent, re-entering on the wheel she late
Had left. That other joyance meanwhile wax'd
A thing to marvel at, in splendour glowing,
Like choicest ruby stricken by the sun.
For, in that upper clime, effulgence comes
Of gladness, as here laughter: and below,
As the mind saddens, murkier grows the shade.

    "God seeth all: and in him is thy sight,"
Said I, "blest spirit! Therefore will of his
Cannot to thee be dark. Why then delays
Thy voice to satisfy my wish untold;
That voice, which joins the inexpressive song,
Pastime of heaven, the which those ardours sing,
That cowl them with six shadowing wings outspread?
I would not wait thy asking, wert thou known
To me, as throughly I to thee am known."

    He, forthwith answering, thus his words began:
"The valley of waters, widest next to that
Which doth the earth engarland, shapes its course,
Between discordant shores, against the sun
Inward so far, it makes meridian there,
Where was before the horizon. Of that vale
Dwelt I upon the shore, 'twixt Ebro's stream
And Macra's, that divides with passage brief
Genoan bounds from Tuscan. East and west
Are nearly one to Begga and my land
Whose haven erst was with its own blood warm.
Who knew my name, were wont to call me Folco;
And I did bear impression of this heaven,
That now bears mine: for not with fiercer flame

THE VISION.

Glow'd Belus' daughter, injuring alike
Sichæus and Creusa, than did I,
Long as it suited the unripen'd down
That fledged my cheek; nor she of Rhodope,
That was beguiled of Demophoon;
Nor Jove's son, when the charms of Iole
Were shrined within his heart. And yet there bides
No sorrowful repentance here, but mirth,
Not for the fault (that doth not come to mind),
But for the virtue, whose o'erruling sway
And providence have wrought thus quaintly. Here
The skill is look'd into, that fashioneth
With such effectual working, and the good
Discern'd, accruing to the lower world
From this above. But fully to content
Thy wishes all that in this sphere have birth,
Demands my further parle. Inquire thou wouldst,
Who of this light is denizen, that here
Beside me sparkles, as the sunbeam doth
On the clear wave. Know then, the soul of Rahab
Is in that gladsome harbour; to our tribe
United, and the foremost rank assign'd.
She to this heaven, at which the shadow ends
Of your sublunar world, was taken up,
First, in Christ's triumph, of all souls redeem'd:
For well behoved, that, in some part of heaven,
She should remain a trophy, to declare
The mighty conquest won with either palm;
For that she favour'd first the high exploit
Of Joshua on the Holy Land, whereof
The Pope recks little now. Thy city, plant
Of him, that on his Maker turn'd the back,
And of whose envying so much woe hath sprung,
Engenders and expands the cursed flower,

That hath made wander both the sheep and lambs,
Turning the shepherd to a wolf. For this,
The gospel and great teachers laid aside,
The decretals, as their stuft margins show,
Are the sole study. Pope and Cardinals,
Intent on these, ne'er journey but in thought
To Nazareth, where Gabriel oped his wings.
Yet it may chance, ere long, the Vatican,
And other most selected parts of Rome,
That were the grave of Peter's soldiery,
Shall be deliver'd from the adulterous bond."

CANTO X.

ARGUMENT.

Their next ascent carries them into the sun, which is the fourth heaven. Here they are encompassed with a wreath of blessed spirits, twelve in number. Thomas Aquinas, who is one of these, declares the names and endowments of the rest.

LOOKING into his first-born with the love
Which breathes from both eternal, the first Might
Ineffable, wherever eye or mind
Can roam, hath in such order all disposed,
As none may see and fail to enjoy. Raise, then,
O reader! to the lofty wheels, with me,
Thy ken directed to the point, whereat
One motion strikes on the other. There begin
Thy wonder of the mighty Architect,
Who loves his work so inwardly, his eye
Doth ever watch it. See, how thence oblique
Brancheth the circle, where the planets roll
To pour their wished influence on the world;
Whose path not bending thus, in heaven above
Much virtue would be lost, and here on earth
All power well nigh extinct; or, from direct
Were its departure distant more or less,
I' the universal order, great defect
Must, both in heaven and here beneath, ensue.

    Now rest thee, reader! on thy bench, and muse
Anticipative of the feast to come;
So shall delight make thee not feel thy toil.
Lo! I have set before thee; for thyself
Feed now: the matter I indite, henceforth
Demands entire my thought. Join'd with the part.

Which late we told of, the great minister
Of nature, that upon the world imprints
The virtue of the heaven, and doles out
Time for us with his beam, went circling on
Along the spires, where each hour sooner comes;
And I was with him, weetless of ascent,
But as a man, that weets him come, ere thinking.

    For Beatrice, she who passeth on
So suddenly from good to better, time
Counts not the act, oh then how great must needs
Have been her brightness! What there was i' th' sun
(Where I had entered), not through change of hue,
But light transparent—did I summon up
Genius, art, practice—I might not so speak,
It should be e'er imagined: yet believed
It may be, and the sight be justly craved.
And if our fantasy fail of such height,
What marvel, since no eye above the sun
Hath ever travel'd? Such are they dwell here,
Fourth family of the Omnipotent Sire,
Who of his spirit and of his offspring shows;
And holds them still enraptured with the view.
And thus to me Beatrice: "Thank, oh thank
The Sun of angels, him, who by his grace
To this perceptible hath lifted thee."

    Never was heart in such devotion bound,
And with complacency so absolute
Disposed to render up itself to God,
As mine was at those words: and so entire
The love for Him, that held me, it eclipsed
Beatrice in oblivion. Nought displeased
Was she, but smiled thereat so joyously,
That of her laughing eyes the radiance brake
And scattered my collected mind abroad.

THE VISION.

  Then saw I a bright band, in liveliness
Surpassing, who themselves did make the crown,
And us their centre: yet more sweet in voice,
Than, in their visage, beaming. Cinctured thus,
Sometime Latona's daughter we behold,
When the impregnate air retains the thread
That weaves her zone. In the celestial court,
Whence I return, are many jewels found,
So dear and beautiful, they cannot brook
Transporting from that realm: and of these lights
Such was the song. Who doth not prune his wing
To soar up thither, let him look from thence
For tidings from the dumb. When, singing thus,
Those burning suns had circled round us thrice,
As nearest stars around the fixed pole;
Then seem'd they like to ladies, from the dance
Not ceasing, but suspense, in silent pause,
Listening, till they have caught the strain anew:
Suspended so they stood: and, from within,
Thus heard I one, who spake: "Since with its beam
The grace, whence true love lighteth first his flame,
That after doth increase by loving, shines
So multiplied in thee, it leads thee up
Along this ladder, down whose hallow'd steps
None e'er descend, and mount them not again;
Who from his phial should refuse thee wine
To slake thy thirst, no less constrained were,
Than water flowing not unto the sea.
Thou fain wouldst hear, what plants are these, that bloom
In the bright garland, which, admiring, girds
This fair dame round, who strengthens thee from heaven.
I, then, was of the lambs, that Dominic
Leads, for his saintly flock, along the way
Where well they thrive, not swoln with vanity.

He, nearest on my right hand, brother was,
And master to me: Albert of Cologne.
Is this; and, of Aquinum, Thomas I.
If thou of all the rest wouldst be assured,
Let thine eye, waiting on the words I speak,
In circuit journey round the blessed wreath.
That next resplendence issues from the smile
Of Gratian, who to either forum lent
Such help, as favour wins in Paradise.
The other, nearest, who adorns our quire,
Was Peter, he that with the widow gave
To holy church his treasure. The fifth light,
Goodliest of all, is by such love inspired,
That all your world craves tidings of his doom:
Within, there is the lofty light, endow'd
With sapience so profound, if truth be truth,
That with a ken of such wide amplitude
No second hath arisen. Next behold
That taper's radiance, to whose view was shown
Clearliest, the nature and the ministry
Angelical, while yet in flesh it dwelt.
In the other little light serenely smiles
That pleader for the Christian temples, he,
Who did provide Augustin of his lore.
Now, if thy mind's eye pass from light to light,
Upon my praises following, of the eighth
Thy thirst is next. The saintly soul, that shows
The world's deceitfulness, to all who hear him,
Is, with the sight of all the good that is,
Blest there. The limbs, whence it was driven, lie
Down in Cieldauro; and from martyrdom
And exile came it here. Lo! further on,
Where flames the ardurous spirit of Isidore;
Of Bede; and Richard, more than man, erewhile,

THE VISION.

In deep discernment. Lastly this, from whom
Thy look on me reverteth, was the beam
Of one, whose spirit, on high musings bent,
Rebuked the lingering tardiness of death.
It is the eternal light of Sigebert,
Who escaped not envy, when of truth he argued,
Reading in the straw-litter'd street." Forthwith,
As clock, that calleth up the spouse of God
To win her bridegroom's love at matin's hour,
Each part of other fitly drawn and urged,
Sends out a tinkling sound, of note so sweet,
Affection springs in well-disposed breast;
Thus saw I move the glorious wheel; thus heard
Voice answering voice, so musical and soft,
It can be known but where day endless shines.

CANTO XI.

ARGUMENT.

Thomas Aquinas enters at large into the life and character of St. Francis; and then solves one of two difficulties which he perceived to have risen in Dante's mind from what he had heard in the last canto.

O FOND anxiety of mortal men!
How vain and inconclusive arguments
Are those, which make thee beat thy wings below.
For statutes one, and one for aphorisms
Was hunting; this the priesthood follow'd; that,
By force or sophistry, aspired to rule;
To rob, another; and another sought,
By civil business, wealth; one, moiling, lay
Tangled in net of sensual delight;
And one to wistless indolence resign'd;
What time from all these empty things escaped,
With Beatrice, I thus gloriously
Was raised aloft, and made the guest of heaven.
    They of the circle to that point, each one,
Where erst it was, had turn'd; and steady glow'd,
As candle in his socket. Then within
The lustre, that erewhile bespake me, smiling
With merer gladness, heard I thus begin:
    "E'en as his beam illumes me, so I look
Into the eternal light, and clearly mark
Thy thoughts from whence they rise. Thou art in doubt,
And wouldst that I should bolt my words afresh
In such plain open phrase, as may be smooth
To thy perception, where I told thee late
That 'well they thrive;' and that 'no second such
Hath risen,' which no small distinction needs.
    "The Providence, that governeth the world,

THE VISION.

In depth of counsel by created ken
Unfathomable, to the end that she,
Who with loud cries was 'spoused in precious blood,
Might keep her footing towards her well-beloved,
Safe in herself and constant unto him,
Hath two ordain'd, who should on either hand
In chief escort her: one, seraphic all
In fervency; for wisdom upon earth,
The other, splendour of cherubic light.
I but of one will tell: he tells of both,
Who one commendeth, which of them soe'er
Be taken: for their deeds were to one end.

"Between Tupino, and the wave that falls
From blest Ubaldo's chosen hill, there hangs
Rich slope of mountain high, whence heat and cold
Are wafted through Perugia's eastern gate:
And Nocera with Gualdo, in its rear,
Mourn for their heavy yoke. Upon that side,
Where it doth break its steepness most, arose
A sun upon the world, as duly this
From Ganges doth: therefore let none, who speak
Of that place, say Ascesi: for its name
Were lamely so deliver'd: but the East,
To call things rightly, be it henceforth styled.
He was not yet much distant from his rising,
When his good influence 'gan to bless the earth.
A dame, to whom none openeth pleasure's gate
More than to death, was, 'gainst his father's will,
His stripling choice: and he did make her his,
Before the spiritual court, by nuptial bonds,
And in his father's sight: from day to day,
Then loved her more devoutly. She, bereaved
Of her first husband, slighted and obscure,
Thousand and hundred years and more, remain'd

Without a single suitor, till he came.
Nor aught avail'd, that, with Amyclas, she
Was found unmoved at rumour of his voice,
Who shook the world: nor aught her constant boldness
Whereby with Christ she mounted on the cross,
When Mary stay'd beneath. But not to deal
Thus closely with thee longer, take at large
The lovers' titles—Poverty and Francis.
Their concord and glad looks, wonder and love,
And sweet regard gave birth to holy thoughts,
So much, that venerable Bernard first
Did bare his feet, and, in pursuit of peace
So heavenly, ran, yet deem'd his footing slow.
O hidden riches! O prolific good!
Egidius bares him next, the next Sylvester,
And follow, both, the bridegroom: so the bride
Can please them. Thenceforth goes he on his way
The father and the master, with his spouse,
And with that family, whom now the cord
Girt humbly: nor did abjectness of heart
Weigh down his eyelids, for that he was son
Of Pietro Bernardone, and by men
In wondrous sort despised. But royally
His hard intention he to Innocent
Set forth: and, from him, first received the seal
On his religion. Then, when numerous flock'd
The tribe of lowly ones, that traced *his* steps,
Whose marvellous life deservedly were sung
In heights empyreal; though Honorius' hand
A second crown, to deck their Guardian's virtues,
Was by the eternal Spirit inwreathed: and when
He had, through thirst of martyrdom, stood up
In the proud Soldan's presence, and there preach'd
Christ and his followers, but found the race

Unripen'd for conversion; back once more
He hasted (not to intermit his toil),
And reap'd Ausonian lands. On the hard rock,
'Twixt Arno and the Tiber, he from Christ
Took the last signet, which his limbs two years
Did carry. Then, the season come that he,
Who to such good had destined him was pleased
To advance him to the meed, which he had earn'd
By his self-humbling; to his brotherhood,
As their just heritage, he gave in charge
His dearest lady: and enjoin'd their love
And faith to her; and, from her bosom, will'd
His goodly spirit should move forth, returning
To its appointed kingdom; nor would have
His body laid upon another bier.

"Think now of one, who were a fit colleague
To keep the bark of Peter, in deep sea,
Helm'd to right point; and such our Patriarch was.
Therefore who follow him as he enjoins,
Thou mayst be certain, take good lading in.
But hunger of new viands tempts his flock;
So that they needs into strange pastures wide
Must spread them: and the more remote from him
The stragglers wander, so much more they come
Home, to the sheep-fold, destitute of milk.
There are of them, in truth, who fear their harm,
And to the shepherd cleave; but these so few,
A little stuff may furnish out their cloaks.

"Now, if my words be clear; if thou have ta'en
Good heed; if that, which I have told, recall
To mind; thy wish may be in part fulfill'd:
For thou wilt see the plant from whence they split;
And he shall see, who girds him, what that means,
'That well they thrive, not swoln with vanity.'"

CANTO XII.

ARGUMENT.

A second circle of glorified souls encompasses the first. Buonaventura, who is one of them, celebrates the praises of Saint Dominic, and informs Dante who the other eleven are that are in this second circle or garland.

SOON as its final word the blessed flame
　　Had raised for utterance, straight the holy mill
　　Began to wheel; nor yet had once revolved,
Or e'er another, circling, compass'd it,
Motion to motion, song to song, conjoining;
Song, that as much our muses doth excel,
Our Syrens with their tuneful pipes, as ray
Of primal splendour doth its faint reflex.
　　As when, if Juno bid her handmaid forth,
Two arches parallel, and trick'd alike,
Span the thin cloud, the outer taking birth
From that within (in manner of that voice
Whom love did melt away, as sun the mist),
And they who gaze, presageful call to mind
The compact, made with Noah, of the world
No more to be o'erflow'd; about us thus,
Of sempiternal roses, bending, wreathed
Those garlands twain; and to the innermost
E'en thus the external answer'd. When the footing,
And other great festivity, of song,
And radiance, light with light accordant, each
Jocund and blythe, had at their pleasure still'd
(E'en as the eyes, by quick volition moved,
Are shut and raised together), from the heart
Of one amongst the new lights moved a voice,

That made me seem like needle to the star,
In turning to its whereabout; and thus
Began: "The love, that makes me beautiful,
Prompts me to tell of the other guide, for whom
Such good of mine is spoken. Where one is,
The other worthily should also be;
That as their warfare was alike, alike
Should be their glory. Slow, and full of doubt,
And with thin ranks, after its banner moved
The army of Christ (which it so dearly cost
To reappoint), when its imperial Head,
Who reigneth ever, for the drooping host
Did make provision, thorough grace alone,
And not through its deserving. As thou heard'st,
Two champions to the succour of his spouse
He sent, who by their deeds and words might join
Again his scatter'd people. In that clime
Where springs the pleasant west-wind to unfold
The fresh leaves, with which Europe sees herself
New-garmented; nor from those billows far
Beyond whose chiding, after weary course,
The sun doth sometimes hide him; safe abides
The happy Callaroga, under guard
Of the great shield, wherein the lion lies
Subjected and supreme. And there was born
The loving minion of the Christian faith,
The hallow'd wrestler, gentle to his own,
And to his enemies terrible. So replete
His soul with lively virtue, that when first
Created, even in the mother's womb,
It prophesied. When, at the sacred font,
The spousals were complete 'twixt faith and him,
Where pledge of mutual safety was exchanged,
The dame, who was his surety, in her sleep

Beheld the wondrous fruit, that was from him
And from his heirs to issue. And that such
He might be construed, as indeed he was,
She was inspired to name him of his owner
Whose he was wholly; and so called him Dominic.
And I speak of him, as the labourer,
Whom Christ in his own garden chose to be
His help-mate. Messenger he seem'd, and friend
Fast-knit to Christ; and the first love he show'd,
Was after the first counsel that Christ gave.
Many a time his nurse, at entering, found
That he had risen in silence, and was prostrate,
As who should say, 'My errand was for this.'
O happy father! Felix rightly named.
O favoured mother! rightly named Joanna;
If that do mean, as men interpret it.
Not for the world's sake, for which now they toil
Upon Ostiense and Taddeo's lore,
But for the real manna, soon he grew
Mighty in learning; and did set himself
To go about the vineyard, that soon turns
To wan and wither'd, if not tended well:
And from the see (whose bounty to the just
And needy is gone by, not through its fault,
But his who fills its basely) he besought,
No dispensation for commuted wrong,
Nor the first vacant fortune, nor the tenths
That to God's paupers rightly appertain,
But, 'gainst an erring and degenerate world,
Licence to fight, in favour of that seed
From which the twice twelve cions gird thee round.
Then, with sage doctrine and good will to help,
Forth on his great apostleship he fared,
Like torrent bursting from a lofty vein;

And, dashing 'gainst the stocks of heresy,
Smote fiercest, where resistance was most stout.
Thence many rivulets have since been turn'd
Over the garden catholic to lead
Their living waters, and have fed its plants.
  "If such, one wheel of that two-yoked car,
Wherein the holy church defended her,
And rode triumphant through the civil broil;
Thou canst not doubt its fellow's excellence,
Which Thomas, ere my coming, hath declared
So courteously unto thee. But the track,
Which its smooth fellies made, is now deserted:
That, mouldy mother is, where late were lees.
His family, that wont to trace his path,
Turn backward, and invert their steps; erelong
To rue the gathering in of their ill crop,
When the rejected tares in vain shall ask
Admittance to the barn. I question not
But he, who search'd our volume, leaf by leaf,
Might still find page with this inscription on't,
'I am as I was wont.' Yet such were not
From Acquasparta nor Casale, whence,
Of those who come to meddle with the text,
One stretches and another cramps its rule.
Bonaventura's life in me behold,
From Bagnoregio; one, who, in discharge
Of my great offices, still laid aside
All sinister aim. Illuminato here,
And Agostino join me: two they were,
Among the first of those barefooted meek ones,
Who sought God's friendship in the cord: with them
Hugues of Saint Victor; Pietro Mangiadore;
And he of Spain in his twelve volumes shining;
Nathan the prophet; Metropolitan

Chrysostom; and Anselmo; and, who deign'd
To put his hand to the first art, Donatus.
Raban is here; and at my side there shines
Calabria's abbot, Joachim, endow'd
With soul prophetic. The bright courtesy
Of friar Thomas and his goodly lore,
Have moved me to the blazon of a peer
So worthy; and with me have moved this throng."

CANTO XIII.

ARGUMENT.

Thomas Aquinas resumes his speech. He solves the other of those doubts which he discerned in the mind of Dante, and warns him earnestly against assenting to any proposition without having duly examined it.

LET him, who would conceive what now I saw,
　　Imagine (and retain the image firm
　　As mountain rock, the whilst he hears me speak),
Of stars, fifteen, from midst the ethereal host
Selected, that, with lively ray serene,
O'ercome the massiest air: thereto imagine
The wain, that, in the bosom of our sky,
Spins ever on its axle night and day,
With the bright summit of that horn, which swells
Due from the pole, round which the first wheel rolls,
To have ranged themselves in fashion of two signs
In heaven, such as Ariadne made,
When death's chill seized her; and that one of them
Did compass in the other's beam; and both
In such sort whirl around, that each should tend
With opposite motion: and conceiving thus,
Of that true constellation, and the dance
Twofold, that circled me, he shall attain
As 'twere the shadow; for things there as much
Surpass our usage, as the swiftest heaven
Is swifter than the Chiana. There was sung
No Bacchus, and no Io Pæan, but
Three persons in the Godhead, and in one
Person that nature and the human join'd.
　　The song and round were measured: and to us

Those saintly lights attended, happier made
At each new ministering. Then silence brake
Amid the accordant sons of Deity,
That luminary, in which the wondrous life
Of the meek man of God was told to me;
And thus it spake: "One ear o' the harvest thresh'd
And its grain safely stored, sweet charity
Invites me with the other to like toil.

"Thou know'st that in the bosom, whence the rib
Was ta'en to fashion that fair cheek, whose taste
All the world pays for; and in that, which pierced
By the keen lance, both after and before
Such satisfaction offer'd as outweighs
Each evil in the scale; whate'er of light
To human nature is allow'd, must all
Have by his virtue been infused, who form'd
Both one and other: and thou thence admirest
In that I told thee, of beatitudes,
A second there is none to him enclosed
In the fifth radiance. Open now thine eyes
To what I answer thee; and thou shalt see
Thy deeming and my saying meet in truth,
As centre in the round. That which dies not,
And that which can die, are but each the beam
Of that idea, which our Sovereign Sire
Engendereth loving; for that lively light,
Which passeth from his splendour, not disjoin'd
From him, nor from his love triune with them,
Doth, through his bounty, congregate itself,
Mirror'd, as 'twere, in new existences;
Itself unalterable, and ever one.

"Descending hence unto the lowest powers,
Its energy so sinks, at last it makes
But brief contingencies; for so I name

Things generated, which the heavenly orbs
Moving, with seed or without seed, produce.
Their wax, and that which molds it, differ much:
And thence with lustre, more or less, it shows
The ideal stamp imprest: so that one tree,
According to his kind, hath better fruit,
And worse: and, at your birth, ye, mortal men,
Are in your talents various. Were the wax
Molded with nice exactness, and the heaven
In its disposing influence supreme,
The brightness of the seal should be complete:
But nature renders it imperfect ever;
Resembling thus the artist, in her work,
Whose faltering hand is faithless to his skill.
Therefore, if fervent love dispose, and mark
The lustrous image of the primal virtue,
There all perfection is vouchsafed; and such
The clay was made, accomplish'd with each gift,
That life can teem with; such the burden fill'd
The virgin's bosom: so that I commend
Thy judgment, that the human nature ne'er
Was, or can be, such as in them it was.

"Did I advance no further than this point;
'How then had he no peer?' thou might'st reply.
But, that what now appears not, may appear
Right plainly, ponder who he was, and what
(When he was bidden 'Ask') the motive, sway'd
To his requesting. I have spoken thus,
That thou mayst see, he was a king, who ask'd
For wisdom, to the end he might be king
Sufficient: not, the number to search out
Of the celestial movers; or to know,
If necessary with contingent e'er
Have made necessity; or whether that

Be granted, that first motion is; or if,
Of the mid circle, can by art be made
Triangle, with its corner blunt or sharp.

"Whence, noting that, which I have said, and this,
Thou kingly prudence and that ken mayst learn,
At which the dart of my intention aims,
And, marking clearly, that I told thee, 'Risen,'
Thou shalt discern it only hath respect
To kings, of whom are many, and the good
Are rare. With this distinction take my words,
And they may well consist with that which thou
Of the first human father dost believe,
And of our well-beloved. And let this
Henceforth be lead unto thy feet, to make
Thee slow in motion, as a weary man,
Both to the 'yea' and to the 'nay' thou seest not.
For he among the fools is down full low,
Whose affirmation, or denial, is
Without distinction, in each case alike.
Since it befalls, that in most instances
Current opinion leans to false: and then
Affection bends the judgment to her ply.

"Much more than vainly doth he loose from shore,
Since he returns not such as he set forth,
Who fishes for the truth and wanteth skill.
And open proofs of this unto the world
Have been afforded in Parmenides,
Melissus, Bryso, and the crowd beside,
Who journey'd on, and knew not whither: so did
Sabellius, Arius, and the other fools,
Who, like to scymitars, reflected back
The scripture-image by distortion marr'd.

"Let not the people be too swift to judge;
As one who reckons on the blades in field,

Or e'er the crop be ripe. For I have seen
The thorn frown rudely all the winter long,
And after bear the rose upon its top;
And bark, that all her way across the sea
Ran straight and speedy, perish at the last
E'en in the haven's mouth. Seeing one steal,
Another bring his offering to the priest,
Let not Dame Birtha and Sir Martin thence
Into heaven's counsels deem that they can pry:
For one of these may rise, the other fall."

CANTO XIV.

ARGUMENT.

Solomon, who is one of the spirits in the inner circle, declares what the appearance of the blest will be after the resurrection of the body. Beatrice and Dante are translated into the fifth heaven, which is that of Mars, and here behold the souls of those who had died fighting for the true faith, ranged in the sign of a cross, athwart which the spirits move to the sound of a melodious hymn.

FROM centre to the circle, and so back
From circle to the centre, water moves
In the round chalice, even as the blow
Impels it, inwardly, or from without.
Such was the image glanced into my mind,
As the great spirit of Aquinum ceased;
And Beatrice, after him, her words
Resumed alternate: "Need there is (though yet
He tells it to you not in words, nor e'en
In thought) that he should fathom to its depth
Another mystery. Tell him, if the light,
Wherewith your substance blooms, shall stay with you
Eternally, as now; and, if it doth,
How, when ye shall regain your visible forms,
The sight may without harm endure the change,
That also tell." As those, who in a ring
Tread the light measure, in their fitful mirth
Raise loud the voice, and spring with gladder bound;
Thus, at the hearing of that pious suit,
The saintly circles, in their tourneying
And wondrous note, attested new delight.

Whoso laments, that we must doff this garb
Of frail mortality, thenceforth to live

Immortally above; he hath not seen
The sweet refreshing of that heavenly shower.
  Him, who lives ever, and for ever reigns
In mystic union of the Three in One,
Unbounded, bounding all, each spirit thrice
Sang, with such melody, as, but to hear,
For highest merit were an ample meed.
And from the lesser orb the goodliest light,
With gentle voice and mild, such as perhaps
The angel's once to Mary, thus replied:
"Long as the joy of Paradise shall last,
Our love shall shine around that raiment, bright
As fervent; fervent as, in vision, blest;
And that as far, in blessedness, exceeding,
As it hath grace, beyond its virtue, great.
Our shape, regarmented with glorious weeds
Of saintly flesh, must, being thus entire,
Show yet more gracious. Therefore shall increase
Whate'er, of light, gratuitous imparts
The Supreme Good; light, ministering aid,
The better to disclose his glory: whence,
The vision needs increasing, must increase
The fervour which it kindles; and that too
The ray, that comes from it. But as the gleed
Which gives out flame, yet in its whiteness shines
More livelily than that, and so preserves
Its proper semblance; thus this circling sphere
Of splendour shall to view less radiant seem,
Than shall our fleshly robe, which yonder earth
Now covers. Nor will such excess of light
O'erpower us, in corporeal organs made
Firm, and susceptible of all delight."
  So ready and so cordial an "Amen"
Follow'd from either choir, as plainly spoke

Desire of their dead bodies; yet perchance
Not for themselves, but for their kindred dear,
Mothers and sires, and those whom best they loved,
Ere they were made imperishable flame.

    And lo! forthwith there rose up round about
A lustre, over that already there;
Of equal clearness, like the brightening up
Of the horizon. As at evening hour
Of twilight, new appearances through heaven
Peer with faint glimmer, doubtfully descried;
So, there, new substances, methought, began
To rise in view beyond the other twain,
And wheeling, sweep their ampler circuit wide.

    O genuine glitter of eternal Beam!
With what a sudden whiteness did it flow,
O'erpowering vision in me. But so fair,
So passing lovely, Beatrice show'd,
Mind cannot follow it, nor words express
Her infinite sweetness. Thence mine eyes regain'd
Power to look up; and I beheld myself,
Sole with my lady, to more lofty bliss
Translated: for the star, with warmer smile
Impurpled, well denoted our ascent.

    With all the heart, and with that tongue which speaks
The same in all, an holocaust I made
To God, befitting the new grace vouchsafed.
And from my bosom had not yet upsteam'd
The fuming of that incense, when I knew
The rite accepted. With such mighty sheen
And mantling crimson, in two listed rays
The splendor shot before me, that I cried,
"God of Sabaoth! that dost prank them thus!"

    As leads the galaxy from pole to pole,
Distinguish'd into greater lights and less,

Its pathway, which the wisest fail to spell;
So thickly studded, in the depth of Mars,
Those rays described the venerable sign,
That quadrants in the round conjoining frame.

    Here memory mocks the toil of genius. Christ
Beam'd on that cross; and pattern fails me now.
But whoso takes his cross, and follows Christ,
Will pardon me for that I leave untold,
When in the flecker'd dawning he shall spy
The glitterance of Christ. From horn to horn,
And 'tween the summit and the base, did move
Lights, scintillating, as they met and pass'd.
Thus oft are seen with ever-changeful glance,
Straight or athwart, now rapid and now slow,
The atomies of bodies, long or short,
To move along the sunbeam, whose slant line
Checkers the shadow interposed by art
Against the noontide heat. And as the chime
Of minstrel music, dulcimer, and harp
With many strings, a pleasant dinning makes
To him, who heareth not the distinct note;
So from the lights, which there appear'd to me,
Gather'd along the cross a melody,
That, indistinctly heard, with ravishment
Possess'd me. Yet I mark'd it was a hymn
Of lofty praises; for there came to me
"Arise," and "Conquer," as to one who hears
And comprehends not. Me such ecstasy
O'ercame that never, till that hour, was thing
That held me in so sweet imprisonment.

    Perhaps my saying overbold appears,
Accounting less the pleasure of those eyes,
Whereon to look fulfilleth all desire.
But he, who is aware those living seals

And I beheld myself,
Sole with my lady, to more lofty bliss
Translated.

Canto XIV., lines 77–79.

Christ
Beam'd on that cross; and pattern fails me now.
Canto XIV., lines 96, 97.

Of every beauty work with quicker force,
The higher they are risen; and that there
I had not turn'd me to them; he may well
Excuse me that, whereof in my excuse
I do accuse me, and may own my truth;
That holy pleasure here not yet reveal'd,
Which grows in transport as we mount aloof.

CANTO XV.

ARGUMENT.

The spirit of Cacciaguida, our Poet's ancestor, glides rapidly to the foot of the cross, tells who he is, and speaks of the simplicity of the Florentines in his days, since then much corrupted.

TRUE love, that ever shows itself as clear
　　In kindness, as loose appetite in wrong,
　　Silenced that lyre harmonious, and still'd
The sacred chords, that are by heaven's right hand
Unwound and tighten'd. How to righteous prayers
Should they not hearken, who, to give me will
For praying, in accordance thus were mute?
He hath in sooth good cause for endless grief,
Who, for the love of thing that lasteth not,
Despoils himself for ever of that love.
　　As oft along the still and pure serene,
At nightfall, glides a sudden trail of fire,
Attracting with involuntary heed
The eye to follow it, erewhile at rest;
And seems some star that shifted place in heaven,
Only that, whence it kindles, none is lost,
And it is soon extinct: thus from the horn,
That on the dexter of the cross extends,
Down to its foot, one luminary ran
From mid the cluster shone there; yet no gem
Dropp'd from its foil: and through the beamy list,
Like flame in alabaster, glow'd its course.
　　So forward stretch'd him (if of credence aught
Our greater muse may claim) the pious ghost
Of old Anchises, in the Elysian bower,

When he perceived his son. "O thou, my blood!
O most exceeding grace divine! to whom,
As now to thee, hath twice the heavenly gate
Been e'er unclosed?" So spake the light: whence I
Turn'd me toward him; then unto my dame
My sight directed: and on either side
Amazement waited me; for in her eyes
Was lighted such a smile, I thought that mine
Had dived unto the bottom of my grace
And of my bliss in Paradise. Forthwith,
To hearing and to sight grateful alike,
The spirit to his proem added things
I understood not, so profound he spake:
Yet not of choice, but through necessity,
Mysterious; for his high conception soar'd
Beyond the mark of mortals. When the flight
Of holy transport had so spent its rage,
That nearer to the level of our thought
The speech descended; the first sounds I heard
Were, "Blest be thou, Triunal Deity!
That hast such favour in my seed vouchsafed."
Then follow'd: "No unpleasant thirst, though long,
Which took me reading in the sacred book,
Whose leaves or white or dusky never change,
Thou hast allay'd, my son! within this light,
From whence my voice thou hear'st: more thanks to her
Who, for such lofty mounting, has with plumes
Begirt thee. Thou dost deem thy thoughts to me
From Him transmitted, who is first of all,
E'en as all numbers ray from unity;
And therefore dost not ask me who I am,
Or why to thee more joyous I appear,
Than any other in this gladsome throng.
The truth is as thou deem'st; for in this life

Both less and greater in that mirror look,
In which thy thoughts, or e'er thou think'st, are shown.
But, that the love, which keeps me wakeful ever,
Urging with sacred thirst of sweet desire,
May be contented fully; let thy voice,
Fearless, and frank, and jocund, utter forth
Thy will distinctly, utter forth the wish,
Whereto my ready answer stands decreed."

    I turn'd me to Beatrice; and she heard
Ere I had spoken, smiling an assent,
That to my will gave wings; and I began:
"To each among your tribe, what time ye kenn'd
The nature, in whom nought unequal dwells,
Wisdom and love were in one measure dealt;
For that they are so equal in the sun,
From whence ye drew your radiance and your heat,
As makes all likeness scant. But will and means,
In mortals, for the cause ye well discern,
With unlike wings are fledge. A mortal, I
Experience inequality like this;
And therefore give no thanks, but in the heart,
For thy paternal greeting. This howe'er
I pray thee, living topaz! that ingemm'st
This precious jewel; let me hear thy name."

    "I am thy root, O leaf! whom to expect
Even, hath pleased me." Thus the prompt reply
Prefacing, next it added: "He, of whom
Thy kindred appellation comes, and who,
These hundred years and more, on its first ledge
Hath circuited the mountain, was my son,
And thy great-grandsire. Well befits, his long
Endurance should be shorten'd by thy deeds.

    "Florence, within her ancient limit-mark,
Which calls her still to matin prayers and noon,

Was chaste and sober, and abode in peace.
She had no armlets and no head-tires then;
No purfled dames; no zone, that caught the eye
More than the person did. Time was not yet,
When at his daughter's birth the sire grew pale,
For fear the age and dowry should exceed,
On each side, just proportion. House was none
Void of its family: nor yet had come
Sardanapalus, to exhibit feats
Of chamber prowess. Montemalo yet
O'er our suburban turret rose; as much
To be surpass'd in fall, as in its rising.
I saw Bellincion Berti walk abroad
In leathern girdle, and a clasp of bone;
And, with no artful colouring on her cheeks,
His lady leave the glass. The sons I saw
Of Nerli, and of Vecchio, well content
With unrobed jerkin; and their good dames handling
The spindle and the flax: O happy they!
Each sure of burial in her native land,
And none left desolate a-bed in France.
One waked to tend the cradle, hushing it
With sounds that lull'd the parent's infancy:
Another, with her maidens, drawing off
The tresses from the distaff, lectured them
Old tales of Troy, and Fesole, and Rome.
A Salterello and Cianghella we
Had held as strange a marvel, as ye would
A Cincinnatus or Cornelia now.

"In such composed and seemly fellowship,
Such faithful and such fair equality,
In so sweet household, Mary at my birth
Bestow'd me, call'd on with loud cries: and there,
In your old baptistery, I was made

Christian at once and Cacciaguida; as were
My brethren Eliseo and Moronto.

"From Valdipado came to me my spouse;
And hence thy surname grew. I follow'd then
The Emperor Conrad: and his knighthood he
Did gird on me; in such good part he took
My valiant service. After him I went
To testify against that evil law,
Whose people, by the shepherd's fault, possess
Your right usurp'd. There I by that foul crew
Was disentangled from the treacherous world
Whose base affection many a spirit soils;
And from the martyrdom came to this peace."

CANTO XVI.

ARGUMENT.

Cacciaguida relates the time of his birth, and, describing the extent of Florence when he lived there, recounts the names of the chief families who then inhabited it. Its degeneracy, and subsequent disgrace, he attributes to the introduction of families from the neighbouring country and villages, and to their mixture with the primitive citizens.

O SLIGHT respect of man's nobility!
I never shall account it marvellous,
That our infirm affection here below
Thou movest to boasting; when I could not chuse,
E'en in that region of unwarp'd desire,
In heaven itself, but make my vaunt in thee.
Yet cloak thou art soon shorten'd; for that Time,
Unless thou be eked out from day to day,
Goes round thee with his shears. Resuming then,
With greeting such as Rome was first to bear,
But since hath disaccustom'd, I began:
And Beatrice, that a little space
Was sever'd, smiled; reminding me of her,
Whose cough embolden'd (as the story holds)
To first offence the doubting Guenever.

"You are my sire," said I: "you give me heart
Freely to speak my thought: above myself
You raise me. Through so many streams with joy
My soul is fill'd, that gladness wells from it;
So that it bears the mighty tide, and bursts not.
Say then, my honour'd stem! what ancestors
Were those you sprang from, and what years were mark'd
In your first childhood? Tell me of the fold,
That hath Saint John for guardian, what was then
Its state, and who in it were highest seated!"

As embers, at the breathing of the wind,
Their flame enliven; so that light I saw
Shine at my blandishments; and, as it grew
More fair to look on, so with voice more sweet,
Yet not in this our modern phrase, forthwith
It answer'd: "From the day, when it was said
'Hail Virgin!' to the throes by which my mother,
Who now is sainted, lighten'd her of me
Whom she was heavy with, this fire had come
Five hundred times and fourscore, to relume
Its radiance underneath the burning foot
Of its own lion. They, of whom I sprang,
And I, had there our birth-place, where the last
Partition of our city first is reach'd
By him that runs her annual game. Thus much
Suffice of my forefathers: who they were,
And whence they hither came, more honourable
It is to pass in silence than to tell.
All those, who at that time were there, betwixt
Mars and the Baptist, fit to carry arms,
Were but the fifth, of them this day alive.
But then the citizen's blood, that now is mix'd
From Campi and Certaldo and Fighine,
Ran purely through the last mechanic's veins.
O how much better were it, that these people
Were neighbours to you; and that at Galluzzo
And at Trespiano ye should have your boundary;
Than to have them within, and bear the stench
Of Aguglione's hind, and Signa's, him,
That hath his eye already keen for bartering.
Had not the people, which of all the world
Degenerates most, been stepdame unto Cæsar,
But, as a mother to her son been kind,
Such one, as hath become a Florentine,

PARADISE.—CANTO XVI.

And trades and traffics, had been turn'd adrift
To Simifonte, where his grandsire plied
The beggar's craft: the Conti were possess'd
Of Montemurlo still: the Cerchi still
Were in Acone's parish: nor had haply
From Valdigrieve past the Buondelmonti.
The city's malady hath ever source
In the confusion of its persons, as
The body's, in variety of food:
And the blind bull falls with a steeper plunge,
Than the blind lamb: and oftentimes one sword
Doth more and better execution,
Than five. Mark Luni; Urbisaglia mark;
How they are gone; and after them how go
Chiusi and Sinigaglia: and 'twill seem
No longer new, or strange to thee, to hear
That families fail, when cities have their end.
All things that appertain to ye, like yourselves,
Are mortal: but mortality in some
Ye mark not; they endure so long, and you
Pass by so suddenly. And as the moon
Doth, by the rolling of her heavenly sphere,
Hide and reveal the strand unceasingly;
So fortune deals with Florence. Hence admire not
At what of them I tell thee, whose renown
Time covers, the first Florentines. I saw
The Ughi, Catilini, and Filippi,
The Alberichi, Greci, and Ormanni,
Now in their wane, illustrious citizens
And great as ancient, of Sannella him,
With him of Arca saw, and Soldanieri,
And Ardinghi, and Bostichi. At the poop
That now is laden with new felony
So cumbrous it may speedily sink the bark,

THE VISION.

The Ravignani sat, of whom is sprung
The County Guido, and whoso hath since
His title from the famed Bellincion ta'en.
Fair governance was yet an art well prized
By him of Pressa: Galigaio show'd
The gilded hilt and pommel, in his house:
The column, clothed with verrey, still was seen
Unshaken; the Sacchetti still were great,
Giouchi, Sifanti, Galli, and Barucci,
With them who blush to hear the bushel named.
Of the Calfucci still the branchy trunk
Was in its strength; and, to the curule chairs,
Sizii and Arrigucci yet were drawn.
How mighty them I saw, whom, since, their pride
Hath undone! And in all their goodly deeds
Florence was, by the bullets of bright gold,
O'erflourish'd. Such the sires of those, who now,
As surely as your church is vacant, flock
Into her consistory, and at leisure
There stall them and grow fat. The o'erweening brood,
That plays the dragon after him that flees,
But unto such as turn and show the tooth,
Ay or the purse, is gentle as a lamb,
Was on its rise, but yet so slight esteem'd,
That Ubertino of Donati grudged
His father-in-law should yoke him to its tribe.
Already Caponsacco had descended
Into the mart from Fesole: and Giuda
And Infangato were good citizens.
A thing incredible I tell, though true:
The gateway, named from those of Pera, led
Into the narrow circuit of your walls.
Each one, who bears the sightly quarterings
Of the great Baron (he whose name and worth

The festival of Thomas still revives),
His knighthood and his privilege retain'd;
Albeit one, who borders them with gold,
This day is mingled with the common herd.
In Borgo yet the Gualterotti dwelt,
And Importuni: well for its repose,
Had it still lack'd of newer neighbourhood.
The house, from whence your tears have had their spring,
Through the just anger, that hath murder'd ye,
And put a period to your gladsome days,
Was honour'd; it, and those consorted with it.
O Buondelmonti! what ill counselling
Prevail'd on thee to break the plighted bond?
Many, who now are weeping, would rejoice,
Had God to Ema given thee, the first time
Thou near our city camest. But so was doom'd:
Florence! on that maim'd stone which guards the bridge,
The victim, when thy peace departed, fell.

"With these and others like to them, I saw
Florence in such assured tranquillity,
She had no cause at which to grieve: with these
Saw her so glorious and so just, that ne'er
The lily from the lance had hung reverse,
Or through division been with vermeil dyed."

CANTO XVII.

ARGUMENT.

Cacciaguida predicts to our Poet his exile and the calamities he had to suffer; and, lastly, exhorts him to write the present poem.

SUCH as the youth, who came to Clymene,
   To certify himself of that reproach
   Which had been fasten'd on him (he whose end
Still makes the fathers chary to their sons),
E'en such was I;. nor unobserved was such
Of Beatrice, and that saintly lamp,
Who had erewhile for me his station moved;
When thus my lady: "Give thy wish free vent,
That it may issue, bearing true report
Of the mind's impress: not that aught thy words
May to our knowledge add, but to the end
That thou mayst use thyself to own thy thirst,
And men may mingle for thee when they hear."
   "O plant, from whence I spring! revered and loved!
Who soar'st so high a pitch, that thou as clear,
As earthly thought determines two obtuse
In one triangle not contain'd, so clear
Dost see contingencies, ere in themselves
Existent, looking at the point whereto
All times are present; I, the whilst I scaled
With Virgil the soul-purifying mount
And visited the nether world of woe,
Touching my future destiny have heard
Words grievous, though I feel me on all sides
Well squared to fortune's blows. Therefore my will

PARADISE.—CANTO XVII.

Were satisfied to know the lot awaits me.
The arrow, seen beforehand, slacks his flight."
    So said I to the brightness, which erewhile
To me had spoken; and my will declared,
As Beatrice will'd, explicitly.
Nor with oracular response obscure,
Such as, or e'er the Lamb of God was slain,
Beguil'd the credulous nations: but, in terms
Precise, and unambiguous lore, replied
The spirit of paternal love, enshrined,
Yet in his smile apparent; and thus spake:
"Contingency, whose verge extendeth not
Beyond the tablet of your mortal mold,
Is all depictured in the eternal sight;
But hence deriveth not necessity,
More than the tall ship, hurried down the flood,
Is driven by the eye that looks on it.
From thence, as to the ear sweet harmony
From organ comes, so comes before mine eye
The time prepared for thee. Such as driven out
From Athens, by his cruel step-dame's wiles,
Hippolytus departed; such must thou
Depart from Florence. This they wish, and this
Contrive, and will ere long effectuate, there,
Where gainful merchandize is made of Christ
Throughout the live-long day. The common cry,
Will, as 'tis ever wont, affix the blame
Unto the party injured: but the truth
Shall, in the vengeance it dispenseth, find
A faithful witness. Thou shalt leave each thing
Beloved most dearly: this is the first shaft
Shot from the bow of exile. Thou shalt prove
How salt the savour is of other's bread;
How hard the passage, to descend and climb

THE VISION.

By other's stairs. But that shall gall thee most,
Will be the worthless and vile company,
With whom thou must be thrown into these straits.
For all ungrateful, impious all, and mad,
Shall turn 'gainst thee: but in a little while,
Theirs, and not thine, shall be the crimson'd brow,
Their course shall so evince their brutishness,
To have ta'en thy stand apart shall well become thee.
 "First refuge thou must find, first place of rest,
In the great Lombard's courtesy, who bears,
Upon the ladder perch'd, the sacred bird.
He shall behold thee with such kind regard,
That 'twixt ye two, the contrary to that
Which 'falls 'twixt other men, the granting shall
Forerun the asking. With him shalt thou see
That mortal, who was at his birth imprest
So strongly from this star, that of his deeds
The nations shall take note. His unripe age
Yet holds him from observance; for these wheels
Only nine years have compast him about.
But, ere the Gascon practise on great Harry,
Sparkles of virtue shall shoot forth in him,
In equal scorn of labours and of gold.
His bounty shall be spread abroad so widely
As not to let the tongues, e'en of his foes,
Be idle in its praise. Look thou to him,
And his beneficence: for he shall cause
Reversal of their lot to many people;
Rich men and beggars interchanging fortunes.
And thou shalt bear this written in thy soul,
Of him, but tell it not:" and things he told
Incredible to those who witness them;
Then added: "So interpret thou, my son,
What hath been told thee.—Lo! the ambushment

That a few circling seasons hide for thee.
Yet envy not thy neighbours: time extends
Thy span beyond their treason's chastisement."

  Soon as the saintly spirit, by silence, mark'd
Completion of that web, which I had stretch'd
Before it, warped for weaving; I began,
As one, who in perplexity desires
Counsel of other, wise, benign, and friendly:
"My father! well I mark how time spurs on
Toward me, ready to inflict the blow,
Which falls most heavily on him who most
Abandoneth himself. Therefore 'tis good
I should forecast, that, driven from the place
Most dear to me, I may not lose myself
All other by my song. Down through the world
Of infinite mourning; and along the mount,
From whose fair height my lady's eyes did lift me;
And, after, through this heaven, from light to light;
Have I learnt that, which if I tell again,
It may with many wofully disrelish:
And, if I am a timid friend to truth,
I fear my life may perish among those,
To whom these days shall be of ancient date."

  The brightness, where enclosed the treasure smiled,
Which I had found there, first shone glisteringly,
Like to a golden mirror in the sun;
Next answered: "Conscience, dimm'd or by its own
Or other's shame, will feel thy saying sharp.
Thou, notwithstanding, all deceit removed,
See the whole vision be made manifest.
And let them wince, who have their withers wrung.
What though, when tasted first, thy voice shall prove
Unwelcome: on digestion, it will turn
To vital nourishment. The cry thou raisest,

Shall, as the wind doth, smite the proudest summits;
Which is of honour no light argument.
For this, there only have been shown to thee,
Throughout these orbs, the mountain, and the deep,
Spirits, whom fame hath note of. For the mind
Of him, who hears, is loth to acquiesce
And fix its faith, unless the instance brought
Be palpable, and proof apparent urge."

But so was doom'd:
Florence! on that maim'd stone which guards the bridge,
The victim, when thy peace departed, fell.

Canto XVI., lines 143–145.

P. P.—50.

So, within the lights,
The saintly creatures flying, sang; and made
Now D, now I, now L, figur'd i' the air.

Canto XVIII., lines 70-72.

Ye host of heaven, whose glory I survey!
O beg ye grace for those, that are, on earth,
All after ill example gone astray.

Canto XVIII., lines 120-122.

Before my sight appear'd, with open wings,
The beauteous image; in fruition sweet,
Gladdening the thronged spirits.

Canto XIX., lines 1-3.

CANTO XVIII.

ARGUMENT.

Dante sees the souls of many renowned warriors and crusaders in the planet Mars, and then ascends with Beatrice to Jupiter, the sixth heaven, in which he finds the souls of those who had administered justice rightly in the world, so disposed, as to form the figure of an eagle. The canto concludes with an invective against the avarice of the clergy, and especially of the Pope.

NOW in his word, sole, ruminating, joy'd
That blessed spirit: and I fed on mine,
Tempering the sweet with bitter. She meanwhile,
Who led me unto God, admonish'd: "Muse
On other thoughts: bethink thee, that near Him
I dwell, who recompenseth every wrong."
 At the sweet sounds of comfort straight I turn'd;
And, in the saintly eyes what love was seen,
I leave in silence here, nor through distrust
Of my words only, but that to such bliss
The mind remounts not without aid. Thus much
Yet may I speak; that, as I gazed on her,
Affection found no room for other wish.
While the everlasting pleasure, that did full
On Beatrice shine, with second view
From her fair countenance my gladden'd soul
Contented; vanquishing me with a beam
Of her soft smile, she spake: "Turn thee, and list.
These eyes are not thy only Paradise."
 As here, we sometimes in the looks may see
The affection mark'd, when that its sway hath ta'en
The spirit wholly; thus the hallow'd light,
To whom I turn'd, flashing, bewray'd its will
To talk yet further with me, and began:

"On this fifth lodgment of the tree, whose life
Is from its top, whose fruit is ever fair
And leaf unwithering, blessed spirits abide,
That were below, ere they arrived in heaven,
So mighty in renown, as every muse
Might grace her triumph with them. On the horns
Look, therefore, of the cross: he whom I name,
Shall there enact, as doth in summer cloud
Its nimble fire." Along the cross I saw,
At the repeated name of Joshua,
A splendour gliding; nor, the word was said,
Ere it was done: then, at the naming, saw,
Of the great Maccabee, another move
With whirling speed; and gladness was the scourge
Unto that top. The next for Charlemain
And for the peer Orlando, two my gaze
Pursued, intently, as the eye pursues
A falcon flying. Last, along the cross,
William, and Renard, and Duke Godfrey drew
My ken, and Robert Guiscard. And the soul
Who spake with me, among the other lights
Did move away, and mix; and with the quire
Of heavenly songsters proved his tuneful skill.

   To Beatrice on my right I bent,
Looking for intimation, or by word
Or act, what next behoved; and did descry
Such mere effulgence in her eyes, such joy,
It passed all former wont. And, as by sense
Of new delight, the man, who perseveres
In good deeds, doth perceive, from day to day,
His virtue growing; I e'en thus perceived,
Of my ascent, together with the heaven,
The circuit widen'd; noting the increase
Of beauty in that wonder. Like the change

In a brief moment on some maiden's cheek,
Which, from its fairness, doth discharge the weight
Of pudency, that stain'd it; such in her,
And to mine eyes so sudden was the change,
Through silvery whiteness of that temperate star,
Whose sixth orb now enfolded us. I saw,
Within that Jovial cresset, the clear sparks
Of love, that reign'd there, fashion to my view
Our language. And as birds, from river banks
Arisen, now in round, now lengthen'd troop,
Array them in their flight, greeting, as seems,
Their new-found pastures; so, within the lights,
The saintly creatures flying, sang; and made
Now D, now I, now L, figured i' the air.
First singing to their notes they moved; then, one
Becoming of these signs, a little while
Did rest them, and were mute. O nymph divine,
Of Pegasean race! whose souls, which thou
Inspirest, makest glorious and long-lived, as they
Cities and realms by thee; thou with thyself
Inform me; that I may set forth the shapes,
As fancy doth present them: be thy power
Display'd in this brief song. The characters,
Vocal and consonant, were five-fold seven.
In order, each, as they appear'd, I mark'd
Diligite Justitiam, the first,
Both verb and noun all blazon'd: and the extreme,
Qui judicatis terram. In the M
Of the fifth word they held their station;
Making the star seem silver streak'd with gold.
And on the summit of the M, I saw
Descending other lights, that rested there,
Singing, methinks, their bliss and primal good.
Then, as at shaking of a lighted brand,

Sparkles innumerable on all sides
Rise scatter'd, source of augury to the unwise;
Thus more than thousand twinkling lustres hence
Seem'd reascending; and a higher pitch
Some mounting, and some less, e'en as the sun,
Which kindleth them, decreed. And when each one
Had settled in his place; the head and neck
Then saw I of an eagle, livelily
Graved in that streaky fire. Who painteth there,
Hath none to guide Him: of Himself he guides:
And every line and texture of the nest
Doth own from Him the virtue fashions it.
The other bright beatitude, that seem'd
Erewhile, with lilied crowning, well content
To over-canopy the M, moved forth,
Following gently the impress of the bird.

 Sweet star! what glorious and thick-studded gems
Declared to me our justice on the earth
To be the effluence of that heaven, which thou,
Thyself a costly jewel, dost inlay.
Therefore I pray the Sovran Mind, from whom
Thy motion and thy virtue are begun,
That He would look from whence the fog doth rise,
To vitiate thy beam; so that once more
He may put forth his hand 'gainst such, as drive
Their traffic in that sanctuary, whose walls
With miracles and martyrdoms were built.

 Ye host of heaven, whose glory I survey!
O beg ye grace for those, that are, on earth,
All after ill example gone astray.
War once had for his instrument the sword:
But now 'tis made, taking the bread away,
Which the good Father locks from none.—And thou,
That writest but to cancel, think, that they,

Who for the vineyard, which thou wastest, died,
Peter and Paul, live yet, and mark thy doings.
Thou hast good cause to cry, "My heart so cleaves
To him, that lived in soltitude remote,
And for a dance was dragg'd to martyrdom,
I wist not of the fisherman nor Paul."

CANTO XIX.

ARGUMENT.

The eagle speaks as with one voice proceeding from a multitude of spirits that compose it, and declares the cause for which it is exalted to that state of glory. It then solves a doubt which our Poet had entertained respecting the possibility of salvation without belief in Christ; exposes the inefficacy of a mere profession of such belief: and prophesies the evil appearance that many Christian potentates will make at the day of judgment.

BEFORE my sight appear'd, with open wings,
   The beauteous image; in fruition sweet,
   Gladdening the thronged spirits. Each did seem
A little ruby, whereon so intense
The sun-beam glow'd, that to mine eyes it came
In clear refraction. And that, which next
Befalls me to pourtray, voice hath not utter'd,
Nor hath ink written, nor in fantasy
Was e'er conceived. For I beheld and heard
The beak discourse; and, what intention form'd
Of many, singly as of one express,
Beginning: "For that I was just and piteous,
I am exalted to this height of glory,
The which no wish exceeds: and there on earth
Have I my memory left, e'en by the bad
Commended, while they leave its course untrod."

   Thus is one heat from many embers felt;
As in that image many were the loves,
And one the voice, that issued from them all:
Whence I address'd them: "O perennial flowers
Of gladness everlasting! that exhale
In single breath your odours manifold;
Breathe now: and let the hunger be appeased,

That with great craving long hath held my soul,
Finding no food on earth. This well I know;
That if there be in heaven a realm, that shows
In faithful mirror the celestial Justice,
Yours without veil reflects it. Ye discern
The heed, wherewith I do prepare myself
To hearken; ye, the doubt, that urges me
With such inveterate craving." Straight I saw,
Like to a falcon issuing from the hood,
That rears his head, and claps him with his wings,
His beauty and his eagerness bewraying;
So saw I move that stately sign, with praise
Of grace divine inwoven, and high song
Of inexpressive joy. "He," it began,
"Who turn'd his compass on the worlds extreme,
And in that space so variously hath wrought,
Both openly and in secret; in such wise
Could not, through all the universe, display
Impression of his glory, that the Word
Of his omniscience should not still remain
In infinite excess. In proof whereof,
He first through pride supplanted, who was sum
Of each created being, waited not
For light celestial; and abortive fell.
Whence needs each lesser nature is but scant
Receptacle unto that Good, which knows
No limit, measured by itself alone.
Therefore your sight, of the omnipresent Mind
A single beam, its origin must own
Surpassing far its utmost potency.
The ken, your world is gifted with, descends
In the everlasting Justice as low down,
As eye doth in the sea; which, though it mark
The bottom from the shore, in the wide main

Discerns it not; and ne'ertheless it is;
But hidden through its deepnesss. Light is none,
Save that which cometh from the pure serene
Of ne'er disturbed ether: for the rest,
'Tis darkness all; or shadow of the flesh,
Or else its poison. Here confess reveal'd
That covert, which hath hidden from thy search
The living Justice, of the which thou madest
Such frequent question; for thou saidst—'A man
Is born on Indus' banks, and none is there
Who speaks of Christ, nor who doth read nor write;
And all his inclinations and his acts,
As far as human reason sees, are good;
And he offendeth not in word or deed:
But unbaptized he dies, and void of faith.
Where is the justice that condemns him? where
His blame, if he believeth not?'—What then,
And who art thou, that on the stool wouldst sit
To judge at distance of a thousand miles
With the short-sighted vision of a span?
To him, who subtilizes thus with me,
There would assuredly be room for doubt
Even to wonder, did not the safe word
Of Scripture hold supreme authority.

"O animals of clay! O spirits gross!
The primal will, that in itself is good,
Hath from itself, the chief Good, ne'er been moved.
Justice consists in consonance with it,
Derivable by no created good,
Whose very cause depends upon its beam."

As on her nest the stork, that turns about
Unto her young, whom lately she hath fed,
Whiles they with upward eyes do look on her;
So lifted I my gaze; and, bending so,

The ever-blessed image waved its wings,
Labouring with such deep counsel. Wheeling round
It warbled, and did say: "As are my notes
To thee, who understand'st them not; such is
The eternal judgment unto mortal ken."

Then still abiding in that ensign ranged,
Wherewith the Romans overawed the world,
Those burning splendours of the Holy Spirit
Took up the strain; and thus it spake again:
"None ever hath ascended to this realm,
Who hath not a believer been in Christ,
Either before or after the blest limbs
Were nail'd upon the wood. But lo! of those
Who call 'Christ, Christ,' there shall be many found,
In judgment, further off from him by far,
Than such to whom his name was never known.
Christians like these the Æthiop shall condemn:
When that the two assemblages shall part;
One rich eternally, the other poor.

"What may the Persians say unto your kings,
When they shall see that volume, in the which
All their dispraise is written, spread to view?
There amidst Albert's works shall that be read,
Which will give speedy motion to the pen,
When Prague shall mourn her desolated realm.
There shall be read the woe, that he doth work
With his adulterate money on the Seine,
Who by the tusk will perish: there be read
The thirsting pride, that maketh fool alike
The English and Scot, impatient of their bound.
There shall be seen the Spaniard's luxury;
The delicate living there of the Bohemian,
Who still to worth has been a willing stranger.
The halter of Jerusalem shall see

A unit for his virtue; for his vices,
No less a mark than million. He, who guards
The isle of fire by old Anchises honour'd,
Shall find his avarice there and cowardice;
And better to denote his littleness,
The writing must be letters maim'd, that speak
Much in a narrow space. All there shall know
His uncle and his brother's filthy doings,
Who so renown'd a nation and two crowns
Have bastardized. And they, of Portugal
And Norway, there shall be exposed, with him
Of Ratza, who hath counterfeited ill
The coin of Venice. O blest Hungary!
If thou no longer patiently abidest
Thy ill-entreating: and, O blest Navarre!
If with thy mountainous girdle thou wouldst arm thee.
In earnest of that day, e'en now are heard
Wailings and groans in Famagosta's streets
And Nicosia's, grudging at their beast,
Who keepeth even footing with the rest."

CANTO XX.

ARGUMENT.

The eagle celebrates the praise of certain kings, whose glorified spirits form the eye of the bird. In the pupil is David, and in the circle round it, Trajan, Hezekiah, Constantine, William II. of Sicily, and Ripheus. It explains to our Poet how the souls of those whom he supposed to have had no means of believing in Christ, came to be in heaven; and concludes with an admonition against presuming to fathom the counsels of God.

WHEN, disappearing from our hemisphere,
The world's enlightener vanishes, and day
On all sides wasteth; suddenly the sky,
Erewhile irradiate only with his beam,
Is yet again unfolded, putting forth
Innumerable lights wherein one shines.
Of such vicissitude in heaven I thought;
As the great sign, that marshalleth the world
And the world's leaders, in the blessed beak
Was silent: for that all those living lights,
Waxing in splendour, burst forth into songs,
Such as from memory glide and fall away.

Sweet Love, that dost apparel thee in smiles!
How lustrous was thy semblance in those sparkles,
Which merely are from holy thoughts inspired.

After the precious and bright beaming stones,
That did ingem the sixth light, ceased the chiming
Of their angelic bells; methought I heard
The murmuring of a river, that doth fall
From rock to rock transpicuous, making known
The richness of his spring-head: and as sound
Of cittern, at the fret-board, or of pipe,
Is, at the wind-hole, modulate and tuned;

THE VISION.

Thus up the neck, as it were hollow, rose
That murmuring of the eagle; and forthwith
Voice there assumed; and thence along the beak
Issued in form of words, such as my heart
Did look for, on whose tables I inscribed them.
　"The part in me, that sees and bears the sun
In mortal eagles," it began, "must now
Be noted steadfastly: for, of the fires,
That figure me, those, glittering in mine eye,
Are chief of all the greatest. This, that shines
Midmost for pupil, was the same who sang
The Holy Spirit's song, and bare about
The ark from town to town: now doth he know
The merit of his soul-impassion'd strains
By their well-fitted guerdon. Of the five,
That make the circle of the vision, he,
Who to the beak is nearest, comforted
The widow for her son: now doth he know,
How dear it costeth not to follow Christ;
Both from experience of this pleasant life,
And of its opposite. He next, who follows
In the circumference, for the over-arch,
By true repenting slack'd the pace of death:
Now knoweth he, that the decrees of heaven
Alter not, when, through pious prayer below,
To-day is made to-morrow's destiny.
The other following, with the laws and me,
To yield the shepherd room, pass'd o'er to Greece;
From good intent, producing evil fruit:
Now knoweth he, how all the ill, derived
From his well doing, doth not harm him aught;
Though it have brought destruction on the world.
That, which thou seest in the under bow,
Was William whom that land bewails, which weeps

For Charles and Frederick living: now he knows
How well is loved in heaven the righteous king;
Which he betokens by his radiant seeming.
Who, in the erring world beneath, would deem
That Trojan Ripheus, in this round, was set,
Fifth of the saintly splendours? now he knows
Enough of that, which the world cannot see;
The grace divine: albeit e'en his sight
Reach not its utmost depth." Like to the lark,
That warbling in the air expatiates long,
Then, trilling out his last sweet melody,
Drops, satiate with the sweetness; such appear'd
That image, stampt by the everlasting pleasure,
Which fashions, as they are, all things that be.

    I, though my doubting were as manifest,
As is through glass the hue that mantles it,
In silence waited not; for to my lips
"What things are these?" involuntary rush'd,
And forced a passage out: whereat I mark'd
A sudden lightening and new revelry.
The eye was kindled; and the blessed sign,
No more to keep me wondering and suspense,
Replied: "I see that thou believest these things,
Because I tell them, but discern'st not how;
So that thy knowledge waits not on thy faith:
As one, who knows the name of thing by rote,
But is a stranger to its properties,
Till other's tongue reveal them. Fervent love,
And lively hope, with violence assail
The kingdom of the heavens, and overcome
The will of the Most High; not in such sort
As man prevails o'er man; but conquers it,
Because 'tis willing to be conquer'd; still,
Though conquer'd, by its mercy, conquering.

THE VISION.

"Those, in the eye who live the first and fifth,
Cause thee to marvel, in that thou behold'st
The region of the angels deck'd with them.
They quitted not their bodies, as thou deem'st,
Gentiles, but Christians; in firm rooted faith,
This, of the feet in future to be pierced,
That, of feet nail'd already to the cross.
One from the barrier of the dark abyss,
Where never any with good will returns,
Came back unto his bones. Of lively hope
Such was the meed; of lively hope, that wing'd
The prayers sent up to God for his release,
And put power into them to bend His will.
The glorious Spirit, of whom I speak to thee,
A little while returning to the flesh,
Believed in him, who had the means to help;
And, in believing, nourish'd such a flame
Of holy love, that at the second death
He was made sharer in our gamesome mirth.
The other, through the riches of that grace,
Which from so deep a fountain doth distil,
As never eye created saw its rising,
Placed all his love below on just and right:
Wherefore, of grace, God oped in him the eye
To the redemption of mankind to come;
Wherein believing, he endured no more
The filth of Paganism, and for their ways
Rebuked the stubborn nations. The three nymphs,
Whom at the right wheel thou beheld'st advancing,
Were sponsors for him, more than thousand years
Before baptizing. O how far removed,
Predestination! is thy root from such
As see not the First Cause entire: and ye,
O mortal men! be wary how ye judge:

For we, who see our Maker, know not yet
The number of the chosen; and esteem
Such scantiness of knowledge our delight:
For all our good is, in that primal good,
Concentrate; and God's will and ours are one."
    So, by that form divine, was given to me
Sweet medicine to clear and strengthen sight.
And, as one handling skilfully the harp,
Attendant on some skilful songster's voice
Bids the chord vibrate; and therein the song
Acquires more pleasure: so the whilst it spake,
It doth remember me, that I beheld
The pair of blessed luminaries move,
Like the accordant twinkling of two eyes,
Their beamy circlets, dancing to the sounds.

CANTO XXI.

ARGUMENT.

Dante ascends with Beatrice to the seventh heaven, which is the planet Saturn; wherein is placed a ladder so lofty, that the top of it is out of his sight. Here are the souls of those who had passed their life in holy retirement and contemplation. Piero Damiano comes near them, and answers questions put to him by Dante; then declares who he was on earth, and ends by declaiming against the luxury of pastors and prelates in those times.

AGAIN mine eyes were fix'd on Beatrice;
And, with mine eyes, my soul that in her looks
Found all contentment. Yet no smile she wore:
And, "Did I smile," quoth she, "thou wouldst be straight
Like Semele when into ashes turn'd:
For, mounting these eternal palace-stairs,
My beauty, which the loftier it climbs,
As thou hast noted, still doth kindle more,
So shines, that, were no tempering interposed,
Thy mortal puissance would from its rays
Shrink, as the leaf doth from the thunderbolt.
Into the seventh splendour are we wafted,
That, underneath the burning lion's breast,
Beams, in this hour, commingled with his might.
Thy mind be with thine eyes; and, in them, mirror'd
The shape, which in this mirror shall be shown."

Whoso can deem, how fondly I had fed
My sight upon her blissful countenance,
May know, when to new thoughts I changed, what joy
To do the bidding of my heavenly guide;
In equal balance, poising either weight.

Within the crystal, which records the name
(As its remoter circle girds the world)

For that all those living lights,
Waxing in splendour, burst forth into songs,
Such as from memory glide and fall away.

Canto XX., lines 10-12.

P. P.—54.   Again mine eyes were fix'd on Beatrice;
And, with mine eyes, my soul that in her looks
Found all contentment.

Canto XXI., lines 1-3.

Down whose steps
I saw the splendours in such multitude
Descending, every light in heaven, methought,
Was shed thence.

Canto XXI., lines 28-31.

Say, then,
Beginning, to what point thy soul aspires:
And meanwhile rest assured, that sight in thee
Is but o'erpower'd a space, not wholly quench'd.

Canto XXVI., lines 7-10.

Of that loved monarch, in whose happy reign
No ill had power to harm, I saw rear'd up,
In colour like to sun-illumined gold,
A ladder, which my ken pursued in vain,
So lofty was the summit; down whose steps
I saw the splendours in such multitude
Descending, every light in heaven, methought,
Was shed thence. As the rooks, at dawn of day,
Bestirring them to dry their feathers chill,
Some speed their way a-field; and homeward some
Returning, cross their flight; while some abide,
And wheel around their airy lodge: so seem'd
That glitterance, wafted on alternate wing,
As upon certain stair it came, and clash'd
Its shining. And one, lingering near us, wax'd
So bright, that in my thought I said: "The love,
Which this betokens me, admits no doubt."

Unwillingly from question I refrain;
To her, by whom my silence and my speech
Are order'd, looking for a sign: whence she,
Who in the sight of Him, that seeth all,
Saw wherefore I was silent, prompted me
To indulge the fervent wish; and I began:
"I am not worthy, of my own desert,
That thou shouldst answer me: but for her sake,
Who hath vouchsafed my asking, spirit blest,
That in thy joy art shrouded! say the cause,
Which bringeth thee so near: and wherefore, say,
Doth the sweet symphony of Paradise
Keep silence here, pervading with such sounds
Of rapt devotion every lower sphere?"
"Mortal art thou in hearing, as in sight;"
Was the reply: "and what forbade the smile
Of Beatrice interrupts our song.

Only to yield thee gladness of my voice,
And of the light that vests me, I thus far
Descend these hallow'd steps: not that more love
Invites me; for, lo! there aloft, as much
Or more of love is witness'd in those flames:
But such my lot by charity assign'd,
That makes us ready servants, as thou seest,
To execute the counsel of the Highest."

"That in this court," said I, "O sacred lamp!
Love no compulsion needs, but follows free
The eternal Providence, I well discern:
This harder find to deem: why, of thy peers,
Thou only, to this office wert foredoom'd."

I had not ended, when, like rapid mill,
Upon its centre whirl'd the light; and then
The love that did inhabit there, replied:
"Splendour eternal, piercing through these folds,
Its virtue to my vision knits; and thus
Supported, lifts me so above myself,
That on the sovran essence, which it wells from,
I have the power to gaze: and hence the joy,
Wherewith I sparkle, equalling with my blaze
The keenness of my sight. But not the soul,
That is in heaven most lustrous, nor the seraph,
That hath his eyes most fix'd on God, shall solve
What thou hast ask'd: for in the abyss it lies
Of th' everlasting statute sunk so low,
That no created ken may fathom it.
And, to the mortal world when thou return'st,
Be this reported: that none henceforth dare
Direct his footsteps to so dread a bourn.
The mind, that here is radiant, on the earth
Is wrapt in mist. Look then if she may do
Below, what passeth her ability

When she is ta'en to heaven." By words like these
Admonish'd, I the question urged no more;
And of the spirit humbly sued alone
To instruct me of its state. "'Twixt either shore
Of Italy, nor distant from thy land,
A stony ridge ariseth; in such sort,
The thunder doth not lift his voice so high.
They call it Catria: at whose foot, a cell
Is sacred to the lonely Eremite;
For worship set apart and holy rites."
A third time thus it spake; then added: "There
So firmly to God's service I adhered,
That with no costlier viands than the juice
Of olives, easily I pass'd the heats
Of summer and the winter frosts; content
In heaven-ward musings. Rich were the returns
And fertile, which that cloister once was used
To render to these heavens: now 'tis fallen
Into a waste so empty, there ere long
Detection must lay bare its vanity.
Pietro Damiano there was I y-clept:
Pietro the sinner, when before I dwelt,
Beside the Adriatic, in the house
Of our blest Lady. Near upon my close
Of mortal life, through much importuning
I was constrained to wear the hat, that still
From bad to worse is shifted.—Cephas came;
He came, who was the Holy Spirit's vessel;
Barefoot and lean; eating their bread, as chanced,
At the first table. Modern Shepherds need
Those who on either hand may prop and lead them,
So burly are they grown; and from behind,
Others to hoist them. Down the palfrey's sides
Spread their broad mantles, so as both the beasts

Are cover'd with one skin. O patience! thou
That look'st on this, and dost endure so long."
   I at those accents saw the splendours down
From step to step alight, and wheel, and wax,
Each circuiting, more beautiful. Round this
They came, and stay'd them; utter'd then a shout
So loud, it hath no likeness here: nor I
Wist what it spake, so deafening was the thunder.

CANTO XXII.

ARGUMENT.

He beholds many other spirits of the devout and contemplative; and amongst these is addressed by St. Benedict, who, after disclosing his own name and the names of certain of his companions in bliss, replies to the request made by our Poet that he might look on the form of the saint without that covering of splendour which then invested it; and then proceeds, lastly, to inveigh against the corruption of the monks. Next Dante mounts with his heavenly conductress to the eighth heaven, or that of the fixed stars, which he enters at the constellation of the Twins; and thence looking back, reviews all the space he has passed between his present station and the earth.

ASTOUNDED, to the guardian of my steps
I turn'd me, like the child, who always runs
Thither for succour, where he trusteth most:
And she was like the mother, who her son
Beholding pale and breathless, with her voice
Soothes him, and he is cheer'd; for thus she spake,
Soothing me: "Know'st not thou, thou art in heaven?
And know'st not thou, whatever is in heaven,
Is holy; and that nothing there is done,
But is done zealously and well? Deem now,
What change in thee the song, and what my smile
Had wrought, since thus the shout had power to move thee;
In which, couldst thou have understood their prayers,
The vengeance were already known to thee,
Which thou must witness ere thy mortal hour.
The sword of heaven is not in haste to smite,
Nor yet doth linger; save unto his seeming,
Who, in desire or fear, doth look for it.
But elsewhere now I bid thee turn thy view;
So shalt thou many a famous spirit behold."

Mine eyes directing, as she will'd, I saw
A hundred little spheres, that fairer grew

By interchange of splendour. I remain'd,
As one, who fearful of o'er-much presuming,
Abates in him the keenness of desire,
Nor dares to question; when, amid those pearls,
One largest and most lustrous onward drew,
That it might yield contentment to my wish;
And, from within it, these the sounds I heard.

"If thou, like me, beheld'st the charity
That burns amongst us: what thy mind conceives,
Were utter'd. But that, ere the lofty bound
Thou reach, expectance may not weary thee;
I will make answer even to the thought,
Which thou hast such respect of. In old days,
That mountain, at whose side Cassino rests,
Was, on its height, frequented by a race
Deceived and ill-disposed: and I it was,
Who thither carried first the name of Him,
Who brought the soul-subliming truth to man.
And such a speedy grace shone over me,
That from their impious worship I reclaim'd
The dwellers round about, who with the world
Were in delusion lost. These other flames,
The spirits of men contemplative, were all
Enliven'd by that warmth, whose kindly force
Gives birth to flowers and fruits of holiness.
Here is Macarius; Romoaldo here;
And here my brethren, who their steps refrain'd
Within the cloisters, and held firm their heart."

I answering thus: "Thy gentle words and kind,
And this the cheerful semblance I behold,
Not unobservant, beaming in ye all,
Have raised assurance in me; wakening it
Full-blossom'd in my bosom, as a rose
Before the sun, when the consummate flower

Has spread to utmost amplitude. Of thee
Therefore intreat I, father, to declare
If I may gain such favour, as to gaze
Upon thine image by no covering veil'd."
  "Brother!" he thus rejoin'd, "in the last sphere
Expect completion of thy lofty aim:
For there on each desire completion waits,
And there on mine; where every aim is found
Perfect, entire, and for fulfilment ripe.
There all things are as they have ever been:
For space is none to bound; nor pole divides.
Our ladder reaches even to that clime;
And so, at giddy distance, mocks thy view.
Thither the patriarch Jacob saw it stretch
Its topmost round; when it appear'd to him
With angels laden. But to mount it now
None lifts his foot from earth: and hence my rule
Is left a profitless stain upon the leaves;
The walls, for abbey rear'd, turned into dens;
The cowls, to sacks choak'd up with musty meal.
Foul usury doth not more lift itself
Against God's pleasure, than that fruit, which makes
The hearts of monks so wanton: for whate'er
Is in the church's keeping, all pertains
To such, as sue for heaven's sweet sake; and not
To those, who in respect of kindred claim,
Or on more vile allowance. Mortal flesh
Is grown so dainty, good beginnings last not
From the oak's birth unto the acorn's setting.
His convent Peter founded without gold
Or silver; I, with prayers and fasting, mine;
And Francis, his in meek humility.
And if thou note the point, whence each proceeds,
Then look what it hath err'd to; thou shalt find

The white grown murky. Jordan was turn'd back:
And a less wonder, than the refluent sea,
May, at God's pleasure, work amendment here."

    So saying, to his assembly back he drew:
And they together cluster'd into one;
Then all rolled upward, like an eddying wind.

    The sweet dame beckon'd me to follow them:
And, by that influence only, so prevail'd
Over my nature, that no natural motion,
Ascending or descending here below,
Had, as I mounted, with my pennon vied.

    So, reader, as my hope is to return
Unto the holy triumph, for the which
I oft-times wail my sins, and smite my breast;
Thou hadst been longer drawing out and thrusting
Thy finger in the fire, than I was, ere
The sign, that followeth Taurus, I beheld,
And enter'd its precinct. O glorious stars!
O light impregnate with exceeding virtue!
To whom whate'er of genius lifteth me
Above the vulgar, grateful I refer;
With ye the parent of all mortal life
Arose and set, when I did first inhale
The Tuscan air; and afterward, when grace
Vouchsafed me entrance to the lofty wheel
That in its orb impels ye, fate decreed
My passage at your clime. To you my soul
Devoutly sighs, for virtue, even now,
To meet the hard emprize that draws me on.

    "Thou art so near the sum of blessedness,"
Said Beatrice, "that behoves thy ken
Be vigilant and clear. And, to this end,
Or ever thou advance thee further, hence
Look downward, and contemplate, what a world

Already stretch'd under our feet there lies:
So as thy heart may, in its blithest mood,
Present itself to the triumphal throng,
Which, through the ethereal concave, comes rejoicing."

I straight obey'd; and with mine eye return'd
Through all the seven spheres; and saw this globe
So pitiful of semblance, that perforce
It moved my smiles: and him in truth I hold
For wisest, who esteems it least; whose thoughts
Elsewhere are fix'd, him worthiest call and best.
I saw the daughter of Latona shine,
Without the shadow, whereof late I deem'd
That dense and rare were cause. Here I sustain'd
The visage, Hyperion, of thy son;
And mark'd, how near him with their circles, round
Move Maia and Dione; here discern'd
Jove's tempering 'twixt his sire and son; and hence,
Their changes and their various aspects,
Distinctly scann'd. Nor might I not descry
Of all the seven, how bulky each, how swift;
Nor, of their several distances, not learn.
This petty area (o'er the which we stride
So fiercely), as along the eternal Twins
I wound my way, appear'd before me all,
Forth from the havens stretch'd unto the hills.
Then, to the beauteous eyes, mine eyes return'd.

CANTO XXIII.

ARGUMENT.

He sees Christ triumphing with his church. The Saviour ascends, followed by his virgin Mother. The others remain with St. Peter.

E'EN as the bird, who midst the leafy bower
   Has, in her nest, sat darkling through the night,
   With her sweet brood; impatient to descry
Their wished looks, and to bring home their food,
In the fond quest unconscious of her toil:
She, of the time prevenient, on the spray,
That overhangs their couch, with wakeful gaze
Expects the sun; nor ever, till the dawn,
Removeth from the east her eager ken:
So stood the dame erect, and bent her glance
Wistfully on that region, where the sun
Abateth most his speed; that, seeing her
Suspense and wondering, I became as one,
In whom desire is waken'd, and the hope
Of somewhat new to come fills with delight.

   Short space ensued; I was not held, I say,
Long in expectance, when I saw the heaven
Wax more and more resplendent; and, "Behold,"
Cried Beatrice, "the triumphal hosts
Of Christ, and all the harvest gather'd in,
Made ripe by these revolving spheres." Meseem'd,
That, while she spake, her image all did burn;
And in her eyes such fulness was of joy,
As I am fain to pass unconstrued by.

   As in the calm full moon, when Trivia smiles,
In peerless beauty, 'mid the eternal nymphs,

That paint through all its gulfs the blue profound;
In bright pre-eminence so saw I there
O'er million lamps a sun, from whom all drew
Their radiance, as from ours the starry train:
And, through the living light, so lustrous glow'd
The substance, that my ken endured it not.

O Beatrice! sweet and precious guide,
Who cheer'd me with her comfortable words:
"Against the virtue, that o'erpowereth thee,
Avails not to resist. Here is the Might,
And here the Wisdom, which did open lay
The path, that had been yearned for so long,
Betwixt the heaven and earth." Like to the fire,
That, in a cloud imprison'd, doth break out
Expansive, so that from its womb enlarged,
It falleth against nature to the ground;
Thus, in that heavenly banqueting, my soul
Outgrew herself; and, in the transport lost,
Holds now remembrance none of what she was.

"Ope thou thine eyes, and mark me: thou hast seen
Things, that empower thee to sustain my smile."
I was as one, when a forgotten dream
Doth come across him, and he strives in vain
To shape it in his fantasy again:
Whenas that gracious boon was proffer'd me,
Which never may be cancel'd from the book
Wherein the past is written. Now were all
Those tongues to sound, that have, on sweetest milk
Of Polyhymnia and her sisters, fed
And fatten'd; not with all their help to boot,
Unto the thousandth parcel of the truth.
My song might shadow forth that saintly smile,
How merely, in her saintly looks, it wrought.
And, with such figuring of Paradise,

The sacred strain must leap, like one that meets
A sudden interruption to his road.
But he, who thinks how ponderous the theme,
And that 'tis laid upon a mortal shoulder,
May pardon, if it tremble with the burden.
The track, our venturous keel must furrow, brooks
No unribb'd pinnace, no self-sparing pilot.
   "Why doth my face," said Beatrice, "thus
Enamour thee, as that thou dost not turn
Unto the beautiful garden, blossoming
Beneath the rays of Christ? Here is the rose,
Wherein the Word Divine was made incarnate;
And here the lilies, by whose odour known
The way of life was follow'd." Prompt I heard
Her bidding, and encounter'd once again
The strife of aching vision. As, erewhile,
Through glance of sun-light, stream'd through broken cloud,
Mine eyes a flower-besprinkled mead have seen;
Though veil'd themselves in shade: so saw I there
Legions of splendours, on whom burning rays
Shed lightnings from above; yet saw I not
The fountain whence they flow'd. O gracious virtue!
Thou, whose broad stamp is on them, higher up
Thou didst exalt thy glory, to give room
To my o'erlabour'd sight; when at the name
Of that fair flower, whom duly I invoke
Both morn and eve, my soul with all her might
Collected, on the goodliest ardour fix'd.
And, as the bright dimensions of the star
In heaven excelling, as once here on earth,
Were, in my eye-balls livelily pourtray'd;
Lo! from within the sky a cresset fell,
Circling in fashion of a diadem;
And girt the star; and, hovering, round it wheel'd.

PARADISE.—CANTO XXIII.

Whatever melody sounds sweetest here,
And draws the spirit most unto itself,
Might seem a rent cloud, when it grates the thunder;
Compared unto the sounding of that lyre,
Wherewith the goodliest sapphire, that inlays
The floor of heaven, was crown'd. "Angelic Love
I am, who thus with hovering flight enwheel
The lofty rapture from that womb inspired,
Where our desire did dwell: and round thee so,
Lady of Heaven! will hover; long as thou
Thy Son shalt follow, and diviner joy
Shall from thy presence gild the highest sphere."

Such close was to the circling melody:
And, as it ended, all the other lights
Took up the strain, and echoed Mary's name.

The robe, that with its regal folds enwraps
The world, and with the nearer breath of God
Doth burn and quiver, held so far retired
Its inner hem and skirting over us,
That yet no glimmer of its majesty
Had stream'd unto me: therefore were mine eyes
Unequal to pursue the crowned flame,
That towering rose, and sought the seed it bore.
And like to babe, that stretches forth its arms
For very eagerness toward the breast,
After the milk is taken; so outstretch'd
Their wavy summits all the fervent band,
Through zealous love to Mary: then, in view,
There halted; and "Regina Cœli" sang
So sweetly, the delight hath left me never.

Oh! what o'erflowing plenty is up-piled
In those rich-laden coffers, which below
Sow'd the good seed, whose harvest now they keep.
Here are the treasures tasted, that with tears

THE VISION.

Were in the Babylonian exile won,
When gold had fail'd them. Here, in synod high
Of ancient council with the new convened,
Under the Son of Mary and of God,
Victorious he his mighty triumph holds,
To whom the keys of glory were assign'd.

CANTO XXIV.

ARGUMENT.

St. Peter examines Dante touching Faith, and is contented with his answers.

"O YE! in chosen fellowship advanced
To the great supper of the blessed Lamb,
Whereon who feeds hath every wish fulfill'd;
If to this man through God's grace be vouchsafed
Foretaste of that, which from your table falls,
Or ever death his fated term prescribe;
Be ye not heedless of his urgent will:
But may some influence of your sacred dews
Sprinkle him. Of the fount ye alway drink,
Whence flows what most he craves." Beatrice spake;
And the rejoicing spirits, like to spheres
On firm-set poles revolving, trail'd a blaze
Of comet splendour: and as wheels, that wind
Their circles in the horologe, so work
The stated rounds, that to the observant eye
The first seems still, and as it flew, the last;
E'en thus their carols weaving variously,
They, by the measure paced, or swift or slow,
Made me to rate the riches of their joy.

From that, which I did note in beauty most
Excelling, saw I issue forth a flame
So bright, as none was left more goodly there.
Round Beatrice thrice it wheel'd about,
With so divine a song, that fancy's ear
Records it not; and the pen passeth on,
And leaves a blank: for that our mortal speech,

Nor e'en the inward shaping of the brain,
Hath colours fine enough to trace such folds.
 "O saintly sister mine! thy prayer devout
Is with so vehement affection urged,
Thou dost unbind me from thy beauteous sphere."
 Such were the accents towards my lady breathed
From that blest ardour, soon as it was stay'd;
To whom she thus: "O everlasting light
Of him, within whose mighty grasp our Lord
Did leave the keys, which of this wondrous bliss
He bare below! tent this man as thou wilt,
With lighter probe or deep, touching the faith,
By the which thou didst on the billows walk.
If he in love, in hope, and in belief,
Be stedfast, is not hid from thee: for thou
Hast there thy ken, where all things are beheld
In liveliest portraiture. But since true faith
Has peopled this fair realm with citizens;
Meet is, that to exalt its glory more,
Thou, in his audience, shouldst thereof discourse."
 Like to the bachelor, who arms himself,
And speaks not, till the master have proposed
The question, to approve, and not to end it;
So I, in silence, arm'd me, while she spake,
Summoning up each argument to aid;
As was behoveful for such questioner,
And such profession: "As good Christian ought,
Declare thee, what is faith?" Whereat I raised
My forehead to the light, whence this had breathed;
Then turn'd to Beatrice; and in her looks
Approval met, that from their inmost fount
I should unlock the waters. "May the grace,
That giveth me the captain of the church
For confessor," said I, "vouchsafe to me

Apt utterance for my thoughts;" then added: "Sire!
E'en as set down by the unerring style
Of thy dear brother, who with thee conspired
To bring Rome in unto the way of life,
Faith of things hoped is substance, and the proof
Of things not seen; and herein doth consist
Methinks its essence."—"Rightly hast thou deem'd,"
Was answer'd; "if thou well discern, why first
He hath defined it substance, and then proof."

"The deep things," I replied, "which here I scan
Distinctly, are below from mortal eye
So hidden, they have in belief alone
Their being; on which credence, hope sublime
Is built: and, therefore substance, it intends.
And inasmuch as we must needs infer
From such belief our reasoning, all respect
To other view excluded; hence of proof
The intention is derived." Forthwith I heard:
"If thus, whate'er by learning men attain,
Were understood; the sophist would want room
To exercise his wit." So breathed the flame
Of love; then added: "Current is the coin
Thou utter'st, both in weight and in alloy.
But tell me, if thou hast it in thy purse."

"Even so glittering and so round," said I,
"I not a whit misdoubt of its assay."

Next issued from the deep-imbosom'd splendour:
"Say, whence the costly jewel, on the which
Is founded every virtue, came to thee."

"The flood," I answer'd, "from the Spirit of God
Rain'd down upon the ancient bond and new,—
Here is the reasoning, that convinceth me
So feelingly, each argument beside
Seems blunt, and forceless, in comparison."

Then heard I: "Wherefore holdest thou that each,
The elder proposition and the new,
Which so persuade thee, are the voice of heaven?"

"The works, that follow'd, evidence their truth,"
I answer'd: "Nature did not make for these
The iron hot, or on her anvil mold them."

"Who voucheth to thee of the works themselves,"
Was the reply, "that they in very deed
Are that they purport? None hath sworn so to thee."

"That all the world," said I, "should have been turn'd
To Christian, and no miracle been wrought,
Would in itself be such a miracle,
The rest were not an hundredth part so great.
E'en thou went'st forth in poverty and hunger
To set the goodly plant, that, from the vine
It once was, now is grown unsightly bramble."

That ended, through the high celestial court
Resounded all the spheres, "Praise we one God!"
In song of most unearthly melody.
And when that Worthy thus, from branch to branch,
Examining, had led me, that we now
Approach'd the topmost bough; he straight resumed:
"The grace, that holds sweet dalliance with thy soul,
So far discreetly hath thy lips unclosed;
That, whatsoe'er has past them, I commend.
Behoves thee to express, what thou believest,
The next; and, whereon, thy belief hath grown."

"O saintly sire and spirit!" I began,
"Who seest that, which thou didst so believe,
As to outstrip feet younger than thine own,
Toward the sepulchre; thy will is here,
That I the tenour of my creed unfold;
And thou, the cause of it, hast likewise ask'd.
And I reply: I in one God believe;

One sole eternal Godhead, of whose love
All heaven is moved, himself unmoved the while.
Nor demonstration physical alone,
Or more intelligential and abstruse,
Persuades me to this faith: but from that truth
It cometh to me rather, which is shed
Through Moses; the rapt Prophets; and the Psalms;
The Gospel; and what ye yourselves did write,
When ye were gifted of the Holy Ghost.
In three eternal Persons I believe;
Essence threefold and one; mysterious league
Of union absolute, which, many a time,
The word of gospel lore upon my mind
Imprints: and from this germ, this firstling spark,
The lively flame dilates; and, like heaven's star,
Doth glitter in me." As the master hears,
Well pleased, and then enfoldeth in his arms
The servant, who hath joyful tidings brought,
And having told the errand keeps his peace;
Thus benediction uttering with song,
Soon as my peace I held, compass'd me thrice
The apostolic radiance, whose behest
Had oped my lips: so well their answer pleased.

CANTO XXV.

ARGUMENT.

St. James questions our Poet concerning Hope. Next St. John appears; and, on perceiving that Dante looks intently on him, informs him that he (St. John) had left his body resolved into earth, upon the earth; and that Christ and the Virgin alone had come with their bodies into heaven.

IF e'er the sacred poem, that hath made
   Both heaven and earth copartners in its toil,
   And with lean abstinence, through many a year,
Faded my brow, be destined to prevail
Over the cruelty, which bars me forth
Of the fair sheep-fold, where, a sleeping lamb,
The wolves set on and fain had worried me;
With other voice, and fleece of other grain,
I shall forthwith return; and, standing up
At my baptismal font, shall claim the wreath
Due to the poet's temples: for I there
First enter'd on the faith, which maketh souls
Acceptable to God: and, for its sake,
Peter had then circled my forehead thus.

   Next from the squadron, whence had issued forth
The first fruit of Christ's vicars on the earth,
Toward us moved a light, at view whereof
My Lady, full of gladness, spake to me:
"Lo! lo! behold the peer of mickle might,
That makes Galicia throng'd with visitants."

   As when the ring-dove by his mate alights;
In circles, each about the other wheels,
And, murmuring, cooes his fondness: thus saw I
One, of the other great and glorious prince,

With kindly greeting, hail'd; extolling, both,
Their heavenly banqueting: but when an end
Was to their gratulation, silent, each,
Before me sat they down, so burning bright,
I could not look upon them. Smiling then,
Beatrice spake: "O life in glory shrined!
Who didst the largess of our kingly court
Set down with faithful pen; let now thy voice,
Of hope the praises, in this height resound.
For well thou know'st, who figurest it as oft,
As Jesus, to ye three, more brightly shone."

"Lift up thy head; and be thou strong in trust:
For that, which hither from the mortal world
Arriveth, must be ripened in our beam."
Such cheering accents from the second flame
Assured me; and mine eyes I lifted up
Unto the mountains, that had bow'd them late
With over-heavy burden. "Sith our Liege
Wills of his grace, that thou, or e'er thy death,
In the most secret council with his lords
Shouldst be confronted, so that having view'd
The glories of our court, thou mayst therewith
Thyself, and all who hear, invigorate
With hope, that leads to blissful end; declare,
What is that hope? how it doth flourish in thee?
And whence thou hadst it?" Thus, proceeding still,
The second light: and she, whose gentle love
My soaring pennons in that lofty flight
Escorted, thus preventing me, rejoin'd:
"Among her sons, not one more full of hope,
Hath the church militant: so 'tis of him
Recorded in the sun, whose liberal orb
Enlighteneth all our tribe: and ere his term
Of warfare, hence permitted he is come,

From Egypt to Jerusalem, to see.
The other points, both which thou hast inquired,
Not for more knowledge, but that he may tell
How dear thou hold'st the virtue; these to him
Leave I: for he may answer thee with ease,
And without boasting, so God give him grace."

    Like to the scholar, practised in his task,
Who, willing to give proof of diligence,
Seconds his teacher gladly; "Hope," said I,
"Is of the joy to come a sure expectance,
The effect of grace divine and merit preceding.
This light from many a star, visits my heart;
But flow'd to me, the first, from him who sang
The songs of the Supreme; himself supreme
Among his tuneful brethren. 'Let all hope
In thee,' so spake his anthem, 'who have known
Thy name;' and, with my faith, who know not that?
From thee, the next, distilling from his spring,
In thine epistle, fell on me the drops
So plenteously, that I on others shower
The influence of their dew." Whileas I spake,
A lamping, as of quick and volley'd lightning,
Within the bosom of that mighty sheen
Play'd tremulous; then forth these accents breathed:
"Love for the virtue, which attended me
E'en to the palm, and issuing from the field,
Glows vigorous yet within me; and inspires
To ask of thee, whom also it delights,
What promise thou from hope, in chief, dost win."

    "Both scriptures, new and ancient," I replied,
"Propose the mark (which even now I view)
For souls beloved of God. Isaias saith,
'That, in their own land, each one must be clad
In twofold vesture;' and their proper land

Is this delicious life. In terms more full,
And clearer far, thy brother hath set forth
This revelation to us, where he tells
Of the white raiment destined to the saints."
And, as the words were ending, from above,
"They hope in thee!" first heard we cried: whereto
Answer'd the carols all. Amidst them next,
A light of so clear amplitude emerged,
That winter's month were but a single day,
Were such a crystal in the Cancer's sign.

  Like as a virgin riseth up, and goes,
And enters on the mazes of the dance;
Though gay, yet innocent of worse intent,
Than to do fitting honour to the bride:
So I beheld the new effulgence come
Unto the other two, who in a ring
Wheel'd, as became their rapture. In the dance,
And in the song, it mingled. And the dame
Held on them fix'd her looks; e'en as the spouse,
Silent, and moveless. "This is he, who lay
Upon the bosom of our pelican;
This he, into whose keeping, from the cross,
The mighty charge was given." Thus she spake:
Yet therefore nought the more removed her sight
From marking them: or e'er her words began,
Or when they closed. As he, who looks intent,
And strives with searching ken, how he may see
The sun in his eclipse, and, through desire
Of seeing, loseth power of sight; so I
Peer'd on that last resplendence, while I heard:
"Why dazzlest thou thine eyes in seeking that,
Which here abides not? Earth my body is,
In earth; and shall be, with the rest, so long,
As till our number equal the decree

Of the Most High. The two that have ascended,
In this our blessed cloister, shine alone
With the two garments. So report below."
    As when, for ease of labour, or to shun
Suspected peril, at a whistle's breath,
The oars, erewhile dash'd frequent in the wave,
All rest: the flamy circle at that voice
So rested; and the mingling sound was still,
Which from the trinal band, soft-breathing, rose.
I turn'd, but ah! how trembled in my thought,
When, looking at my side again to see
Beatrice, I descried her not; although,
Not distant, on the happy coast she stood.

CANTO XXVI.

ARGUMENT.

St. John examines our Poet touching Charity. Afterwards Adam tells when he was created, and placed in the terrestial Paradise; how long he remained in that state; what was the occasion of his fall; when he was admitted into heaven; and what language he spake.

WITH dazzled eyes, whilst wondering I remain'd;
Forth of the beamy flame, which dazzled me,
Issued a breath, that in attention mute
Detain'd me; and these words it spake: "'Twere well,
That, long as till thy vision, on my form
O'erspent, regain its virtue, with discourse
Thou compensate the brief delay. Say then,
Beginning, to what point thy soul aspires:
And meanwhile rest assured, that sight in thee
Is but o'erpower'd a space, not wholly quench'd;
Since thy fair guide and lovely, in her look
Hath potency, the like to that, which dwelt
In Ananias' hand."—I answering thus:
"Be to mine eyes the remedy, or late
Or early, at her pleasure; for they were
The gates, at which she enter'd, and did light
Her never-dying fire. My wishes here
Are centred: in this palace is the weal,
That Alpha and Omega is, to all
The lessons love can read me." Yet again
The voice, which had dispersed my fear when dazed
With that excess, to converse urged, and spake:
"Behoves thee sift more narrowly thy terms;
And say, who levell'd at this scope thy bow."

"Philosophy," said I, "hath arguments,
And this place hath authority enough,
To imprint in me such love: for, of constraint,
Good, inasmuch as we perceive the good,
Kindle our love; and in degree the more,
As it comprises more of goodness in 't.
The essence then, where such advantage is,
That each good, found without it, is nought else
But of his light the beam, must needs attract
The soul of each one, loving, who the truth
Discerns, on which this proof is built. Such truth
Learn I from him, who shows me the first love
Of all intelligential substances
Eternal: from his voice I learn, whose word
Is truth; that of himself to Moses saith,
'I will make all my good before thee pass:'
Lastly, from thee I learn, who chief proclaim'st
E'en at the outset of thy heralding,
In mortal ears the mystery of heaven."

"Through human wisdom, and the authority
Therewith agreeing," heard I answer'd, "keep
The choicest of thy love for God. But say,
If thou yet other cords within thee feel'st,
That draw thee towards him; so that thou report
How many are the fangs, with which this love
Is grappled to thy soul." I did not miss,
To what intent the eagle of our Lord
Had pointed his demand; yea, noted well
The avowal which he led to; and resumed:
"All grappling bonds, that knit the heart to God,
Confederate to make fast our charity.
The being of the world; and mine own being;
The death which He endured, that I should live;
And that, which all the faithful hope, as I do;

To the foremention'd lively knowledge join'd;
Have from the sea of ill love saved my bark,
And on the coast secured it of the right.
As for the leaves, that in the garden bloom,
My love for them is great, as is the good
Dealt by the eternal hand, that tends them all."

    I ended: and therewith a song most sweet
Rang through the spheres; and "Holy, holy, holy,"
Accordant with the rest, my lady sang.
And as a sleep is broken and dispersed
Through sharp encounter of the nimble light,
With the eye's spirit running forth to meet
The ray, from membrane on to membrane urged;
And the upstartled wight loathes that he sees;
So, at his sudden waking, he misdeems
Of all around him, till assurance waits
On better judgment: thus the saintly dame
Drove from before mine eyes the motes away,
With the resplendence of her own, that cast
Their brightness downward, thousand miles below.
Whence I my vision, clearer than before,
Recover'd; and well nigh astounded, ask'd
Of a fourth light, that now with us I saw.

    And Beatrice: "The first living soul,
That ever the first virtue framed, admires
Within these rays his Maker." Like the leaf,
That bows its lithe top till the blast is blown;
By its own virtue rear'd, then stands aloof:
So I, the whilst she said, awe-stricken bow'd.
Then eagerness to speak embolden'd me;
And I began: "O fruit! that wast alone
Mature, when first engender'd; ancient father!
That doubly seest in every wedded bride
Thy daughter, by affinity and blood;

THE VISION.

Devoutly as I may, I pray thee hold
Converse with me: my will thou seest: and I,
More speedily to hear thee, tell it not."
    It chanceth oft some animal bewrays,
Through the sleek covering of his furry coat,
The fondness, that stirs in him, and conforms
His outside seeming to the cheer within:
And in like guise was Adam's spirit moved
To joyous mood, that through the covering shone,
Transparent, when to pleasure me it spake:
"No need thy will be told, which I untold
Better discern, than thou whatever thing
Thou hold'st most certain: for that will I see
In Him, who is truth's mirror; and Himself,
Parhelion unto all things, and nought else,
To Him. This wouldst thou hear: how, long since, God
Placed me in that high garden, from whose bounds
She led me up this ladder, steep and long;
What space endured my season of delight;
Whence truly sprang the wrath that banish'd me;
And what the language, which I spake and framed.
Not that I tasted of the tree, my son,
Was in itself the cause of that exile,
But only my transgressing of the mark
Assign'd me. There, whence at thy lady's hest
The Mantuan moved him, still was I debarr'd
This council, till the sun had made complete,
Four thousand and three hundred rounds and twice,
His annual journey; and, through every light
In his broad pathway, saw I him return,
Thousand save seventy times, the whilst I dwelt
Upon the earth. The language I did use
Was worn away, or ever Nimrod's race
Their unaccomplishable work began.

For nought, that man inclines to, e'er was lasting:
Left by his reason free, and variable
As is the sky that sways him. That he speaks,
Is nature's prompting: whether thus, or thus,
She leaves to you, as ye do most affect it.
Ere I descended into hell's abyss,
El was the name on earth of the Chief Good,
Whose joy enfolds me: Eli then 'twas call'd.
And so beseemeth: for, in mortals, use
Is as the leaf upon the bough: that goes,
And other comes instead. Upon the mount
Most high above the waters, all my life,
Both innocent and guilty, did but reach
From the first hour, to that which cometh next
(As the sun changes quarter) to the sixth."

CANTO XXVII.

ARGUMENT.

St. Peter bitterly rebukes the covetousness of his successors in the apostolic see, while all the heavenly host sympathize in his indignation; they then vanish upwards. Beatrice bids Dante again cast his view below. Afterwards they are borne into the ninth heaven, of which she shows him the nature and properties; blaming the perverseness of man, who places his will on low and perishable things.

THEN "Glory to the Father, to the Son,
And to the Holy Spirit," rang aloud
Throughout all Paradise; that with the song
My spirit reel'd, so passing sweet the strain.
And what I saw was equal ecstasy:
One universal smile it seem'd of all things;
Joy past compare; gladness unutterable;
Imperishable life of peace and love;
Exhaustless riches, and unmeasured bliss.

    Before mine eyes stood the four torches lit:
And that, which first had come, began to wax
In brightness; and, in semblance, such became,
As Jove might be, if he and Mars were birds,
And interchanged their plumes. Silence ensued,
Through the blest quire; by Him, who here appoints
Vicissitude of ministry, enjoin'd;
When thus I heard: "Wonder not, if my hue
Be changed; for, while I speak, these shalt thou see
All in like manner change with me. My place
He who usurps on earth (my place, ay, mine,
Which in the presence of the Son of God
Is void), the same hath made my cemetery
A common sewer of puddle and of blood:

PARADISE.—CANTO XXVII.

The more below his triumph, who from hence
Malignant fell." Such colour, as the sun,
At eve or morning, paints an adverse cloud,
Then saw I sprinkled over all the sky.
And as the unblemish'd dame, who, in herself
Secure from censure, yet at bare report
Of other's failing, shrinks with maiden fear;
So Beatrice, in her semblance, changed:
And such eclipse in heaven, methinks, was seen,
When the Most Holy suffer'd. Then the words
Proceeded, with voice, alter'd from itself
So clean, the semblance did not alter more.
"Not to this end was Christ's spouse with my blood,
With that of Linus, and of Cletus, fed;
That she might serve for purpose of base gold:
But for the purchase of this happy life,
Did Sextus, Pius, and Callixtus bleed,
And Urban; they, whose doom was not without
Much weeping seal'd. No purpose was of ours,
That on the right hand of our successors,
Part of the Christian people should be set,
And part upon their left; nor that the keys,
Which were vouchsafed me, should for ensign serve
Unto the banners, that do levy war
On the baptized: nor I, for sigil-mark,
Set upon sold and lying privileges:
Which makes me oft to bicker and turn red.
In shepherd's clothing, greedy wolves below
Range wide o'er all the pastures. Arm of God!
Why longer sleep'st thou? Cahorsines and Gascons
Prepare to quaff our blood. O good beginning!
To what a vile conclusion must thou stoop.
But the high providence, which did defend,
Through Scipio, the world's empery for Rome,

Will not delay its succour: and thou, son,
Who through thy mortal weight shalt yet again
Return below, open thy lips, nor hide
What is by me not hidden." As a flood
Of frozen vapours streams adown the air,
What time the she-goat with her skiey horn
Touches the sun; so saw I there stream wide
The vapours, who with us had linger'd late,
And with glad triumph deck the ethereal cope.
Onward my sight their semblances pursued;
So far pursued, as till the space between
From its reach sever'd them: whereat the guide
Celestial, marking me no more intent
On upward gazing, said, "Look down, and see
What circuit thou hast compast." From the hour
When I before had cast my view beneath,
All the first region overpast I saw,
Which from the midmost to the boundary winds;
That onward, thence, from Gades, I beheld
The unwise passage of Laertes' son;
And hitherward the shore, where thou, Europa,
Madest thee a joyful burden; and yet more
Of this dim spot had seen, but that the sun,
A constellation off and more, had ta'en
His progress in the zodiac underneath.

    Then by the spirit, that doth never leave
Its amorous dalliance with my lady's looks,
Back with redoubled ardour were mine eyes
Led unto her: and from her radiant smiles,
Whenas I turn'd me, pleasure so divine
Did lighten on me, that whatever bait
Or art or nature in the human flesh,
Or in its limn'd resemblance, can combine,
Through greedy eyes to take the soul withal,

Were, to her beauty, nothing. Its boon influence
From the fair nest of Leda rapt me forth,
And wafted on into the swiftest heaven.

    What place for entrance Beatrice chose,
I may not say; so uniform was all,
Liveliest and loftiest. She my secret wish
Divined; and, with such gladness, that God's love
Seem'd from her visage shining, thus began:
"Here is the goal, whence motion on his race
Starts: motionless the centre, and the rest
All moved around. Except the soul divine,
Place in this heaven is none; the soul divine,
Wherein the love, which ruleth o'er its orb,
Is kindled, and the virtue, that it sheds:
One circle, light and love, enclasping it,
As this doth clasp the others; and to Him,
Who draws the bound, its limit only known.
Measured itself by none, it doth divide
Motion to all, counted unto them forth,
As by the fifth or half ye count forth ten.
The vase, wherein time's roots are plunged, thou seest:
Look elsewhere for the leaves. O mortal lust!
That canst not lift thy head above the waves
Which whelm and sink thee down. The will in man
Bears goodly blossoms; but its ruddy promise
Is, by the dripping of perpetual rain,
Made mere abortion: faith and innocence
Are met with but in babes; each taking leave,
Ere cheeks with down are sprinkled: he, that fasts
While yet a stammerer, with his tongue let loose
Gluts every food alike in every moon:
One, yet a babbler, loves and listens to
His mother; but no sooner hath free use
Of speech, than he doth wish her in her grave.

THE VISION.

So suddenly doth the fair child of him,
Whose welcome is the morn and eve his parting,
To negro blackness change her virgin white.
 "Thou, to abate thy wonder, note, that none
Bears rule in earth; and its frail family
Are therefore wanderers. Yet before the date,
When, through the hundredth in his reckoning dropt,
Pale January must be shoved aside
From winter's calendar, these heavenly spheres
Shall roar so loud, that fortune shall be fain
To turn the poop, where she hath now the prow;
So that the fleet run onward: and true fruit,
Expected long, shall crown at last the bloom."

CANTO XXVIII.

ARGUMENT.

Still in the ninth heaven, our Poet is permitted to behold the divine essence; and then sees, in three hierarchies, the nine choirs of angels. Beatrice clears some difficulties which occur to him on this occasion.

SO she, who doth imparadise my soul,
    Had drawn the veil from off our present life,
    And bared the truth of poor mortality:
When lo! as one who, in a mirror, spies
The shining of a flambeau at his back,
Lit sudden ere he deem of its approach,
And turneth to resolve him, if the glass
Have told him true, and sees the record faithful
As note is to its metre; even thus,
I well remember, did befall to me,
Looking upon the beauteous eyes, whence love
Had made the leash to take me. As I turn'd:
And that which none, who in that volume looks,
Can miss of, in itself apparent, struck
My view; a point I saw, that darted light
So sharp, no lid, unclosing, may bear up
Against its keenness. The least star we ken
From hence, had seem'd a moon; set by its side,
As star by side of star. And so far off,
Perchance, as is the halo from the light
Which paints it, when most dense the vapour spreads;
There wheel'd about the point a circle of fire,
More rapid than the motion which surrounds,

Speediest, the world. Another this enring'd;
And that a third; the third a fourth, and that
A fifth encompass'd; which a sixth next bound;
And over this, a seventh, following, reach'd
Circumference so ample, that its bow,
Within the span of Juno's messenger,
Had scarce been held entire. Beyond the seventh,
Ensued yet other two. And every one,
As more in number distant from the first,
Was tardier in motion: and that glow'd
With flame most pure, that to the sparkle of truth,
Was nearest; as partaking most, methinks,
Of its reality. The guide beloved
Saw me in anxious thought suspense, and spake:
"Heaven, and all nature, hangs upon that point.
The circle thereto most conjoin'd observe;
And know, that by intenser love its course
Is, to this swiftness, wing'd." To whom I thus:
"It were enough; nor should I further seek,
Had I but witness'd order, in the world
Appointed, such as in these wheels is seen.
But in the sensible world such difference is,
That in each round shows more divinity,
As each is wider from the centre. Hence
If in this wondrous and angelic temple,
That hath, for confine, only light and love,
My wish may have completion, I must know,
Wherefore such disagreement is between
The exemplar and its copy: for myself,
Contemplating, I fail to pierce the cause."

"It is no marvel, if thy fingers foil'd
Do leave the knot untied: so hard 'tis grown
For want of tenting." Thus she said: "But take,"
She added, "if thou wish thy cure, my words,

And entertain them subtly. Every orb,
Corporeal, doth proportion its extent
Unto the virtue through its parts diffused.
The greater blessedness preserves the more.
The greater is the body (if all parts
Share equally) the more is to preserve.
Therefore the circle, whose swift course enwheels
The universal frame, answers to that
Which is supreme in knowledge and in love.
Thus by the virtue, not the seeming breadth
Of substance, measuring, thou shalt see the heavens,
Each to the intelligence that ruleth it,
Greater to more, and smaller unto less,
Suited in strict and wondrous harmony."

As when the north blows from his milder cheek
A blast, that scours the sky, forthwith our air,
Clear'd of the rack that hung on it before,
Glitters; and, with his beauties all unveil'd,
The firmament looks forth serene, and smiles:
Such was my cheer, when Beatrice drove
With clear reply the shadows back, and truth
Was manifested as a star in heaven.
And when the words were ended, not unlike
To iron in the furnace, every cirque,
Ebullient, shot forth scintillating fires:
And every sparkle shivering to new blaze,
In number did outmillion the account
Reduplicate upon the chequer'd board.
Then heard I echoing on, from choir to choir,
"Hosanna," to the fixed point, that holds,
And shall for ever hold them to their place,
From everlasting, irremovable.

Musing awhile I stood: and she, who saw
My inward meditations, thus began:

THE VISION.

"In the first circles, they, whom thou beheld'st,
Are seraphim and cherubim. Thus swift
Follow their hoops, in likeness to the point,
Near as they can, approaching; and they can
The more, the loftier their vision. Those
That round them fleet, gazing the Godhead next,
Are thrones; in whom the first trine ends. And all
Are blessed, even as their sight descends
Deeper into the truth, wherein rest is
For every mind. Thus happiness hath root
In seeing, not in loving, which of sight
Is aftergrowth. And of the seeing such
The meed, as unto each, in due degree,
Grace and good-will their measure have assign'd.
The other trine, that with still opening buds
In this eternal springtide blossom fair,
Fearless of bruising from the nightly ram,
Breathe up in warbled melodies threefold
Hosannas, blending ever; from the three,
Transmitted, hierarchy of gods, for aye
Rejoicing; dominations first; next them,
Virtues; and powers the third; the next to whom
Are princedoms and archangels, with glad round
To tread their festal ring; and last, the band
Angelical, disporting in their sphere.
All, as they circle in their orders, look
Aloft; and, downward, with such sway prevail,
That all with mutual impulse tend to God.
These once a mortal view beheld. Desire,
In Dionysius, so intensely wrought,
That he, as I have done, ranged them; and named
Their orders, marshal'd in his thought. From him,
Dissentient, one refused his sacred read.
But soon as in this heaven his doubting eyes

Were open'd, Gregory at his error smiled.
Nor marvel, that a denizen of earth
Should scan such secret truth; for he had learnt
Both this and much beside of these our orbs,
From an eye-witness to heaven's mysteries."

CANTO XXIX.

ARGUMENT.

Beatrice beholds, in the mirror of divine truth, some doubts which had entered the mind of Dante. These she resolves; and then digresses into a vehement reprehension of certain theologians and preachers in those days, whose ignorance or avarice induced them to substitute their own inventions for the pure word of the Gospel.

NO longer, than what time Latona's twins
   Cover'd of Libra and fleecy star,
   Together both, girding the horizon hang;
In even balance, from the zenith poised;
Till from that verge, each, changing hemisphere,
Part the nice level; e'en so brief a space
Did Beatrice's silence hold. A smile
Sat painted on her cheek; and her fix'd gaze
Bent on the point, at which my vision fail'd:
When thus, her words resuming, she began:
"I speak, nor what thou wouldst inquire, demand;
For I have mark'd it, where all time and place
Are present. Not for increase to himself
Of good, which may not be increased, but forth
To manifest his glory by its beams;
Inhabiting his own eternity,
Beyond time's limit or what bound soe'er
To circumscribe his being; as he will'd,
Into new natures, like unto himself,
Eternal love unfolded: nor before,
As if in dull inaction, torpid, lay,
For, not in process of before or aft,
Upon these waters moved the Spirit of God.
Simple and mix'd, both form and substance, forth

PARADISE.—CANTO XXIX.

To perfect being started, like three darts
Shot from a bow three-corded. And as ray
In crystal, glass, and amber, shines entire,
E'en at the moment of its issuing; thus
Did, from the eternal Sovran, beam entire
His threefold operation, at one act
Produced coeval. Yet, in order, each
Created his due station knew: those highest,
Who pure intelligence were made; mere power,
The lowest; in the midst, bound with strict league,
Intelligence and power, unsever'd bond.
Long tract of ages by the angels past,
Ere the creating of another world,
Described on Jerome's pages, thou hast seen.
But that what I disclose to thee is true,
Those penmen, whom the Holy Spirit moved,
In many a passage of their sacred book,
Attest; as thou by diligent search shalt find:
And reason, in some sort, discerns the same,
Who scarce would grant the heavenly ministers,
Of their perfection void, so long a space.
Thus when and where these spirits of love were made,
Thou know'st, and how: and, knowing, hast allay'd
Thy thirst, which from the triple question rose.
Ere one had reckon'd twenty, e'en so soon,
Part of the angels fell: and, in their fall,
Confusion to your elements ensued.
The others kept their station: and this task,
Whereon thou look'st, began, with such delight,
That they surcease not ever, day nor night,
Their circling. Of that fatal lapse the cause
Was the curst pride of him, whom thou hast seen
Pent with the world's incumbrance. Those, whom here
Thou seest, were lowly to confess themselves

THE VISION.

Of his free bounty, who had made them apt
For ministries so high: therefore their views
Were, by enlightening grace and their own merit,
Exalted; so that in their will confirm'd
They stand, nor fear to fall. For do not doubt,
But to receive the grace, which Heaven vouchsafes,
Is meritorious, even as the soul
With prompt affection welcometh the guest.
Now, without further help, if with good heed
My words thy mind have treasured, thou henceforth
This consistory round about mayst scan,
And gaze thy fill. But, since thou hast on earth
Heard vain disputers, reasoners in the schools,
Canvass the angelic nature, and dispute
Its powers of apprehension, memory, choice;
Therefore, 'tis well thou take from me the truth,
Pure and without disguise; which they below,
Equivocating, darken and perplex.

"Know thou, that, from the first, these substances,
Rejoicing in the countenance of God,
Have held unceasingly their view, intent
Upon the glorious vision, from the which
Nought absent is nor hid: where then no change
Of newness, with succession, interrupts,
Remembrance, there, needs none to gather up
Divided thought and images remote.

"So that men, thus at variance with the truth,
Dream, though their eyes be open; reckless some
Of error; others well aware they err,
To whom more guilt and shame are justly due.
Each the known track of sage philosophy
Deserts, and has a by-way of his own:
So much the restless eagerness to shine,
And love of singularity, prevail.

Yet this, offensive as it is, provokes
Heaven's anger less, than when the book of God
Is forced to yield to man's authority,
Or from its straightness warp'd: no reckoning made
What blood the sowing of it in the world
Has cost; what favour for himself he wins,
Who meekly clings to it. The aim of all
Is how to shine: e'en they, whose office is
To preach the gospel, let the gospel sleep,
And pass their own inventions off instead.
One tells, how at Christ's suffering the wan moon
Bent back her steps, and shadow'd o'er the sun
With intervenient disk, as she withdrew:
Another, how the light shrouded itself
Within its tabernacle, and left dark
The Spaniard, and the Indian, with the Jew.
Such fables Florence in her pulpit hears,
Bandied about more frequent, than the names
Of Bindi and of Lapi in her streets.
The sheep, meanwhile, poor witless ones, return
From pasture, fed, with wind: and what avails
For their excuse, they do not see their harm?
Christ said not to his first conventicle,
'Go forth and preach impostures to the world,'
But gave them truth to build on; and the sound
Was mighty on their lips: nor needed they,
Beside the gospel, other spear or shield,
To aid them in their warfare for the faith.
The preacher now provides himself with store
Of jests and gibes; and, so there be no lack
Of laughter, while he vents them, his big cowl
Distends, and he has won the meed he sought:
Could but the vulgar catch a glimpse the while
Of that dark bird which nestles in his hood,

THE VISION.

They scarce would wait to hear the blessing said,
Which now the dotards hold in such esteem,
That every counterfeit, who spreads abroad
The hands of holy promise, finds a throng
Of credulous fools beneath. Saint Anthony
Fattens with this his swine, and others worse
Than swine, who diet at his lazy board,
Paying with unstampt metal for their fare.
   "But (for we far have wander'd) let us seek
The forward path again; so as the way
Be shorten'd with the time. No mortal tongue,
Nor thought of man, hath ever reach'd so far,
That of these natures he might count the tribes.
What Daniel of their thousands hath reveal'd,
With finite number, infinite conceals.
The fountain, at whose source these drink their beams,
With light supplies them in as many modes,
As there are splendours that it shines on: each
According to the virtue it conceives,
Differing in love and sweet affection.
Look then how lofty and how huge in breadth
The eternal might, which, broken and dispersed
Over such countless mirrors, yet remains
Whole in itself and one, as at the first."

P. P.—57.   Then "Glory to the Father, to the Son,
And to the Holy Spirit," rang aloud
Throughout all Paradise; that with the song
My spirit reel'd, so passing sweet the strain.

Canto XXVII., lines 1-4.

Not unlike
To iron in the furnace, every cirque,
Ebullient, shot forth scintillating fires.

Canto XXVIII., lines 80-82.

CANTO XXX.

ARGUMENT.

Dante is taken up with Beatrice into the empyrean; and there having his sight strengthened by her aid, and by the virtue derived from looking on the river of light, he sees the triumph of the angels and of the souls of the blessed.

NOON'S fervid hour perchance six thousand miles
From hence is distant; and the shadowy cone
Almost to level on our earth declines;
When, from the midmost of this blue abyss,
By turns some star is to our vision lost.
And straightway as the handmaid of the sun
Puts forth her radiant brow, all, light by light,
Fade; and the spangled firmament shuts in,
E'en to the loveliest of the glittering throng.
Thus vanish'd gradually from my sight,
The triumph, which plays ever round the point,
That overcame me, seeming (for it did)
Engirt by that it girdeth. Wherefore love,
With loss of other object, forced me bend
Mine eyes on Beatrice once again.

If all, that hitherto is told of her,
Were in one praise concluded, 'twere too weak
To furnish out this turn. Mine eyes did look
On beauty, such, as I believe in sooth,
Not merely to exceed our human; but,
That save its Maker, none can to the full
Enjoy it. At this point o'erpower'd I fail;
Unequal to my theme; as never bard
Of buskin or of sock hath fail'd before.
For as the sun doth to the feeblest sight,

309

THE VISION.

E'en so remembrance of that witching smile
Hath dispossest my spirit of itself.
Not from that day, when on this earth I first
Beheld her charms, up to that view of them,
Have I with song applausive ever ceased
To follow; but now follow them no more;
My course here bounded, as each artist's is,
When it doth touch the limit of his skill.

    She (such as I bequeath her to the bruit
Of louder trump than mine, which hasteneth on,
Urging its arduous matter to the close)
Her words resumed, in gesture and in voice
Resembling one accustom'd to command:
"Forth from the last corporeal are we come
Into the heaven, that is unbodied light;
Light intellectual, replete with love;
Love of true happiness, replete with joy;
Joy, that transcends all sweetness of delight.
Here shalt thou look on either mighty host
Of Paradise; and one in that array,
Which in the final judgment thou shalt see."

    As when the lightning, in a sudden spleen
Unfolded, dashes from the blinding eyes
The visive spirits, dazzled and bedimm'd;
So, round about me, fulminating streams
Of living radiance play'd, and left me swathed
And veil'd in dense impenetrable blaze.
Such weal is in the love, that stills this heaven;
For its own flame the torch thus fitting ever.

    No sooner to my listening ear had come
The brief assurance, than I understood
New virtue into me infused, and sight
Kindled afresh, with vigour to sustain
Excess of light however pure. I look'd;

And, in the likeness of a river, saw
Light flowing, from whose amber-seeming waves
Flash'd up effulgence, as they glided on
'Twixt banks, on either side, painted with spring,
Incredible how fair: and, from the tide,
There ever and anon, outstarting, flew
Sparkles instinct with life; and in the flowers
Did set them, like to rubies chased in gold:
Then, as if drunk with odours, plunged again
Into the wondrous flood; from which, as one
Re-enter'd, still another rose. "The thirst
Of knowledge high, whereby thou art inflamed,
To search the meaning of what here thou seest,
The more it warms thee, pleases me the more.
But first behoves thee of this water drink,
Or e'er that longing be allay'd." So spake
The day-star of mine eyes: then thus subjoin'd:
"This stream; and these, forth issuing from its gulf,
And diving back, a living topaz each;
With all this laughter on its bloomy shores;
Are but a preface, shadowy of the truth
They emblem: not that, in themselves, the things
Are crude; but on thy part is the defect,
For that thy views not yet aspire so high."

    Never did babe that had outslept his wont,
Rush, with such eager straining, to the milk,
As I toward the water bending me,
To make the better mirrors of mine eyes
In the refining wave and as the eaves
Of mine eyelids did drink of it, forthwith
Seem'd it unto me turned from length to round.
Then as a troop of maskers, when they put
Their vizors off, look other than before;
The counterfeited semblance thrown aside:

So into greater jubilee were changed
Those flowers and sparkles; and distinct I saw,
Before me either court of heaven display'd.
    O prime enlightener! thou who gavest me strength
On the high triumph of thy realm to gaze,
Grant virtue now to utter what I kenn'd.
    There is in heaven a light, whose goodly shine
Makes the Creator visible to all
Created, that in seeing him alone
Have peace; and in a circle spreads so far,
That the circumference were too loose a zone
To girdle in the sun. All is one beam,
Reflected from the summit of the first,
That moves, which being hence and vigour takes.
And as some cliff, that from the bottom eyes
His image mirror'd in the crystal flood,
As if to admire his brave apparelling
Of verdure and of flowers; so, round about,
Eying the light, on more than million thrones,
Stood, eminent, whatever from our earth
Has to the skies return'd. How wide the leaves,
Extended to their utmost, of this rose,
Whose lowest step embosoms such a space
Of ample radiance! Yet, nor amplitude
Nor height impeded, but my view with ease
Took in the full dimensions of that joy.
Near or remote, what there avails, where God
Immediate rules, and Nature, awed, suspends
Her sway? Into the yellow of the rose
Perennial, which, in bright expansiveness,
Lays forth its gradual blooming, redolent
Of praises to the never-wintering sun,
As one, who fain would speak yet holds his peace,
Beatrice lead me; and, "Behold," she said,

"This fair assemblage; stoles of snowy white,
How numberless. The city, where we dwell,
Behold how vast; and these our seats so throng'd,
Few now are wanting here. In that proud stall,
On which, the crown, already o'er its state
Suspended, holds thine eyes—or e'er thyself
Mayst at the wedding sup,—shall rest the soul
Of the great Harry, he who, by the world
Augustus hail'd, to Italy must come,
Before her day be ripe. But ye are sick,
And in your tetchy wantonness as blind
As is the bantling, that of hunger dies,
And drives away the nurse. Nor may it be,
That he, who in the sacred forum sways,
Openly or in secret, shall with him
Accordant walk: whom God will not endure
I' the holy office long; but thrust him down
To Simon Magus, where Alagna's priest
Will sink beneath him: such will be his meed."

CANTO XXXI.

ARGUMENT.

The Poet expatiates further on the glorious vision described in the last Canto. On looking round for Beatrice, he finds that she has left him, and that an old man is at his side. This proves to be St. Bernard, who shows him that Beatrice has returned to her throne, and then points out to him the blessedness of the Virgin Mother.

IN fashion, as a snow white rose, lay then
   Before my view the saintly multitude,
   Which in his own blood Christ espoused. Meanwhile,
That other host, that soar aloft to gaze
And celebrate his glory, whom they love,
Hover'd around; and, like a troop of bees,
Amid the vernal sweets alighting now,
Now, clustering, where their fragrant labour glows,
Flew downward to the mighty flower, or rose
From the redundant petals, streaming back
Unto the stedfast dwelling of their joy.
Faces had they of flame, and wings of gold;
The rest was whiter than the driven snow;
And, as they flitted down into the flower,
From range to range, fanning their plumy loins
Whisper'd the peace and ardour, which they won
From that soft winnowing. Shadow none, the vast
Interposition of such numerous flight
Cast, from above, upon the flower, or view
Obstructed aught. For, through the universe,
Whatever merited, celestial light
Glides freely, and no obstacle prevents.
   All there, who reign in safety and in bliss,
Ages long past or new, on one sole mark

Their love and vision fix'd. O trinal beam
Of individual star, that charm'st them thus!
Vouchsafe one glance to gild our storm below.

If the grim brood, from Arctic shores that roam'd
(Where Helice for ever, as she wheels,
Sparkles a mother's fondness on her son),
Stood in mute wonder 'mid the works of Rome,
When to their view the Lateran arose
In greatness more than earthly; I, who then
From human to divine had passed, from time
Unto eternity, and out of Florence
To justice and to truth, how might I chuse
But marvel too? 'Twixt gladness and amaze,
In sooth no will had I to utter aught,
Or hear. And, as a pilgrim, when he rests
Within the temple of his vow, looks round
In breathless awe, and hopes some time to tell
Of all its goodly state; e'en so mine eyes
Coursed up and down along the living light,
Now low, and now aloft, and now around,
Visiting every step. Looks I beheld,
Where charity in soft persuasion sat;
Smiles from within, and radiance from above;
And, in each gesture, grace and honour high.

So roved my ken, and in its general form
All Paradise survey'd: when round I turn'd
With purpose of my lady to inquire
Once more of things, that held my thought suspense,
But answer found from other than I ween'd;
For, Beatrice when I thought to see,
I saw instead a senior, at my side,
Robed, as the rest, in glory. Joy benign
Glow'd in his eye, and o'er his cheek diffused,
With gestures such as spake a father's love.

And, "Whither is she vanish'd?" straight I asked.
  "By Beatrice summon'd," he replied,
"I come to aid thy wish. Looking aloft
To the third circle from the highest, there
Behold her on the throne, wherein her merit
Hath placed her." Answering not, mine eyes I raised,
And saw her, where aloof she sat, her brow
A wreath reflecting of eternal beams.
Not from the centre of the sea so far
Unto the region of the highest thunder,
As was my ken from hers; and yet the form
Came through that medium down, unmix'd and pure.
  "O lady! thou in whom my hopes have rest;
Who, for my safety, hast not scorn'd, in hell
To leave the traces of thy footsteps mark'd;
For all mine eyes have seen, I to thy power
And goodness, virtue owe and grace. Of slave
Thou hast to freedom brought me: and no means,
For my deliverance apt, hast left untried.
Thy liberal bounty still toward me keep:
That, when my spirit, which thou madest whole,
Is loosen'd from this body, it may find
Favour with thee." So I my suit preferr'd:
And she, so distant, as appear'd, look'd down,
And smiled; then towards the eternal fountain turn'd.
  And thus the senior, holy and revered:
"That thou at length mayst happily conclude
Thy voyage (to which end I was dispatch'd,
By supplication moved and holy love),
Let thy upsoaring vision range, at large,
This garden through: for so, by ray divine
Kindled, thy ken a higher flight shall mount;
And from heaven's queen, whom fervent I adore
All gracious aid befriend us; for that I

In fashion, as a snow-white rose, lay then
Before my view the saintly multitude,
Which in his own blood Christ espoused.

Canto XXXI., lines 1–3.

Answering not, mine eyes I raised,
And saw her, where aloof she sat, her brow
A wreath reflecting of eternal beams.

Canto XXXI., lines 64–66.

Am her own faithful Bernard." Like a wight,
Who haply from Croatia wends to see
Our Veronica; and the while 'tis shown,
Hangs over it with never-sated gaze,
And, all that he hath heard revolving, saith
Unto himself in thought: "And didst thou look
E'en thus, O Jesus, my true Lord and God?
And was this semblance thine?" So gazed I then
Adoring; for the charity of him,
Who musing, in this world *that* peace enjoy'd,
Stood livelily before me. "Child of grace!"
Thus he began: "thou shalt not knowledge gain
Of this glad being, if thine eyes are held
Still in this depth below. But search around
The circles, to the furthest, till thou spy
Seated in state, the queen, that of this realm
Is sovran." Straight mine eyes I raised; and bright,
As, at the birth of morn, the eastern clime
Above the horizon, where the sun declines;
So to mine eyes, that upward, as from vale
To mountain sped, at the extreme bound, a part
Excell'd in lustre all the front opposed.
And as the glow burns ruddiest o'er the wave,
That waits the ascending team, which Phaeton
Ill knew to guide, and on each part the light
Diminish'd fades, intensest in the midst;
So burn'd the peaceful oriflamb, and slack'd
On every side the living flame decay'd.
And in that midst their sportive pennons waved
Thousands of angels; in resplendence each
Distinct, and quaint adornment. At their glee
And carol, smiled the Lovely One of heaven,
That joy was in the eyes of all the blest.

Had I a tongue in eloquence as rich,

THE VISION.

As is the colouring in fancy's loom,
'Twere all too poor to utter the least part
Of that enchantment. When he saw mine eyes
Intent on her, that charm'd him; Bernard gazed
With so exceeding fondness, as infused
Ardour into my breast, unfelt before.

CANTO XXXII.

ARGUMENT.

St. Bernard shows him, on their several thrones, the other blessed souls, both of the Old and New Testament; explains to him that their places are assigned them by grace, and not according to merit; and lastly, tells him that if he would obtain power to descry what remained of the heavenly vision, he must unite with him in supplication to Mary.

FREELY the sage, though wrapt in musings high,
   Assumed the teacher's part, and mild began:
"The wound that Mary closed she open'd first,
Who sits so beautiful at Mary's feet.
The third in order, underneath her, lo!
Rachel with Beatrice: Sarah next;
Judith; Rebecca; and the gleaner-maid,
Meek ancestress of him, who sang the songs
Of sore repentance in his sorrowful mood.
All, as I name them, down from leaf to leaf,
Are, in gradation, throned on the rose.
And from the seventh step successively,
Adown the breathing tresses of the flower,
Still doth the file of Hebrew dames proceed.
For these are a partition wall, whereby
The sacred stairs are sever'd, as the faith
In Christ divides them. On this part, where blooms
Each leaf in full maturity, are set
Such as in Christ, or e'er he came, believed.
On the other, where an intersected space
Yet shows the semicircle void, abide
All they, who look'd to Christ already come.
And as our Lady on her glorious stool,

THE VISION.

And they who on their stools beneath her sit,
This way distinction make; e'en so on his,
The mighty Baptist that way marks the line
(He who endured the desert, and the pains
Of martyrdom, and, for two years, of hell,
Yet still continued holy), and beneath,
Augustin; Francis; Benedict; and the rest,
Thus far from round to round. So heaven's decree
Forecasts, this garden, equally to fill,
With faith in either view, past or to come.
Learn too, that downward from the step, which cleaves,
Midway, the twain compartments, none there are
Who place obtain for merit of their own,
But have through others' merit been advanced,
On set conditions; spirits all released,
Ere for themselves they had the power to chuse.
And, if thou mark and listen to them well,
Their childish looks and voice declare as much.
  "Here, silent as thou art, I know thy doubt;
And gladly will I loose the knot, wherein
Thy subtil thoughts have bound thee. From this realm
Excluded, chance no entrance here may find;
No more than hunger, thirst, or sorrow can.
A law immutable hath stablish'd all;
Nor is there aught thou seest, that doth not fit,
Exactly, as the finger to the ring.
It is not, therefore, without cause, that these,
O'erspeedy comers to immortal life,
Are different in their shares of excellence.
Our Sovran Lord, that settleth this estate
In love and in delight so absolute,
That wish can dare no further, every soul,
Created in his joyous sight to dwell,
With grace, at pleasure, variously endows,

And for a proof the effect may well suffice.
And 'tis moreover most expressly mark'd
In holy Scripture, where the twins are said
To have struggled in the womb. Therefore, as grace
Inweaves the coronet, so every brow
Weareth its proper hue of orient light.
And merely in respect to his prime gift,
Not in reward of meritorious deed,
Hath each his several degree assign'd.
In early times with their own innocence
More was not wanting, than the parents' faith,
To save them: those first ages past, behoved
That circumcision in the males should imp
The flight of innocent wings: but since the day
Of grace hath come, without baptismal rites
In Christ accomplish'd, innocence herself
Must linger yet below. Now raise thy view
Unto the visage most resembling Christ:
For, in her splendour only, shalt thou win
The power to look on him." Forthwith I saw
Such floods of gladness on her visage shower'd,
From holy spirits, winging that profound;
That, whatsoever I had yet beheld,
Had not so much suspended me with wonder,
Or shown me such similitude of God.
And he, who had to her descended, once,
On earth, now hail'd in heaven; and on poised wing,
"Ave, Maria, gratia plena," sang:
To whose sweet anthem all the blissful court,
From all parts answering, rang: that holier joy
Brooded the deep serene. "Father revered!
Who deign'st, for me, to quit the pleasant place
Wherein thou sittest, by eternal lot;
Say, who that angel is, that with such glee

Beholds our queen, and so enamour'd glows
Of her high beauty, that all fire he seems."
   So I again resorted to the lore
Of my wise teacher, he, whom Mary's charms
Embellish'd, as the sun the morning star;
Who thus in answer spake: "In him are summ'd,
Whate'er of buxomness and free delight
May be in spirit, or in angel, met:
And so beseems: for that he bare the palm
Down unto Mary, when the Son of God
Vouchsafed to clothe him in terrestrial weeds.
Now let thine eyes wait heedful on my words;
And note thou of this just and pious realm
The chiefest nobles. Those, highest in bliss,
The twain, on each hand next our empress throned,
Are as it were two roots unto this rose:
He to the left, the parent, whose rash taste
Proves bitter to his seed: and, on the right,
That ancient father of the holy church,
Into whose keeping Christ did give the keys
Of this sweet flower; near whom behold the seer,
That, ere he died, saw all the grievous times
Of the fair bride, who with the lance and nails
Was won. And, near unto the other, rests
The leader, under whom, on manna, fed
The ungrateful nation, fickle, and perverse.
On the other part, facing to Peter, lo!
Where Anna sits, so well content to look
On her loved daughter, that with moveless eye
She chants the loud hosanna: while, opposed
To the first father of your mortal kind,
Is Lucia, at whose hest thy lady sped,
When on the edge of ruin closed thine eye.
   "But (for the vision hasteneth to an end)

Here break we off, as the good workman doth,
That shapes the cloak according to the cloth;
And to the primal love our ken shall rise;
That thou mayst penetrate the brightness, far
As sight can bear thee. Yet, alas! in sooth
Beating thy pennons, thinking to advance,
Thou backward fall'st. Grace then must first be gain'd;
Her grace, whose might can help thee. Thou in prayer
Seek her: and, with affection, whilst I sue,
Attend, and yield me all thy heart." He said;
And thus the saintly orison began.

CANTO XXXIII.

ARGUMENT.

St. Bernard supplicates the Virgin Mary that Dante may have grace given him to contemplate the brightness of the Divine Majesty, which is accordingly granted; and Dante then himself prays to God for ability to show forth some part of the celestial glory in his writings. Lastly, he is admitted to a glimpse of the great mystery; the Trinity, and the union of man with God.

"O VIRGIN mother, daughter of thy Son!
Created beings all in lowliness
Surpassing, as in height above them all;
Term by the eternal counsel pre-ordain'd;
Ennobler of thy nature, so advanced
In thee, that its great Maker did not scorn,
To make himself his own creation;
For in thy womb rekindling shone the love
Reveal'd, whose genial influence makes now
This flower to germin in eternal peace:
Here thou to us, of charity and love,
Art, as the noon-day torch; and art, beneath,
To mortal men, of hope a living spring.
So mighty art thou, lady, and so great,
That he, who grace desireth, and comes not
To thee for aidance, fain would have desire
Fly without wings. Not only him, who asks,
Thy bounty succours; but doth freely oft
Forerun the asking. Whatsoe'er may be
Of excellence in creature, pity mild,
Relenting mercy, large munificence,
Are all combined in thee. Here kneeleth one,
Who of all spirits hath review'd the state,
From the world's lowest gap unto this height.

Suppliant to thee he kneels, imploring grace
For virtue yet more high, to lift his ken
Toward the bliss supreme. And I, who ne'er
Coveted sight, more fondly, for myself,
Than now for him, my prayers to thee prefer
(And pray they be not scant), that thou wouldst drive
Each cloud of his mortality away,
Through thine own prayers, that on the sovran joy
Unveil'd he gaze. This yet, I pray thee, Queen,
Who canst do what thou wilt; that in him thou
Wouldst, after all he hath beheld, preserve
Affection sound, and human passions quell.
Lo! where, with Beatrice, many a saint
Stretch their clasp'd hands, in furtherance of my suit."

    The eyes, that heaven with love and awe regards,
Fix'd on the suitor, witness'd, how benign
She looks on pious prayers: then fasten'd they
On the everlasting light, wherein no eye
Of creature, as may well be thought, so far
Can travel inward. I, meanwhile, who drew
Near to the limit, where all wishes end,
The ardour of my wish (for so behoved)
Ended within me. Beckoning smiled the sage
That I should look aloft: but, ere he bade,
Already of myself aloft I look'd;
For visual strength, refining more and more,
Bare me into the ray authentical
Of sovran light. Thenceforward, what I saw,
Was not for words to speak, nor memory's self
To stand against such outrage on her skill.

    As one, who from a dream awaken'd, straight
All he hath seen forgets; yet still retains
Impression of the feeling in his dream;
E'en such am I: for all the vision dies,

As 'twere, away; and yet the sense of sweet,
That sprang from it, still trickles in my heart.
Thus in the sun-thaw is the snow unseal'd;
Thus in the winds on flitting leaves was lost
The Sibyl's sentence. O eternal beam!
(Whose height what reach of mortal thought may soar?)
Yield me again some little particle
Of what thou then appearedst; give my tongue
Power, but to leave one sparkle of thy glory,
Unto the race to come, that shall not lose
Thy triumph wholly, if thou waken aught
Of memory in me, and endure to hear
The record sound in this unequal strain.

    Such keenness from the living ray I met,
That, if mine eyes had turn'd away, methinks,
I had been lost; but, so embolden'd, on
I pass'd, as I remember, till my view
Hover'd the brink of dread infinitude.

    O grace, unenvying of thy boon! that gavest
Boldness to fix so earnestly my ken
On the everlasting splendour, that I look'd,
While sight was unconsumed; and, in that depth,
Saw in one volume clasp'd of love, whate'er
The universe unfolds; all properties
Of substance and of accident, beheld,
Compounded, yet one individual light
The whole. And of such bond methinks I saw
The universal form; for that whene'er
I do but speak of it, my soul dilates
Beyond her proper self; and, till I speak,
One moment seems a longer lethargy,
Than five-and-twenty ages had appear'd
To that emprize, that first made Neptune wonder
At Argo's shadow darkening on his flood.

PARADISE.—CANTO XXXIII.

With fixed heed, suspense and motionless,
Wondering I gazed; and admiration still
Was kindled as I gazed. It may not be,
That one, who looks upon that light, can turn
To other object, willingly, his view.
For all the good, that will may covet, there
Is summ'd; and all elsewhere defective found,
Complete. My tongue shall utter now, no more
E'en what remembrance keeps, than could the babe's
That yet is moisten'd at his mother's breast.
Not that the semblance of the living light
Was changed (that ever as at first remain'd),
But that my vision quickening, in that sole
Appearance, still new miracles descried,
And toil'd me with the change. In that abyss
Of radiance, clear and lofty, seem'd, methought,
Three orbs of triple hue, clipt in one bound:
And, from another, one reflected seem'd,
As rainbow is from rainbow: and the third
Seem'd fire, breathed equally from both. O speech!
How feeble and how faint art thou, to give
Conception birth. Yet this to what I saw
Is less than little. O eternal light!
Sole in thyself that dwell'st; and of thyself
Sole understood, past, present, or to come;
Thou smiledst, on that circling, which in thee
Seem'd as reflected splendour, while I mused;
For I therein, methought, in its own hue
Beheld our image painted: stedfastly
I therefore pored upon the view. As one,
Who versed in geometric lore, would fain
Measure the circle; and, though pondering long
And deeply, that beginning, which he needs,
Finds not: e'en such was I, intent to scan

THE VISION.

The novel wonder, and trace out the form,
How to the circle fitted, and therein
How placed: but the flight was not for my wing;
Had not a flash darted athwart my mind,
And, in the spleen, unfolded what it sought.
    Here vigour fail'd the towering fantasy:
But yet the will roll'd onward, like a wheel
In even motion, by the love impell'd,
That moves the sun in heaven and all the stars.

THE END.

More books from CGR Publishing:
www.CGRpublishing.com

1939 New York World's Fair: The World of Tomorrow in Photographs

San Francisco 1915 World's Fair: The Panama-Pacific International Expo.

1904 St. Louis World's Fair: The Louisiana Purchase Exposition in Photographs

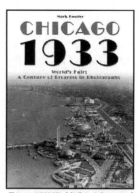
Chicago 1933 World's Fair: A Century of Progress in Photographs

19th Century New York: A Dramatic Collection of Images

The American Railway: The Trains, Railroads, and People Who Ran the Rails

The Clock Book: A Detailed Illustrated Collection of Classic Clocks

The World's Fair of 1893 Ultra Massive Photographic Adventure Vol. 1

The World's Fair of 1893 Ultra Massive Photographic Adventure Vol. 2

The World's Fair of 1893 Ultra Massive Photographic Adventure Vol. 3

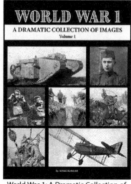
World War 1: A Dramatic Collection of Images

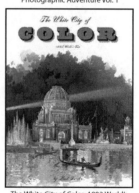
The White City of Color: 1893 World's Fair

Ethel the Cyborg Ninja Book 1

Ethel they Cyborg Ninja 2

How To Draw Digital by Mark Bussler

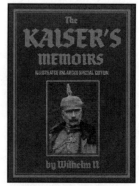
The Kaiser's Memoirs: Illustrated Enlarged Special Edition

Visit our complete catalog at:
www.CGRpublishing.com

Ultra Massive Video Game Console Guide Volume 1

Ultra Massive Video Game Console Guide Volume 2

Ultra Massive Video Game Console Guide Volume 3

Ultra Massive Sega Genesis Guide

The Illustrated History of the 1876 Centennial Exhibition Volume 1

Chicago's White City Cookbook

The Art of World War 1

How To Grow Mushrooms: A 19th Century Approach

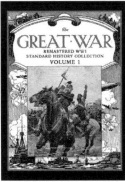
The Great War Remastered WW1 Standard History Collection Vol. 1

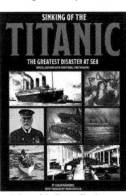
Sinking of the Titanic: The Greatest Disaster at Sea

All Hail the Vectrex Ultimate Collector's Guide

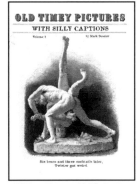
Old Timey Pictures with Silly Captions Volume 1

P.T. Barnum The Greatest Showman on Earth

Electricity at the World's Fair of 1893 Columbian Exposition

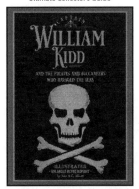
Captain William Kidd and the Pirates and Buccaneers Who Ravaged the Seas

The Aeroplane Speaks: Illustrated Historical Guide to Airplanes

Gustave Doré
Retro Restored Collection

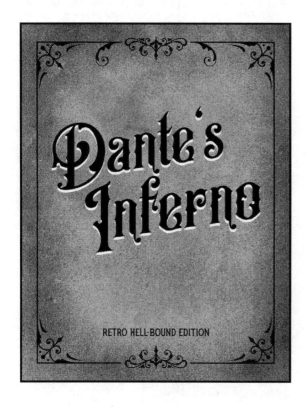 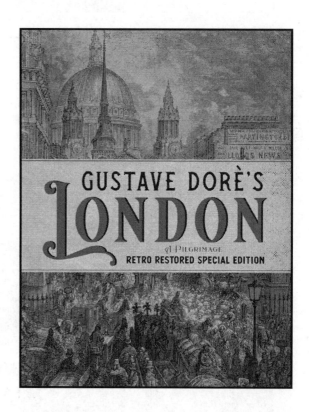

From CGR Publishing at
www.CGRpublishing.com

Made in the USA
Las Vegas, NV
02 November 2024

b9c39763-90e6-41b4-ad11-e43f357ebdf7R01